The Lady's Code
As It Pleases God®

Dr. Y. Bur

AVAILABLE TITLES

ASITPLEASESGOD.COM

THE LADY'S CODE
As It Pleases God®

Copyright © 2024 by Dr. Y. Bur. All rights reserved.

Visit www.RoarPublishingGroup.com for more information. No part of this publication may be reproduced, stored in a retrieval system, or transmitted in any way by any means, electronic, mechanical, photocopy, recording, or otherwise, without the prior permission of the author, except as provided by USA copyright law.

Book design copyright ©2024 by R.O.A.R. International Group. All rights reserved.

R.O.A.R. Publishing Group
581 N. Park Ave. Ste. #725
Apopka, FL 32704
www.RoarPublishingGroup.com

Published in the United States of America
ISBN: 978-1-948936-87-3
$22.88

ASITPLEASESGOD.COM

PLEASE SEND PRAYERS, TESTIMONIES, DONATIONS, OR ORDERS TO:

Dr. Y. Bur
R.O.A.R. Publishing Group
581 N. Park Ave. Ste. #725
Apopka, FL 32704
ROAR-58-2316
762-758-2316

✉ Dr.YBur@gmail.com

Visit Us At:
📷 **AsItPleasesGodMovement**
▶ **AsItPleasesGod**

🖥 **DrYBur.com**
🖥 **AsItPleasesGod.com**

Please Donate

Please DONATE to this *Missionable Movement of God* as a GIVE-BACK to the Kingdom. Thanks for your support. Many Blessings.

AIPG Donation Link

Scan to Pay

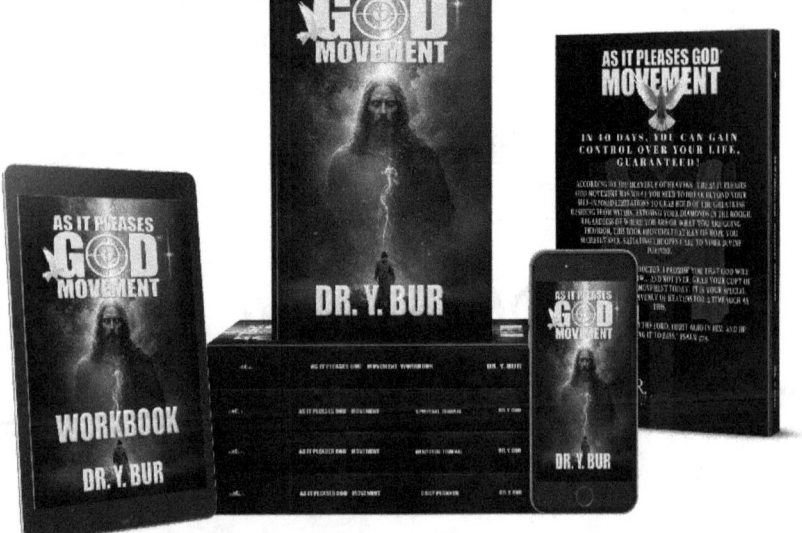

TABLE OF CONTENTS

INTRODUCTION 11

CHAPTER 1 17
  THE PLAYING FIELD 17
    Established Order 22
    Stepping Into 24
    Spiritual Alignment 27
    Inner Genius 33
    The Ironclad Seed 38
    Kindness, Love, and Togetherness 45
    Path to Mastery in Challenging Times 46

CHAPTER 2 49
  WRITING ON THE WALL 49
    Wall of Prophecy 52
    Wall of Thinking 55
    Wall of a Proper Perspective 64
    Wall of Busyness 67
    Wall of Creativity 73

CHAPTER 3 75
  UPFRONT AND HONEST 75
    Territorial Control 83
    The Streets of Gold Revelation 86
    Eyes Wide Open 95
    The Secrets of the Garden 98
    Avoiding Dullness 101
    Embracing Teachability 104

CHAPTER 4 107
THE BAGGAGE 107
- Wall of Forgiveness 112
- Wall of the Breaking Process 115
- Wall of Letting Go 118

CHAPTER 5 121
THE LADY'S CODE 121
- Wall of Divorce 126
- Wall of Dead Ends 128
- Wall of Relational Assets 132

CHAPTER 6 139
OPPOSITES ATTRACT 139
- Wall of Rebound 142
- Wall of Being Equally or Unequally Yoked 146
- The Warning - Silvia's Writing on the Wall 150
- Wall of Restoration 163

CHAPTER 7 179
FEAR OR FREEDOM 179
- Peace, Purpose, and Passion 181
- Spiritually Impoverished 186
- Relational Dating or Mating 189
- Story of Fears – Pam's Writing on the Wall 194
- Crushing Fear 205

CHAPTER 8 209
WALL OF PRETENSE 209
- Woman of Deceit 212
- Clueless Dating 215
- The Eye-Opener - Alice's Writing on the Wall 217

CHAPTER 9 229
RELATIONSHIP 80/20 RULE 229

    Divine Wisdom...235
    Distracted...242
    The Real Daisyrella - Daisy's Writing on the Wall........................250
    Love on Layaway - Malcolm's Writing on the Wall.....................255
    Wall of Overcoming..262
    Hunger Pains' Writing on the Wall...267

CHAPTER 10..269
  WHERE IS THE LOVE...269
    The Forbidden Fruit - Carrie's Writing on the Wall......................272
    Wall of Friends – Pat and Frank's Writing on the Wall................278
    Friends with Benefits Theory – Spiritual Transfers......................282
    Friends Without Benefits..288

CHAPTER 11..293
  SETTING STANDARDS..293
    Who Is Really Winning...298
    Wall of Masks..300
    Standing In The Gap...305

CHAPTER 12..307
  WALL OF TEMPTATION..307
    The Psyche's Attempt To Control...309
    Weighing the Risk - Jim and Lucy's Writing on the Wall.............312
    The Cheater Within - Brad's Writing on the Wall........................316
    Wall of Relations...322

INTRODUCTION

We have a relationship phenomenon going on, one that has undergone a seismic shift, leaving us perplexed about what is normal and what is not. The ease of connections through technology has transformed how we approach love as we unawaringly overlook the fundamental aspects of building meaningful relations, *As It Pleases God*. Due to this oversight, it is leading us to jump into and out of relationships, go on wild dates, and rush into and out of marriages without giving it a second thought or fully contemplating the consequences.

According to the Heavenly of Heavens, our swipe-right or to-the-left culture sets an unhealthy trend for those looking to get their groove on, shack up, get married, or kick someone to the curb with zero accountability. Then again, we use DIVORCE as our Plan B to jump out as quickly as we jumped in, while not putting in the necessary work to sustain a good relationship. And still have the audacity to say, 'I do not understand why they are leaving me.' In the *Lady's Code: As It Pleases God*®, this question underscores the deeper issues at play.

The matter at hand is...What do we do in these confusing times of dating, mating, and relating? First, we must reclaim our understanding of love, *As It Pleases God*. Secondly, we must define our own normal in a way that promotes accountability and healthy connections to uplift and empower, rather than engaging in those that drain and deplete. Lastly, we must know the difference, and this is where *The Lady's Code* comes in, providing viable information and roadmaps guiding us into our next.

Introduction

Above all, you have free will to do whatever you want, whenever, however, and with whomever, but the question is, 'Are you losing your feminine power?' If you do not know about your feminine power, then this book is designed just for you.

The Lady's Code: As It Pleases God is our hidden SUPERPOWER to find or attract the right person who keeps the phenomenon phenomenal. The moment we break the CODE when dealing with matters of the heart, it can become used to our detriment personally, professionally, and Spiritually.

The best psychologists, dating gurus, and sex therapists have spent many years trying to dissect *The Lady's Code*, as well as exploring the development or impulses of the human psyche to discover the precepts behind successful, long-term relationships...be it personal, professional, or Spiritual. Yet, the divorce rate still has an 80% failure rate. At the same time, *The Lady's Code* is shattered beyond measure. So, one must ask, 'Is this system broken? Or, 'Have we forgotten who we are?'

The central query now emerges in the Eye of God that something is definitely wrong. Conversely, based on Spiritual Duality for a time such as this, let us change the language on this matter: Something is definitely RIGHT. As life would have it, as the Divine Messenger of the Most High God, I have the Divine Secrets to successful relations, *As It Pleases Him*. In addition, in this book, I also include the reasons why we need love on our level, the importance of dating, mating, or relating, and why we should not break *The Lady's Code*!

As *Women of Stature*, we often break *The Lady's Code* due to our known or unknown unstable thoughts, actions, reactions, words, biases, and the lack of understanding, particularly if we do not add God into our equational efforts. As a result, it prevents us from having the WISDOM needed to avoid wreaking havoc or satiating a vendetta. One of the most painful experiences one can face is being jilted or ghosted by someone we care about, only to watch them move on with someone else.

In moments of heartache, rejection, and loss, it becomes all too easy to let our emotions spiral out of control, causing us to do

Introduction

things we later regret. The feelings of betrayal and anger are real, and a natural human response may be to seek revenge, whether through passive-aggressive behavior, slandering, gossip, or other means of retribution. When we are reckless in this manner, perpetuating a cycle of negativity, it levies bondage from within and generational curses, with an all-consuming fire.

To avoid vengeance from clouding our sense of good judgment, we must become cognizant of our thoughts, actions, and triggers, especially the areas we tend to sleep on, ignore, or downplay. Truthfully, no one is exempt from experiencing this, but as *Women of Stature*, it is essential to MASTER the ability to PAUSE and REFLECT to counteract our impulses. When we allow ourselves the space to grieve, the time to process our real emotions, and the opportunity to regulate our self-talk, we heal quicker. Plus, this is not only a healthy thing to do for ourselves, but it is necessary for our sanity, our well-being, and a renewed perspective. In this book, *The Lady's Code: As It Pleases God*®, it shares how to do so and why.

According to the Heavenly of Heavens, it is time to forget about the *Girl's Code*; it is time out for the cat and mouse or tit for tat games. They are leading us into the Abyss with a one-way ticket. For this reason, in this book, as *Women of Stature*, we are dealing with *The Lady's Code: As It Pleases God*® to gain SKILLS...Spiritual Skills, to be exact. Once and for all, we are getting off the milk and getting to the crux of the MEAT of how we are designed to operate, *As It Pleases Him*.

Suppose you are single, married, or anything in between. In this case, you know how difficult it is to find good, sound advice about dating, developing new relationships, maintaining the relationships that you already have, or building a *Spirit to Spirit* Relationship with your Heavenly Father. In the Eye of God, the plug-and-play advice is not going to get it!

In the grand tapestry of living real life, many have formulas or strategies for dating, mating, and relating without God. In the end, all of it leads us back to Him anyway, sometimes wounded, traumatized, or disoriented. Whether ingesting the right or wrong

Introduction

information, without God, it may get our Spiritual Wires crossed in more ways than one. So, in this book, *The Lady's Code*, it bears mentioning that for me, Dr. Y. Bur, The WHY Doctor, I just have questions. Yes, the Divinely Loaded questions with the potential of leveling *The Playing* Field on any level.

How is it humanly possible to invoke the Leveling Process for Believers and non-believers alike? Being that God is no respecter of persons, according to Romans 2:11, we selflessly focus on incorporating Him, our Heavenly Father, *As It Pleases Him*, into the equational efforts of all things from a Divine Perspective. At the same time, we use relatable Writing on the Wall stories to drive the point home!

As The WHY Doctor, my Divine Purpose is not to provide you with a mere ten steps to find the perfect soul mate, or to present myself as a dating or relationship guru. Instead, I am here to EMPOWER you with a new perspective that is realistic, practical, profound, usable, and proven to work according to God's Divine Will. In essence, I will also share with you the gist of what is really happening from a Spiritual Perspective and how we get caught up. Albeit difficult, and we are all different, these Divine Perspectives are not for everyone, nor are they applicable in every given situation. Still, the gleanable information should not be overlooked or underestimated.

In this book, *The Lady's Code: As It Pleases God*®, we are going to keep dating, mating, and relating really simple. We are not going with the statistics...We are going with the *Writing on the Wall* Principles, according to the Heavenly of Heavens, bridging the gap between where you are and where you are going.

The plan is to share ways to read the *Writing on the Wall* about yourself or others, and how to not waste precious time with Mental, Physical, Emotional, or Spiritual contradictions that lead you away from the Kingdom. In addition, it will also help you drop *The Baggage* of negativity, debauchery, and confusion, causing you to get a side-eye from God Almighty.

Now, the different *Walls of Reality* that we will discuss will better prepare you to become the ultimate best version of who God has

Introduction

created you to be. The walls are thought-provoking, as they are designed to get you to think inside, outside, around, and through the box of life, leaving no stone unturned. Regardless of whether you are single, dating, married, divorced, separated, or straddling the fence, this book has something for you. Nevertheless, you are required to be *Upfront and Honest* with God, yourself, and others.

As we all know, being single can become a challenging and lonely place with daunting or isolating experiences. Nevertheless, I would say that it is an even worse place to be married, living a lonely life with secrets, caught between *Fear or Freedom* and staying within the confines of a commitment, with zero communication.

What is more heart-wrenching is when you have vowed before God to love someone for the rest of your life, and they do not want you anymore. To add insult to injury, the reason why they do not want you is that you are not what they expected, you have gained weight, you have disagreeable goals, you do not have enough money in your bank account, your credit score is not high enough, you do not speak proper grammar, you have gotten sick, and the list goes on with negative excuses.

To put it simply, it hurts worse when you are sleeping with the enemy in your own home with a *Wall of Pretense*. At the same time, knowing that your time is limited in the relationship, and you cannot tell anyone you are internally *Distracted* or fragmented. Nor can you admit that you were not equally yoked in the first place.

Meanwhile, you were convinced that the *Opposite Attracts*, not realizing it also repels when you are unequally yoked. So, where do you go from here, especially with *Setting Standards*? You can only go up with your hands lifted to the Heavens, surrendering all of your weaknesses and your *Wall of Trophies*.

If you dare to take a look at *The Lady's Code: As It Pleases God*, I will take you on a Spiritual Journey that will revolutionize your life, putting the *Relationship Games* to boot to become a *Woman of Stature*, GUARANTEED.

As the Spiritually Anointed WHY Doctor, I am passionate about the transformational power of understanding our motivations and values, especially when it comes to building

Introduction

quality relationships. One Divine Principle I stand by is that there is absolutely NO LIMIT to what we can achieve when we are confident in our abilities and equipped with *The Lady's Code*. This Divine Framework of SOUND DOCTRINE not only enhances our interpersonal connections. It also aligns our actions, thoughts, beliefs, and desires with our Divinely Blueprinted Purpose, *As It Pleases God*, with confidence, grace, authenticity, respect, empathy, and integrity.

Do we really need *The Lady's Code* to be in Purpose on purpose? Frankly, we do not need anything because we were not created as robots. Plus, we have free will to accept or decline *The Lady's Code* to remain regular or in a state of mediocrity, grappling with an identity crisis, lacking a sense of self-worth, and seeking approval from others. But at the core of it all, if we attempt to live life without *The Lady's Code: As It Pleases God*®, rest assured, the Spiritual Access to Divine Wisdom, Understanding, Secrets, Treasures, and Powers from the Kingdom of Heaven will be denied until we align ourselves, *As It Pleases Him*.

Simply put, we have various paths to choose from. Some may prefer to take the long road, indulging in every twist and turn unnecessarily. Others might lean toward the shorter route, aiming for efficiency, speed, patchwork, and quick fixes. Some feel compelled to carve their own unique paths, forging ahead with personal beliefs, experiences, and on their own terms to please themselves or others. However, amid all, there is another route that we all knowingly or unknowingly seek...The Proven Way. This path is the Spiritually Stamped and Approved Way, recognized by the Heavenly of Heavens, leading to true fulfillment and enlightenment. What is the difference between them all? The element of the TIME it takes to learn, grow, and sow back into the Kingdom, *As It Pleases God*. So, whether we waste it or maximize it, the Divine Blueprint does not change; we must do the changing!

Without further ado, as a *Woman of Stature*, prepare yourself to seize control and experience a metamorphosis that will leave you feeling empowered, courageous, and fulfilled beyond what you could ever imagine. *Spirit to Spirit*, let's do it, for real, for real!

CHAPTER 1

THE PLAYING FIELD

Are you playing yourself short? Are you content with *Playing the Field*? Then again, is the *Field Playing* you? As life continues to move forward with or without us, as *Women of Stature*, the WHY questions become more legitimate for us to ask. To play to win, we must learn how to play accordingly because *The Lady's Code: As It Pleases God* is Team Me, and Team You.

Life has various levels and playing fields that require different levels of preparation, *As It Pleases God*. However, it is crucial to remember that this does not justify mistreating or sabotaging others who are either above or below our levels. Why? Fortunately, there are Spiritual Rules and Principles governing our thoughts, actions, behaviors, biases, and words, especially as *Women of Stature*. All of these are designed to keep us from biting the hand that feeds us or wearing our emotions on our shoulders.

According to *The Lady's Code*, it is also designed to put us on an even playing field. If we are playing out of our league, we will set ourselves up for defeat; therefore, it is always best to get an understanding of who we are and why we are. If we are not up-to-date with this ideology, we will become embroiled in many

The Playing Field

relationship traumas that could have been avoided. Suppose we have a desire to level *The Playing Field*. In this case,

- ☐ We must *Establish Order* in our relationships or dating agendas.
- ☐ We must know when to *Step In* or Out of whatever with whomever.
- ☐ We must know the precise moment to *Spiritually Align* ourselves, *As It Pleases God*.
- ☐ We must unveil our *Inner Genius*.
- ☐ We must know and understand *The Seeds* associated with our engagements or endeavors.

In this book, you are not left on your own to figure out how to accomplish these items. I will walk you through them step by step to prepare the groundwork of your *Playing Field* without having to play dirty.

We can tiptoe around mating, dating, baiting, fating, or anything in between. Still, it does not change what the *Writing on the Wall* says, nor does it give us the right to break *The Lady's Code*, regardless of what it says about them or us.

In *The Playing Field*, it does not matter how much we think we DO NOT need anyone; we are not the lone rangers. As fate would have it, we cannot date or mate with ourselves. Surely, we can spend time alone; in reality, it takes two to date, two to become mates, two to commune, two to procreate, and two to generate. Yes, I said, generate…This is how we get generation! They all work together; we are wired a certain way, and this book is going to answer some of the questions we secretly ask ourselves when no one is looking.

As Spiritual Beings having a human experience, there are certain things we crave in relationships that go beyond physical needs. Listed below are a few of our needs, desires, and wants, but not limited to such:

The Playing Field

- ☐ We need Connection.
- ☐ We desire Authenticity.
- ☐ We want Honesty.
- ☐ We need to Trust.
- ☐ We safeguard our Vulnerability.
- ☐ We desire Empathy.
- ☐ We need Understanding.
- ☐ We want Respect.
- ☐ We desire Support.
- ☐ We seek Encouragement.
- ☐ We need Growth.
- ☐ We desire Acceptance.
- ☐ We need Forgiveness.
- ☐ We must exhibit Gratitude.
- ☐ We want internal Joy.
- ☐ We need Love.
- ☐ We desire Compassion.
- ☐ We seek Intimacy.
- ☐ We enjoy Playfulness.
- ☐ We need Freedom.

Even though we are all subject to error on occasion, these things are essential for a healthy and fulfilling relationship that nourishes our Spiritual Growth and well-being. When we prioritize these things in our relationships, we create a strong foundation for love, growth, and happiness. If not, we are more apt to break *The Lady's Code: As It Pleases God.*

We often would like to think about everyone being our equal and giving everyone a fair chance at our love, but what we have is not for everyone. They may not be ready for us, or we may not be ready for them; therefore, we must determine who fits into our lives and who does not.

Suppose we are not careful about who we allow into our circles. In this case, our relationships will become plagued with jealousy, envy, anger, revenge, insecurity, covetousness, and malice, especially when dealing with defeated or rejected foes.

The Playing Field

The competition is fierce when you are dating, when you are in a relationship, or when you are married, but it is indeed a fair game. Now, the question is, 'What are you going to do that is so different that it will put the ball in your court?' Even if loving on your level may appear complicated, and there may be twenty women to every one man, it does not matter. When you follow the Spiritual Rules, Principles, and Concepts and do not break *The Lady's Code: As It Pleases God*, you will always get the upper hand. Really? Yes, really! *"Who can find a virtuous wife? For her worth is far above rubies."* Proverbs 31:10.

While online dating has gone absolutely bonkers, it does work for some. However, I prefer the old-fashioned way of communicating with a potential mate, but whatever works for you—do you! Of course, it is okay to meet people randomly; however, it is better to meet them where you both have a common interest via hobbies, classes, social events, the gym, etc. Even if you do not meet someone immediately in the activity of your interest, you can make new friends.

When determining the first level of compatibility or the *Playing Field*, simply strike up a conversation with someone, getting them to talk. Why do we need to get them to talk? People will tell you everything you need to know if you ask the right questions or embark upon the proper conversation. If you do not know how to start a conversation, just talk about the weather or compliment someone. Is it that easy? Yes, it is!

Find something positive about that person and compliment them. Hint, hint, people love to talk about themselves, their children, and their pets. If you master this, you will become a master at starting a conversation with anyone, even if they do not appear approachable. Remember, everybody knows somebody, and there is someone for everybody!

Now that we have cutting-edge technological services to date online, as with everything, there are positives and negatives. However, you must determine if old-fashioned or new-age dating will work for you. Some consider it a blessing, some consider it a curse, some think it is magic, and some believe it is unwise; regardless of how anyone sees it, it is here to stay.

The Playing Field

The online way of dating has pretty much replaced the back-in-the-day dating services, which match you up with people according to your profile. As we get with the program regarding the new wave of dating, people become who they want, real or fake, to lure you in. Therefore, one must exercise extreme caution when doing so, and one must not become desperate, or the vultures will swoop in to eat lunch. Of course, this is not you, right?

Online dating is convenient for some but a nightmare for others, so you have to really determine the best way for you to meet people. Keep in mind that you still must become active in the relationship in order for it to grow. If you are not willing to build a relationship, become transparent, put away selfishness, or put in the work, then you must reevaluate why you need love on your level in the first place.

In addition to deciding to date online, as a rule of thumb, you must be ever so cognizant of who you are meeting online before meeting them in person. Also, be very careful about what personal information you put on the internet. *The Lady's Code* advises that you should not list your address, phone number, or where you work. Why should we become ever so cautious about this? Unrecognizable predators online are waiting for you to slip!

Listen, they use false dating profiles and fake pictures to draw you in. Therefore, it is best to save yourself a little time by getting out and doing the legwork of real dating. While simultaneously reading the *Writing on the Wall* to prevent yourself from meeting a hellion or chameleon, loving below your level, or outright settling.

This book, *The Lady's Code: As It Pleases God*, provides you with the *Wall of Questions* to save a lot of time with dead-end dating or dead-end relationships, therefore giving you the platform to spend more time on the people, places, and things that are more conducive to your true self. Remember, in all things, the grass will always appear greener on the other side. Still, greener pastures must be maintained as well. The greener the grass, requires more work. So, work on the grass where you are and make sure it is up to par before you move on to a pasture that you may be unequipped for.

Of course, you are going to kiss a few frogs...okay, you may kiss a lot of frogs. But it allows you to weed out those who are looking for something different than what you have to offer and those who are unequally yoked with you. Your best bet is always to keep it real with the people you love, and never think that you are too good or too whatever for them.

According to *The Lady's Code*, a successful relationship depends on the quality of time you spend together. Although every situation or relationship is unique, communication illuminates and bonds the uniqueness of the relationship together. When you ask the right questions of yourself and others, whether it is short-term, long-term, or a lifetime commitment, you are able to become crystal clear about the commitment level and the direction of the relationship. Even if a relationship is not an option for you, exhibit love while helping everyone within reason, while *Establishing Order*.

Established Order

In *Establishing Order* on *The Playing Field*, I am beginning this with the most prominent yet most hidden downfall of man, which lies in the Spirit of Jezebel. The controlling and manipulative Spirit of Jezebel is not just in women, breaking *The Lady's Code* as most would think. The reason why this is a hidden kryptonite to humanity is that this Spirit resides in men as well. We believe, or better yet, we are being taught that the Spirit that possessed Jezebel is limited to women, but we are sadly mistaken. In all reality, this Spirit has no gender...all it needs is a willing, weak, or naive vessel.

The Jezebel Spirit has enough power to consume us all, primarily if we do not recognize it, cast it down, and replace it with the appropriate positive Spiritual Character Traits, *As It Pleases God*. When we find ourselves eating, sexing, bullying, social media-ing our way through our hidden pains, or continually breaking *The Lady's Code*, this is the very moment one must cast this Spirit out.

Although one would never think they are Spiritually Bound...however, if one is saying, 'What is wrong with me?' or 'Why do I keep doing this?' It is an automatic sign of an inner war

The Playing Field

between the Mind, Body, Soul, and Spirit. We can play around with the Jezebel Spirit all we want, but when it ensnares someone we love, then what do we do?

Now, the question is, 'How can this Spirit ensnare others when we are dealing with it, or is it our very own personal battle?' When dealing with a Jezebel Spirit, the goal is to bully, manipulate, scheme, and curse others. If we do not think it is accurate, CHECK OUR THOUGHTS when we do not get what we want. Do we bless someone, or do we find a way to curse them, dig up dirt, or air out their flaws? Once we carry out negative thoughts and behaviors, they have consequences and repercussions that may bypass us and fall upon our loved ones.

Every time we knowingly do evil, there is a price or sacrifice attached to it, whether we realize it or not. Also, we must become conscious of our thoughts as well. It is through our thoughts that our actions are formed and carried out. For the innocent men who are dealing with women who are consumed with this Spirit, here is what Revelation 2:20 has to say: *"But I have this against you, that you tolerate that woman Jezebel, who calls herself a prophetess and is teaching and seducing my servants to practice sexual immorality and to eat food sacrificed to idols."*

According to the Heavenly of Heavens, we are accountable for the behaviors we tolerate. In my opinion, it is like the guilt-by-association concept, but in the Spiritual Realm. Can we be held accountable for another person's actions? The answer is yes. Ephesians 5:11 says, *"Take no part in the unfruitful works of darkness, but instead expose them."* We must kindly bring awareness to the situation. *"Do not be deceived: Bad company ruins good morals."* 1 Corinthians 15:33. We do not have to wait around for someone to exhibit lousy behavior; all we need to do is make them aware of their folly. If they do not make the corrections necessary, it is our responsibility to redirect the expended energy. Then again, there are times when we may need to find an exit.

In the Eye of God, we cannot think it is okay for a woman to become a ruler in a house when there is a man present; it contradicts scripture, and it is totally out of order, breaking *The*

The Playing Field

Lady's Code. Unfortunately, this is the number one reason why men cheat, and our divorce rate is at 80%!

Do we think for a minute that a man would correct his out-of-control wife who would make his life a living hell? Absolutely not! *"It is better to live on a corner of the roof than share a house with a quarrelsome wife."* Proverbs 21:9. When this happens, most men will cut women off emotionally by ignoring them, or they will cheat, if not physically, but definitely mentally, emotionally, or cyberly.

So, for all the women out there embracing *The Lady's Code: As It Pleases God*, it is time out for insecurity; we are an anchor to our men. We need to be able to hold them down or have their back. We do not need to be in their face, confronting them, or all over their back with chains and whips as if they were a child. According to Ephesians 4:2, *"With all humility and gentleness, with patience, bearing with one another in love"* is our Power Play. There is no reason for a woman to treat her man like a little child, and if this is the case, they are unequally yoked.

Stepping Into

How does it feel when you *Step Into* your home? How do others feel about *Stepping Into* your domain? Regardless of whether you *Step Into* or out of something, it is designed to build your Stature, *As It Pleases God*.

Home is where the heart is. If our hearts are not in our homes, then we will experience some form of abandonment on our behalf or the behalf of someone else. We often do not think about abandonment as much if it is not pointed out; however, it does have extreme ties to our hearts. Besides, the sting of neglect does not affect us unless it becomes tied to our emotions, to an experience, or an open wound.

In my opinion, it is not the act of abandonment that affects us; it is how we feel about the act of abandonment and by whom. In all actuality, we are abandoned all the time based on our beliefs, cultures, and lifestyles.

The Playing Field

If we are not able to handle the abandonment or the rejection of our past, we are not ready for *The Lady's Code: As It Pleases God*. In order for us to *Step Into* our Destined Greatness, we are going to experience a lot of haters along the way. If we are not able to handle it mentally or emotionally, we will retreat or have a pity party at the first sign of resistance.

When we are emotionally and mentally ready to become a *Woman of Stature*, we will not have to retreat or lash out when we are rejected, hurt, laughed at, or abused. We can stand our ground through obstacles, stand against the enemy, stand our ground with the dream killers, or stand our ground with a sense of peace beyond all human understanding!

In my opinion, some of us allow our emotional or mental states to determine if we are ready for something or someone; however, it could be very misleading. I would say that we are better off going with our instincts or our inner knowing, which requires us to tap into our Spirituality. For me, it is a surefire way I can peacefully live without regrets. Do I make mistakes? Absolutely!

Those mistakes are usually made when I mentally rationalize or emotionally stigmatize my decisions, answers, perceptions, or analyses. Nevertheless, *The Lady's Code: As It Pleases God* is always on point, truthful, relentless, sleepless, and faithful while always having my best interest at heart.

When *Stepping In* or stepping up to the plate, we can prevent ourselves from getting stepped on. Our Level of Stature may be different from the next person, but we are not all here on this earth for the same reason. According to the Heavenly of Heavens, there is a reason for our madness, our struggles, our hurts, our abuses, our betrayals, and the list goes on. In the Eye of God, they are designed to help us *Step Into* our rightful places in the Kingdom.

On the other hand, if we make a conscious decision to break *The Lady's Code*, wallow, complain, downplay, or hide what we are going through, and judge others for their imperfections while secretly discriminating against others based on power, money, sex, status, job title, or where they live, we corrupt the code of our

The Playing Field

psyche. Really? Yes, really! So, instead of us being in control, it controls us, causing us to turn on ourselves.

We are all in a state of denial when it comes down to the element of judgment and discrimination. The moment someone says to me that they do not have a judgmental or discriminatory bone in their body, I do not trust that person at all. Listen, we are all subject to error on occasion, and we are all a work-in-progress. If they had prefaced that statement, 'I do my best not to _____,' 'It depends upon the situation,' or 'I have to protect my livelihood,' I would extend a level of trust toward that individual based upon the Fruits of the Spirit or their Level of Positivity.

With all of our flaws or imperfections, we are secretly hoping for change when the change is already within. When we make the sacrifice to change our lives, it is going to feel different. As a matter of fact, it will feel as if we are losing our grip or as if people are walking away. All of these feelings are normal because we are willing to break the cycle.

For example, if we have a desire to erect a new building in place of the old one. We must first get rid of the old building or gut it first, and then remodel or build a new building, right? Of course! Well, this is the same concept, but it is going to apply to our thoughts, feelings, and emotions. They will appear conflicting from time to time; it does not always mean that we are digressing unless one is willfully doing so. However, if one is on the right track, one is expected to experience the feelings of turning back. Typically, this is why we need to plan, focus, and pursue. If not, the elements of life will toss us to and fro, especially if we are full of doubt, fear, rebellion, disobedience, or double-mindedness.

In dealing with *The Lady's Code: As It Pleases God*, we cannot allow negative emotions to consume us. We must counteract them with positive affirmations, along with scripture, if possible. Clearly, no one is immune to negative thoughts, emotions, triggers, or seeds; however, it is our responsibility to cast them down or cancel them immediately. Here are a few examples:

The Playing Field

- ☐ I cast down the Spirit of ABANDONMENT, and I replace it with the Spirit of RELATIONSHIP, STRENGTH, PURPOSE, and DIRECTION. *"Though my father and mother forsake me, the LORD will receive me. Teach me Your way, LORD; lead me in a straight path because of my oppressors."* Psalm 27:10-11. *"I have been young, and now am old; yet have I not seen the righteous forsaken, nor his seed begging bread."* Psalm 37:25.

- ☐ I cast down the Spirit of ANGER, and I replace it with the Spirit of CALMNESS and RATIONALITY. For *"A soft answer turneth away wrath: but grievous words stir up anger."* Proverbs 15:1. And, *"He that is slow to anger is better than the mighty, and he that ruleth his spirit than he that taketh a city."* Proverbs 16:32.

- ☐ I cast down the Spirit of ANXIETY, and I replace it with the Spirit of PEACE and CALMNESS. *"I will not be anxious about anything, but in every situation, by prayer and petition, with thanksgiving, present my requests to God. And the peace of God, which transcends all understanding, will guard my heart and my mind in Christ Jesus."* Philippians 4:6-7.

What is the purpose of counteracting negativity? If there is no counteraction, it remains with us, with the probability of growth. In my opinion, it is like a weed growing up; if we do not pluck it up, it grows like wildflowers. For this reason, *The Lady's Code: As It Pleases God* requires *Spiritual Alignment*.

Spiritual Alignment

In *The Lady's Code*, the act of *Spiritual Alignment* refers to being in harmony with our own Spiritual Beliefs and Values, as well as being in tune with the Holy Trinity (The Father, Son, and Holy Spirit). While the society in which we live defines this in many

The Playing Field

different ways, we are not most people; we are an Elite Group of Women heeding the Spiritual Demands set forth by the Heavenly of Heavens.

The Lady's Code: As It Pleases God must align itself with the Biblical Principles we tend to overlook or attempt to justify and rationalize. Even if we think they do not apply to us or are a little dated, they are still PROFOUND and ENFORCEABLE in or out of the Kingdom of God. At the crux of this matter, for some odd reason, I find we take the portions of the Bible we like, overlook the other parts we need, or downplay what is designed to convict the conscience to tame the flesh. Nonetheless, this book is not about Bible Study here; it is about developing *Spiritual Alignment* according to our Predestined Blueprinted Purpose, *As It Pleases God*.

Once we align ourselves with the things of the Spirit, *As It Pleases God*, we will find our lives may become shaken to the core. Some would say their lives were turned upside down, some would say their lives went crazy, and some would say their lives spiraled out of control. When it comes down to the Divine Things of the Spirit or when gaining Kingdom Credentials, this is possible. Let me assure you that it is only a TEST, preparing you for what is next or delivering you from your past! In short, this happens to most of us to see if we are serious about our Spiritual Walk with God. Unfortunately, this is usually where most people turn around and go back to their old habits or old ways of living to please themselves, instead of just stepping into the Spiritual Classroom, *As It Pleases God*.

Why are we tested to the max, especially when we are sold out to the Kingdom of God, doing what we were called to do, and loving God with all our hearts? Just because we love Him with all our hearts does not mean that He is ruling our thoughts, desires, propensities, actions, biases, or whatever.

Rest assured, when on *The Playing Field*, if we are being TESTED in the Eye of God, there is an underlying Judas (Sell-Out) Spirit, a Haman (Plotting) Spirit, or a Jezebel (Manipulative) Spirit at the table. How do we know if one of these is within us? It is really simple...We are human, and Spiritual Duality (The knowledge of

The Playing Field

good and evil, right and wrong, just and unjust) will remain as long as the Earth remains, paving the way to the SAINT or the BEAST within us. As a rule of thumb, we do not know or realize what is in us or which one dominates until we are pressed, squeezed, triggered, or pushed to the max. Unfortunately, this is why some people just CLICK! But of course, this is not you, right?

The SAINT or the BEAST likes to hide in plain sight, hidden under layers of something else. As Women of Stature, if we know about DUALISM, *As It Pleases God*, we can do something to change the trajectory, redirecting all intents to become positive, productive, winning, and fruitful while self-correcting at the drop of a dime. Conversely, if we do not know anything about the SAINT or the BEAST and Dualism, we will get got by the enemy's wiles for not knowing what we should. In addition, we will also find ourselves wallowing in the negative, becoming unproductive, suffering many losses, battling with the unfruitful, and becoming more self-destructive, while appearing right in our own eyes.

The moment we say that we do not possess any of the above character traits, it is a silent indicator that we are lying to ourselves, and cannot be trusted with Kingdom Credentials, Divine Wisdom, Heavenly Secrets, and Supernatural Power, *As It Pleases God*. For those who pride themselves on saying God said, and He did not say; God did, what He did not do; and God gave, what He did not give, exercise extreme caution. Why must Believers tread carefully when doing this? There are Spiritual Laws, Principles, and Protocols guarding the DIVINE, and if we think we can selfishly bypass them, then have at it.

Who am I to judge who has Divine Access to what, right? No judgment intended. Let me say this before moving on: There is a reason that we have the Blood of Jesus for SALVATION and CLEANSING. Also, there is a reason that we have the Holy Spirit to guide us, the Fruits of the Spirit to help build our character, forgiveness to purge our hearts, and repentance and grace to help us reset ourselves on a moment-by-moment basis.

Above all, if we are proclaiming to be Heaven-Sent with corrupt character traits or having zero knowledge about positive and negative character traits, then we have work to do. Moreover, I

The Playing Field

am just the Messenger, designed to level the Playing Field, exposing the lies that the psyche tends to hide from us, yet it is revealed in our character traits.

The *Spiritual Alignment* surrounding *The Lady's Code* for *Women of Stature* is determined by:

- ☐ Our responsibility.
- ☐ Our discipline.
- ☐ Our proactiveness.
- ☐ Our personal, private, professional, or communal Fruits of the Spirit.
- ☐ Our Level of Respect for ourselves and others.
- ☐ Our ability to repent and forgive.
- ☐ Our ability to show compassion.
- ☐ Our ability to understand and apply Spiritual Laws and Principles, *As It Pleases God*.

Without being tested, we will not know our strengths or weaknesses. Theoretically, we must become proactive in *Spiritually Aligning* ourselves to ensure we do not crumble when pressure is applied or when the issues of life come upon us. Not to give the devil any credit, but he will have a field day with those who are pretending to be Spiritually Sound but secretly unsound. Regrettably, this is where the division, battles, and prejudices are taking place to keep us from understanding that it is not about us. What is it about then, especially if it is not about us or our four and no more? It is about exhibiting the Fruits of the Spirit and living in Purpose on purpose with a balance between the Mind, Body, Soul, and Spirit, *As It Pleases God*.

When embarking upon a journey of *Spiritual Alignment*, it may require us to seek out time alone. The elements of being alone and being lonely are often intertwined as being the same when they are indeed different. When we are alone, it means the absence of people. It is definitely possible to be alone and not feel the sting of loneliness. On the other hand, we can be surrounded by tons of

The Playing Field

people and still feel lonely because it is an emotional or mental state of being, whereas being alone is the physical aspect.

Is it possible to be alone and lonely? The answer is yes. But it does not have to be that way...we can choose not to be lonely based on our thoughts, actions, beliefs, and reactions. Most of the time, people resort to being alone when people or even a job violates their right to privacy. This world has come to an ultimate state of violating our constitutional rights to privacy and our rights to be who we are.

When we are placed in a box to be like everyone else, we become limited, enslaved, or easily bullied. Furthermore, if one is doing great things, we do not get the same rights or treatment as those who do not want anything or those who are content with mediocrity.

We can tiptoe around this issue all we would like, but major corporations are the most guilty of this behavior. They are giving way to their employees to violate the privacy of others with no consequences or repercussions. They would reason that they are choosing the best candidates as employees for the company. Let me say that is so far from the truth of what they are getting. They are still hiring wayward and corrupt employees who have learned how to beat the system and who lack positive character traits.

In my opinion, the violation of privacy is the ultimate level of discrimination known to man because it allows people to place their ungoverned perception over an individual. Listen, the psychological mind games to get into people's lives were all created by man, for man! Therefore, we are all subject to err on occasion, and no one is perfect, not even one!

Unjustifiable deprivation or mistreatment out of envy or jealousy is the ultimate cause for most to seek to be alone. There are times when this is used as a means of protection, as a peaceful alternative to stay ahead of the game, or as a form of *Spiritual Alignment.*

Who does not want to stay on their toes when it comes down to life, right? Well, there are times when we overlook the vital elements of our Spirituality when it comes down to doing, seeing, becoming, and maximizing the Greatness from Within. Some do

The Playing Field

not believe Greatness resides from within, and some do not know how to Spiritually Align with their Greatness.

In *The Lady's Code*, our daily regime opens the floodgate of what tomorrow is going to bring. As we mold and shape our destiny to build good, solid relationships, we cannot forget about the impact of what we are doing right now. Of course, we all have hope for tomorrow, but our tomorrow has the hope of what we are doing today in order to set in motion its very own agenda.

Now, if for some reason we fall short, we do not need people in our lives to kick us when we are down. If they do...leave them alone. Our setbacks are basically our setup for a real BLESSING if we do not give up on ourselves.

I firmly believe in leaving no stone unturned, and I ran into someone else who thinks the same way: Lisa was considered to be a profound risk-taker; as a result, she found herself living on the edge, dealing with a lot of failures. Of course, with each endeavor, her risk became a little higher until she fell flat on her face, losing everything. The friends she thought she had did not call, nor did they check on her. Lisa was totally abandoned by everyone, including her family.

She became the talk of the town. It seemed as if everyone was waiting for the opportunity to laugh and talk about her. In Lisa's moment of loneliness, she began to question her purpose in life. What she found out about herself was astounding. As a result of her failure, she realized she was a people pleaser. She allowed herself to become driven by the opinions and the influences of her friends, therefore clouding her judgment regarding what she was really supposed to be doing, *As It Pleased God*. As a result, Lisa became very strategic in her thoughts, actions, reactions, words, and most of all, her time.

In my opinion, this woman began to manage her time like it was a full-time job. She turned off the television and the radio so she could listen to her thoughts and the lack thereof. After several months of listening to life and asking questions, she began to receive dynamic answers. She realized her input determined her output, and if she was not putting out the right things, she changed her thoughts.

The Playing Field

Lisa took one block of her life and began to build an EMPIRE. Although it did not happen overnight, she continued to build her life as if she had a systematic plan. She discovered that if you find the WHAT in life, the how-to develops. When she sets a goal for herself, she asks herself the who, what, when, where, how, and why questions. She firmly believes your effectiveness is increased when you know what you want and why you want it.

Of course, no one likes to be wrong, and self-correction can become difficult at times. However, when we do not know or understand the reason behind our ineffectiveness, we become resistant to change, especially when our backs are up against the wall.

It was through the bumps and bruises that Lisa gained her strength, wisdom, know-how, and Spiritual Alignment, *As It Pleased God*. To my amazement, Lisa built an Empire that blew my mind. I could not believe what she built in the midst of what people considered her downfall.

In essence, this woman secretly built an EMPIRE while people laughed, talked, ridiculed, mistreated, dogged her out, and ignored her, and the most amazing thing about it was that she did not try to defend herself. When they realized what she had accomplished, it was too late—the damage was already done. They were already on the AVOID list.

As *Women of Stature*, if you ever find yourself on the wrong road or at a dead-end, quickly re-evaluate the situation, find out where you went wrong, and turn around. But, more importantly, if life knocks you down, GET BACK UP AGAIN!

Inner Genius

The most valuable Possessions of the Spirit are GUARDED. One would say, guarded by what? It is more like, by WHOM! The Elements of LIFE...the Laws of Life..., and the Laws of the Spirit guard it. According to *The Lady's Code*, our *Inner Genius* is guarded as well. So, before we get into the *Writing on the Wall*, we need an understanding of our *Inner Genius* first, while on the *Playing Field*.

The Playing Field

Most often, we look for Spiritual Alignment, Guidance, or the Genius in others, yet we fail to realize our remarkable capabilities or creativity. Why would this happen to us? We are not being taught that we are Geniuses when we are born. Instead, we are dumbed down with limitations or spoken down to as if we are incapable of learning or grasping knowledge.

How can we make the *Inner Genius* make sense? The *Inner Genius* is like a mechanism hidden within our conscience or Spiritual Compass that comes forth by ACKNOWLEDGMENT and USE. If we do not know about it, we cannot use it properly, we cannot come into agreement with it, nor can we place a Spiritual Demand on it.

For example, we exhibit Genius capabilities within our mother's womb, such as being born at the appropriate time and functioning only with instincts until we are taught otherwise. I am pretty sure we can all agree that we do see the Genius capabilities in babies. We think their behavior is cute and funny, not realizing the impact or its power. If we dare to flip the switch, to teach them about their *Inner Genius* from conception, training them after birth to adapt to the Spiritual way of living, while preparing them for the world that we live in, we would be amazed at the creativity that would come forth.

We are so busy trying to save our kids from the world or keeping them safe from predators. While totally forgetting how to train or prepare them to live in this world, Mentally, Physically, Emotionally, and Spiritually.

Once the child becomes older, then we try to backtrack in our training process, especially when the *Inner Genius* has gone into its dormant state. Once this happens, it is guaranteed to be covered with layers of bad habits, negative debris, selfish character traits, intrusive traumas, or wayward behaviors. Unbeknown to most, this is why when we try to align ourselves Spiritually, chaos finds a way to wreak havoc in our lives.

Based upon many experiences, when we regraft our lives, all that debris, all of those bad habits, or negativity, we do not want to leave. They (meaning habits or vices) will fight for their territory. If we do not realize that we have power over them, they

The Playing Field

will control the psyche. For this reason, we must stay strong when deciding to move forward in our pursuit of Spiritual Awareness.

I know there are times when we cannot see the forest for the trees when the issues of life are upon us. If we allow our *Inner Genius* to guide us, *As It Pleases God*, we will find that the tools, information, provisions, and know-how will come freely.

In all simplicity, we must then work on ourselves, *As It Pleases God*, which means we cannot pick and choose what we want to work on. We must bring ourselves into proper alignment, Mentally, Physically, and Emotionally, using the Fruits of the Spirit. In addition, it works even better when using positive affirmations along with scripture to back it up. Once the two are in alignment, we must gear up our Spiritual Instincts with our Spiritual Eyes to see, our Spiritual Ears to hear, and with a Spiritual Guard over our mouths to understand and know when God is using others to:

- ☐ Speak life.
- ☐ Provide lessons.
- ☐ Provide correction.
- ☐ Provide wisdom.
- ☐ Provide guidance.
- ☐ Provide discernment of the wolves in sheep's clothing.

If we do not conduct or approach our Inner Genius in this manner with God first, self, and others, we will find that people will begin to use our flaws against us to create elements of insecurity to tarnish our self-esteem. Although we all have flaws, when we are in our genius moments, the enemy will use us or others to hinder or place doubt in the process. The blemishes of the inner self-talk can corrupt our positive thinking process, especially if we do not learn how to counteract it with positive affirmations or Biblical scriptures.

Once we are in this place, we do not have to worry about open or closed doors. All we need to worry about is being prepared and ready for our windows of opportunity. If we are prepared in this manner, the right doors will open, and the wrong doors will close. We cannot get emotionally angry, depressed, or frustrated when we do not get what we want. Just know that we will have everything we need in due time.

The moment we become big-headed or arrogant about being perfect, the conscience will give us a MENTAL FLASHBACK as a warning to correct our behaviors. If it is not corrected, we may get a few notches knocked off our belts. If still left uncorrected, the issues of life will bring us down to reality, exposing some, if not all of our skeletons.

Please do not allow your skeletons, weaknesses, or hang-ups to cause you to fall by the wayside because of a deaf ear to wisdom, a desire to make others feel bad, or to simply pick on them. Here is a story that touched me: As a child, Tina suffered from a reading disorder. She would read words that were not there, and her comprehension skills were extremely poor. If this was not enough, little Tina had a stutter as well. She was able to hide her flaws most of the time by staying silent, but when she did speak, she stumbled over her words.

This little child was already afraid of people, and now she has to deal with her classmates laughing at her, picking on her, and judging her because she could not articulate words very well. Although she was a brilliant little girl, her flaws made her feel inferior to those who appeared not to have any flaws at all. As a result, Tina shut down when she was around people; it was hard to get her to communicate. One would think this child was illiterate, but she was so far from that; she was an Honor Roll Student who graduated in the top 10% of her class.

I was puzzled by this little girl, but she said that if she opened her mouth, people would not think she was smart, so she would rather just 'BE SMART' instead. She said that she was not going to allow another child to stop her from getting her education, because she was tired of having to go to work after school and on the weekends picking oranges in the hot sun, then coming home dirty and stink. This was enough embarrassment for her, and she did not want to deal with anyone who did not understand her situation.

The Playing Field

To my dismay, this little girl never had a day off. She did not have the luxury of playing like an average child, and the only way God could change her life was through her ability to learn. Therefore, there was no need to talk or respond to anyone who was not more intelligent than her or who could not help her with her situation.

As time progressed, she learned how to respect her flaws while developing the discipline to become better. Her first step of discipline came when she started reading the Bible every day. As she read the Bible aloud, she would ask God to polish up her reading and comprehension skills. She did not become an expert reader overnight, but her discipline paid off quite well. She is now a speed reader with excellent comprehension skills that are a step above the rest. Oh, by the way, she no longer has a stutter. She prayed her stutter away by reciting, '*My tongue is a pen of a ready writer*' over and over until her stutter ceased. Today, this woman is so well-spoken; it is unbelievable how her respect and discipline enabled her to top the charts with her written and spoken words of wisdom.

The twist to the story was that she did not have a reading disorder; it was a GIFT! This child's mind was auto-correcting the words that should have been there. She was correcting mistakes as a child without realizing what she was doing. She was reading material like she would have written it, and the teacher yelling at her made her nervous.

Once Tina learned what she was doing, she was better able to correct it. Tina also learned that impediments are designed to drive greatness out of us, regardless of how it may seem at the time. As she looked back at the classmates who picked on her, she now realized that it was only a distraction to keep her from learning, as it was indeed her BLESSING IN DISGUISE.

An impediment is basically an obstruction or hindrance that will create a superficial image of weakness. When a weakness is exposed to others, most often, we retreat out of shame instead of taking our weaknesses and turning them into something extraordinary.

The Playing Field

A weakness exposed is better than a weakness covered up. As a matter of fact, an exposed weakness will give us more of an incentive to work on that area. But on the other hand, when our weakness is covered up, it is easier to overlook or make excuses for it. The truth is that we all have some form of impediment. Some are able to cover them up better than others, but in all reality, we all fall short.

According to *The Lady's Code*, an impediment cannot keep you blocked if you look for the BENEFIT, and most often, our *Inner Genius* is hidden under it. When you do this, greatness is inevitable, creating an open door of opportunity for you to take advantage of.

With this sort of faith, it will be tested! If we fail, we have to repeat the process until we get it right. In *The Lady's Code* or on *The Playing Field*, we cannot get caught up with frivolous people, places, and things that distract us from what we need to do, *As It Pleases God*. Why must we avoid them as Believers? Everything has a SEED.

The Ironclad Seed

To truly embrace *The Playing Ground* or *The Seed*, we must understand that no one is absolutely perfect; we are born into a world of sin, and we are all subject to human nature. If we look around us, we will see that we will never have to train a child to do wrong. They will naturally do the wrong thing, for *"Foolishness is bound up in the heart of a child."* Proverbs 22:15. Yet, it is our responsibility to teach them how to do right!

In *The Lady's Code: As It Pleases God*, this same concept applies to us as well...our minds will naturally gravitate to the negative until we train the mind to look for the positive automatically. How can *Women of Stature* break this cycle? By grabbing the IRON Cutters who do not mind sharing their iron-sharpening skills to mold us in Spirit and in Truth. *"As iron sharpens iron, So a man sharpens the countenance of his friend."* Proverbs 27:17.

The Playing Field

While on *The Playing Field*, let me ask an IRONCLAD question: If we were not able to speak a word or had a stutter, how would we make our voices heard? Wait, wait, wait, take a moment to think about that! Here is another IRONCLAD question: How would our lives reflect our passions from within if we could not say a word? If one can truthfully answer these questions and develop a plan without opening their mouth to say one word, they would find their hidden PURPOSE. How is this humanly possible? When we stop speaking verbally, our Inner Voice is still chatting away, whether we listen to it, silence it, or maximize it, positively or negatively, building us up, watering our seeds, or drowning us out.

From a Spiritual Perspective in *The Lady's Code*, when dealing with IRON Cutters or *Women of Stature*, we are forced to look within to use other parts of the brain we would not usually use. Then again, we may be encouraged to TAP into the Spiritual Essence of who we truly are in the Eye of God. How do we make this make sense? Our Spirit Man is *The Ironclad Seed* that is more powerful than any physical seed known to man. Unfortunately, we do not recognize it as such due to the lack of understanding or exposure, *As It Pleases God*.

Why do we need God to tap into *The Ironclad Seed*? Selfishness and debauchery without the Holy Trinity will forbid its exposure. Frankly, we are taught to downplay the Elements of the Spirit or depend on others for their anointing. In reality, we can also TAP into the anointing from within ourselves by following the rules of engagement, *As It Pleases God*.

Tap into what? I would say it is more like tapping into WHOM! By Divine Design, we must TAP into God first, and then into ourselves to extract the ANOINTED Gifts, Talents, Creativity, or Blueprint for our God-Given Mission. And sometimes, we cannot get to this point because we are running our mouths too much, overthinking, or making things complicated, drowning out His Spiritual Voice.

Here is the deal: We have *The Ironclad Seed* (accessed only through the Holy Trinity), and we have the ordinary seeds

The Playing Field

(accessed by anyone). Thus, we are going to deal with both interchangeably. In *The Lady's Code*, what can we do to have the best of both, *As It Pleases God*? Here is a list, but not limited to such:

- ☐ First, we need to become aware of our Spiritual Power.
- ☐ Secondly, we must own our truth by becoming transparent.
- ☐ Thirdly, we need to cast down vain thoughts, negativity, and confusion.
- ☐ Fourthly, we must utilize the Fruits of the Spirit with no exceptions to this rule.
- ☐ Fifthly, we must forgive, repent, pray, and have mercy on ourselves and others.
- ☐ Sixthly, we must become humbly thankful for everything, regardless of how it may appear.
- ☐ Seventhly, we must align our lives with scripture while creating a win-win to seal the Promises of God and govern our conversations accordingly.

It may seem as if it is a lot to do, but take one step at a time, mastering each one. Rest assured, after doing so, one would be able to contend with the Spiritual Elites on their level or above due to the OPENING of our Spiritual Eyes, Ears, and Mouth. And, when it comes down to *The Lady's Code*, it will create the *Iron Sharpening Love* that is equitable and unbreakable.

The value of our diversified seed lies in our ability to communicate effectively, positively, humbly, caringly, and openly. When we communicate, we must take the element of selfishness out of the equation to better understand everyone's right to their thoughts and individuality. Why is it important to remove selfishness? Our perceptions can become a hindrance to *The Ironclad Seed* if we allow our biased opinions to cast a negative cloud over the situation, circumstance, or event.

When it comes down to *The Ironclad Seed*, responsibility and opportunity work hand in hand, whether we like it or not. Most

The Playing Field

of us want opportunities in life without having to work or plant good, fruitful seeds. Psalm 22:30 states, "*A seed shall serve him; it shall be accounted to the Lord for a generation.*" Whatever seeds we are planting today, we pass down to our children positively or negatively. I hope that we stay on the positive side of the spectrum with the seeds we are sowing; if not, it could become detrimental to the innocent, who may pass the seeds on to the next generation.

If, for some reason, we are dealing with unfruitful or negative seeds, we have the opportunity to regraft the process of that seed. But before we do, we must understand the WHY of our seeds. If not, the growth will continue affecting *The Lady's Code* or our ability to read and interpret the *Writing on the Wall*. Then again, it could make our Spiritual Wall unstable, depending on the type of seed sown.

There is no competition when it comes down to digging deep within the depths of our souls for fact-finding information. In my opinion, no one can tell our story better than we can. No one can tell our truth better than we can. For this reason, when it comes down to self-analysis, self-deception is out of the equation. If, for some reason, we find ourselves superficially deceiving ourselves with fallacies, then we must question who else we are deceiving.

There is POWER in being true to thyself. Besides, when it comes down to the mind, we can make a lot of things appear real when they are not! Self-deception has become one of the biggest downfalls of the human race. Once this happens, our perceptions will kick into high gear, making everything appear real, when it is our way of superficially healing a hidden void, pain, abuse, or trauma. For the most part, this is why some are becoming super-sensitive about everything.

When we refuse to deal with our hidden issues, we subconsciously lash out at others about things that may not concern us, simply because they may have inadvertently touched a hidden place of pain, trauma, or insecurity. We can tiptoe around this issue all we like, but when it comes down to the seeds we are sowing, we must take a different approach with a positive twist.

Of course, no one is 100% right or 100% wrong all the time, which leaves room for imperfections in some areas of our lives. All

The Playing Field

in all, this is precisely why we all have strengths and weaknesses; if we have not noticed them by now, then live a little longer. For this reason, we need to extend mercy, compassion, and forgiveness into our seeds, around our seeds, through our seeds, over our seeds, and beneath our seeds. What is a seed? A seed can be our actions, reactions, thoughts, words, attitude, character, money, etc. Is it that serious? Yes, it is that serious! The seeds we are sowing today will determine our harvests for the future, with or without permitting them.

If we make it our business to exhibit the Fruits of the Spirit consistently, it will help us through the emotional hurt or trauma we do not understand. I do not expect everyone to be perfect at analyzing every thought, action, reaction, etc. I am expecting the Fruits of the Spirit to fill in the gap between what we know and what we do not. In *The Lady's Code*, the Fruits of the Spirit are similar to gap insurance, which covers us when we fall short.

When it is all said and done, if one knows they have unresolved issues from within, it behooves them to master the Fruits of the Spirit as a form of leverage before tackling the elements of real life. Is this a shortcut? Absolutely! As *Women of Stature*, we cannot go wrong with exhibiting Love, Joy, Peace, Patience, Kindness, Goodness, Faithfulness, Gentleness, and Self-Control. The Spiritual Default mechanisms hidden within *The Seed* will work in our favor if we simply use them, *As It Pleases God*!

How do we make the Fruits of the Spirit work for us? God has given us specific *Spiritual Tools* to assist us with everyday living. It is our responsibility to know what they are, why they are available to us, when to use them, how to apply them effectively, and where to use them. Plus, when our seeds are on the line, one must not tread on uncharted territory unequipped. Why should we avoid treading in such a manner? Unwarranted vendettas or undercover doxing sought to disrupt the Will of God or His Spiritual Decrees would cause the Spirit of Saul to fall upon us.

What is the Spirit of Saul? The Spirit of Saul refers to the evil Spirit that tormented King Saul in the Old Testament of the Bible. According to scripture, God sent the Spirit to Saul as a punishment for his disobedience, arrogance, and recklessness. Unfortunately,

The Playing Field

the Spirit caused Saul to feel anxious, unstable, troubled, aloof, and paranoid, depriving him of his happiness, joy, patience, self-control, and peace. Can this really happen to us if we break *The Lady's Code*? Absolutely. In short, this is why God is bringing this to the forefront to preserve the *Women of Stature*.

As the Spirit of the Lord is upon us, when it comes down to our seeds, breaking *The Lady's Code* by creating a roadblock for others out of spite, jealousy, envy, anger, fear, bias, or hatred, we will subject ourselves to invisible internal or external blockages that will appear when we least expect them.

Nevertheless, on the other hand, if we have a desire for our seeds to bear good fruit, we must positively clear the way for others as we clear our conscience of all negativity, deceit, debauchery, or attempts to railroad people for the same things we are guilty of.

What is the big deal, especially when we have free will? For a time such as this, sitting on the bench plotting to whitewash our faults or wrongdoings is not a good look in the Eye of God. Plus, we do not want to play around with any form of ill-willed intentions, causing LADY JUSTICE to reign down on us, reversing the plots, especially when throwing rocks and hiding our hands.

Even though we pretend to be innocent because we have leverage over the fallen or those who made mistakes, we have zero rights to break *The Lady's Code*, mainly when it covers us temporarily when we were dropping it like it was hot. Still, know this: In the Eye of God, He sees all and knows what our mouths have yet to admit.

Before going to the next chapter, *Writing on the Wall*, in the same way, I am reaching my hand out to you through this book. Do not DARE kick another sister when she is down...you help her back up and keep it moving in the Spirit of Excellence. Nor should you ever give way to the idiom: *'Hell hath no fury like a woman scorned.'*

Why should we avoid this idiom? First, it breaks *The Lady's Code*. Secondly, you can lose your Kingdom Status as a *Woman of Stature*. Thirdly, you forfeit your credibility and integrity. And lastly, due to rotten fruits, you will get a side-eye from God Almighty until repentance and forgiveness occur.

The Playing Field

To put it simply, do not play dirty because the Spiritual Veil has been lifted. So, *"Whoever digs a pit will fall into it, And he who rolls a stone will have it roll back on him."* Proverbs 26:27. If you think this is a joke, rest assured that God will make an example out of you. So, beware! You do not get free passes when plotting, scheming, or outing the personal private lives of others for personal gain or selfishness to satiate a vendetta or to avoid assuming responsibility for a wrongness.

Above all, we as women have gone through too much to turn against each other. For this reason, as *Women of Stature*, we stick together, *As It Pleases God*. Here are a few things that do not require a lot from us:

- ☐ Greet people.
- ☐ Smile often.
- ☐ Make eye contact when speaking to someone.
- ☐ Verbalize appreciation or love.
- ☐ Give gifts of appreciation or love.
- ☐ Proactively think about an individual's needs.
- ☐ Pay attention to the moods and offer positive encouragement.
- ☐ An appropriate, subtle, natural touch.
- ☐ A kiss, hug, or tickle works well.
- ☐ Holding someone when appropriate.
- ☐ The surprises are great.
- ☐ Notes are awesome.
- ☐ Eat together.
- ☐ Pray together.
- ☐ Play together.
- ☐ Never appear busy, even if you are. Patience is GOLDEN.
- ☐ Set aside time for a person, place, or thing.
- ☐ Communicate often.
- ☐ Play or have fun often.
- ☐ Do not be afraid to grab someone's hand.
- ☐ Sincerely ask about a person's well-being.
- ☐ Look for ways to be a BLESSING.
- ☐ Always be hopeful.

The Playing Field

☐ Be warm and sincere with others.

What does this checklist have to do with anything? When life is lifing, we all need subtle reminders of ways to extend acts of kindness, love, and togetherness.

Kindness, Love, and Togetherness

When on *The Playing Field*, can acts of kindness, love, and togetherness really work on our behalf as Believers? In today's fast-paced world, where division, disrespectfulness, and discord often capture our attention negatively, the timeless virtues of kindness, love, and togetherness have never been more crucial for the human race than right now. For many Believers, these qualities are not just moral imperatives; they are POWERFUL TOOLS and COMPONENTS that can shape the psyche, our relationships, homes, families, communities, and, ultimately, the world if we dare to master the ability to read the *Writing on the Wall*.

Scientifically, within both the giver and the receiver, love is the most profound and potent force in our faith. Without it, we become openly or privately dysfunctional due to the lack of oxytocin (The Love or Bonding Hormone) being released into the brain.

What if we do not need this love hormone, or we are sick of this love thing? Fortunately, we were prewired with this hormonal chemical for the sake of our Heaven on Earth Experience, in addition to the need for safety and security. From a Divine Perspective, we would definitely want this hormone to flow properly, connecting us to God, *Spirit to Spirit*. By far, in my opinion, it keeps us from approaching Him grumpily, hatefully, ungratefully, selfishly, pompously, or rudely.

Above all, the release of oxytocin aids in our transformative efforts, helping us break down barriers, heal wounds, overcome trauma, inspire hope in even the most challenging situations, bridge divides, promote unity, and serve as a beacon of light during dark, challenging times. Unbeknown to most, it also aids in the release of other positive chemicals within the body, such as the release of dopamine, which is associated with pleasure and reward, and serotonin, which helps regulate our moods. Additionally, oxytocin can promote the release of other neuropeptides and hormones, such as vasopressin, which is linked to social behavior and bonding. The interactions between these chemicals contribute to feelings of trust, empathy, and social connection.

In the Eye of God, it is always best to begin with oxytocin. Why should we focus on this before all of the other chemicals? First, it has a direct connection to the Fruits of the Spirit through the use of them. Secondly, it is associated with the touch and connection needed to seal the Supernatural Components of our DNA that Science has yet to crack the code on. Lastly, it is CONNECTED to the Breath of Life, having enough power to combat or contain the release of cortisol within the human body.

What does cortisol have to do with what we are discussing here? Although cortisol is essential for survival, regulating our metabolism, blood sugar levels, and immune responses, it must still be understood and regulated. Unfortunately, most of our issues and health problems are related to the untimely or over-release of cortisol within the human body due to chronic stress or fatigue. In *The Lady's Code: As It Pleases God*, we must familiarize ourselves with this stress hormone to ensure that an overproduction or prolonged release of cortisol does not lead to a range of health issues. For this reason, the Fruits of the Spirit provide us with a way of escape if we MASTER using them when reading *The Writing on the Wall*.

Path to Mastery in Challenging Times

When on *The Playing Field* of life, it can become a little tricky in the navigational process when we are both a player and a spectator. Spiritually Speaking, as we maneuver through life, it is only wise to get all of our ducks in a row to ensure we do not become swept away by the issues of life.

The Playing Field

Why must we get our ducks in a row as Believers, especially when we are not a duck? Regardless of what we are, our instincts, discernment, responses, and decision-making skills will be put to the ultimate test. If we do not learn how to read the *Writing on the Wall*, the unexpected shifts will catch us off guard with chaos, confusion, and disbelief.

What does all of this mean? As *Women of Stature*, when on any *Path of Mastery*, organization, proactiveness, and preparation are a must to preserve the human psyche. For this reason, in *The Lady's Code*, my goal is to prepare you to turn your internal alignment into Divine Alignment, *As It Pleases God*. When dealing with or engaging in relational support systems with the Holy Trinity, yourself, and others, you cannot afford to drop the ball on the playing field, not now, not ever!

Every stepping stone has a lesson or message of Divine Wisdom attached to it, and if our duckies are ducking out, we will miss the vital information needed for our next step. More importantly, if we do not step up our game, *As It Pleases God*, the invitation to grow, understand, and evolve cannot be extended.

What is the purpose of not receiving an invite as a faithful Believer? Most often, an invitation cannot be extended due to our unreadiness, distractions, or disobedience. So, it behooves us to learn how to read *The Writing on the Wall* in every aspect of our lives to ensure our people skills are on point, balanced, and Spiritually Cued up, ready to go despite any challenges headed our way.

In this Spiritual Stance, we must pay attention with a discerning eye to our surroundings, relationships, behaviors, conversations, beliefs, and thoughts to ensure our emotional undercurrents are not drowning out our Spiritual Voice with quacking. Why is this so important when on The Playing Field? When quacking like a duck, in the Eye of God, this is similar to babbling with a misunderstanding in communication of what is expected of us. If this is the case while attempting to outsmart Him, He will change the language on us at the drop of a dime, similar to what happened in the story of the Tower of Babel found in Genesis 11:1-9.

The Playing Field

According to the Heavenly of Heavens, there are limits placed on our self-made or self-induced determination and get-up-and-go, especially when thinking we are smarter than our Creator. We must remember that God's sovereignty overrides our human endeavors any day of the week. Therefore, it is only wise to add Him into the equation proactively. But do not worry; in *The Lady's Code*, I will share how to do things God's way to prevent any form of scattering, Mentally, Physically, Emotionally, or Spiritually.

So, if you are ready to step up your game with Divine Intervention, *As It Pleases God*, let us get a better understanding of *The Writing on the Wall* from a Divine Perspective.

CHAPTER 2

WRITING ON THE WALL

In every relationship, be it personal, professional, or Spiritual, there will always be a paper trail. If we fail to read it, we cannot blame anyone for its content. Is it that we choose the wrong individuals over and over again? Is it that we have bad taste in choosing a mate? Is it that we are settling for less? Is it that we are looking for love in all the wrong places? Is it that we are attracting people who are too much like us? Is it that we behave in a particular way that makes a perfectly great mate leave us? Is it that we are downright destructive in a relationship?

The answers to our questions in life or a relationship will always be *Written on the Wall* with a paper trail. Amazingly, no one is exempt from these writings. However, as *Women of Stature*, it is our responsibility to OWN our truth by paying attention to what is being written, why it is being written, how it is written, where it is written, and when it is written to avoid breaking *The Lady's Code*.

What makes *The Lady's Code* so important? As *Women of Stature*, we are held to a higher standard in the Eye of God. In light of this, we must pay attention, listen, learn, grow, and help others, *As It Pleases Him* with kindness, grace, mercy, compassion, and forgiveness. Here is *The Lady's Code*'s expectation: *"She opens her mouth with wisdom, and on her tongue is the law of kindness."* Proverbs 31:26. Rest assured, if we attempt to read the *Writing on the Wall* with unaddressed or unrepentant anger, hatefulness, rudeness, and debauchery, we will read it wrong. Why would we read it wrong? It is CODED. Exhibiting the Fruits of the Spirit and Christlike Character, *As It Pleases God*, helps us to defrag, decode, or remove the veil. Unfortunately, this is how we get relationships wrong while appearing right.

As life would have it, after a failure in a relationship, some would think that it is a matter of misfortune, a generational curse, or a matter of emotional or mental dysfunction. Now, it is a possibility that those factors may have an element of truth to them, depending upon the seeds that we have sown throughout our past. But, for the most part, failure and success are from the same seed; it is merely a matter of owning our actions, reactions, and thoughts and overcoming our superficial limitations or perceptions.

In other words, our failed relationships really prepare us for successful ones if we learn from them and allow them to have a positive effect on us. As the *Writing on the Wall* will concur, once we accept this type of positive mindset, we will unawaringly draw goodness toward us.

The art of our true success is based on the Biblical Principles of Seedtime and Harvest, or the Law of Reciprocity. For this reason, we must plant our seeds of good relations in our time of harvest to ensure that our blessings remain.

The Lady's Code firmly believes that living life is no joke, and it is a shame to allow an unused or misused blessing, gift, or calling to fall by the wayside of our inability to relate to others. So, every wall in this book allows you to embrace the art of successful living by learning how to motivate others through your wisdom, creativity, ambitions, or skills without allowing bragging or boasting to cloud your end result.

The *Writing on the Wall* Principle is basically a forewarning of things to come before we get caught up. It is often said that warning comes before destruction. *"Surely the Lord God does nothing, unless He reveals His secret to His servants the prophets."* Amos 3:7. If one

Writing On The Wall

has not noticed by now, God warns us about everything that will bring about harm to us; most often, we do not listen or take heed to it. Therefore, it is my reasonable service to share the concept of the *Writing on the Wall* Principle, *As It Pleases God*.

If one builds a house, what is it that holds the roof on the house? Of course, it is the walls that keep it from caving in. Well, this same concept applies to our TEMPLES (the body). A house with a shaky foundation, a house without walls, a house that leaves the door open, a house without a roof, and a house without a Spiritual Relationship with God will become a problematic household by default. When our house becomes prone to problems, we will begin to look for things on the outside to fill the void, as opposed to bringing some sort of resolve to the situation, circumstance, or event.

In order to build the best relationships ever, you must offer encouragement to yourself and others while making your house a home by focusing, building, and maintaining your own house without condemning others for what they have chosen to do behind closed doors. If someone is not bringing kindness, love, and peace to your home, it is a possibility that you may need to show them to the door. It would be best if you had walls built, not to block you in, but to protect your well-being.

The key takeaway is that *The Lady's Code* maintains its STANCE on 4 Divine Principles:

- ☐ **Wall of Prophecy**: *"Before destruction the heart of a man is haughty, And before honor is humility."* Proverbs 18:12.
- ☐ **Wall of Thinking**: *"He who answers a matter before he hears it, It is folly and shame to him."* Proverbs 18:13.
- ☐ **Wall of A Proper Perspective**: *'The spirit of a man will sustain him in sickness, But who can bear a broken spirit?"* Proverbs 18:14.
- ☐ **Wall of Busyness**: *"The heart of the prudent acquires knowledge, And the ear of the wise seeks knowledge."* Proverbs 18:15.

Writing On The Wall

What is the purpose of these 4 Principles of *The Lady's Code*? As *Women of Stature*, we want to illuminate this Spiritual Seal: *"A man's gift makes room for him, And brings him before great men."* Proverbs 18:16. Therefore, if we humbly pay attention to the nudges of God while thinking, listening, learning, and growing, *As It Pleases Him*, using the Fruits of the Spirit and behaving Christlike, nothing or no one can hold us back.

Wall of Prophecy

We often do not realize that we are a self-fulfilling prophecy. It is said, *"Life and death are in the power of the tongue and those who love it will eat its fruit."* Proverbs 18:21. Although most individuals do not believe this Proverbial Scripture. Why would they not believe it? If they did, they would not speak certain things over themselves, as well as their spouse, children, friends, etc.

The truth is that we are defeated in a relationship by what we secretly say or think to ourselves. This back-and-forth conversation we have, or the mental chatter, must come to an abrupt end. People are able to pick up on damaging thoughts, emotions, insecurities, as well as negative energy, even if they are trying to hide them. Our *Wall of Prophecy* is revealed in our body language, gestures, eye contact, facial expressions, tone of voice, etc.; they are all powerful forms of communication that reveal our prophecy without us having to say one word.

Your inner dialogue must become positive if you want people to become magnets to you or what you have to offer. Trust that positive body language speaks volumes by merely adding in great posture, making eye contact, standing straight, not crossing our arms or legs, smiling, or a simple nod of affirmation. Simple gestures, as such, indicate confidence, friendliness, affluence, and self-assurance. Regardless of how you may or may not feel about dating or mating, exhibiting confident behavior will put your insecurities at bay, especially if you have a habit of second-guessing yourself.

Writing On The Wall

What does our body language have to do with the *Wall of Prophecy*? In the Kingdom, our body language must align with our members; if not, we will appear dull or cold. *"For as we have many members in one body, but all the members do not have the same function, so we, being many, are one body in Christ, and individually members of one another. Having then gifts differing according to the grace that is given to us, let us use them: if prophecy, let us prophesy in proportion to our faith."* Romans 12:4-6.

The Lady's Code in the *Wall of Prophecy* is predicated on faith. In all simplicity, little faith limits prophecy, but a lot of faith equates to more prophecy. To say the least, it is imperative to develop our faith, *As It Pleases God*.

What is faith? In the Eye of God, faith is a deep and unwavering trust in God's character, His promises, and His Divinely Blueprinted Plan for our lives. It is the belief that God is who He says He is and that He will do what He promises to do. Spiritually, we have no reason to doubt Him. Faith is often described as a GIFT from God that keeps on giving as long as we BELIEVE and take ACTION.

According to the Heavenly of Heavens, faith is the foundation of our *Spirit to Spirit* Relationship with God. Now, my question is, 'What are your thoughts on faith?' 'Do you use your faith like God intended?' When we face trials, adversities, or hardships, it is our faith that can give us the courage to persevere. In addition, the comfort of knowing that we are not alone assures our hope, growth, and transformation. As a part of *The Lady's Code: As It Pleases God*, here are practical tips on how to build faith, but not limited to such:

- ☐ Develop a *Spirit to Spirit* Relationship with your Heavenly Father.
- ☐ Pray, forgive, meditate, and repent regularly.
- ☐ Read and study the Bible.
- ☐ Use the Fruits of the Spirit to understand God's charactorial expectations.
- ☐ Attend church services.

Writing On The Wall

- ☐ Worship God through music, art, and other creative expressions.
- ☐ Share your faith with others.
- ☐ Unselfishly serve others through acts of kindness and compassion.
- ☐ Seek reconciliation with others.
- ☐ Live a life of integrity and honesty.
- ☐ Trust in God's plan for your life.
- ☐ Surrender your will to His Divine Will.
- ☐ Develop an attitude of gratitude and thankfulness.
- ☐ Practice humility and avoid pride and arrogance.
- ☐ Build relationships with other Believers.
- ☐ Seek accountability by taking responsibility.
- ☐ Seek to glorify and give thanks to God in all that you do.
- ☐ Overcome fear and anxiety.
- ☐ Trust in God's protection and provision.
- ☐ Persevere through trials and hardships by pinpointing the win-win.
- ☐ Reverse negativity with positivity.
- ☐ Use positive affirmations.
- ☐ Develop obedience to God.
- ☐ Create a positive mental mindset, *As It Pleases God*.

Will this list help build faith? With this checklist, it is indeed a great start. Once again, faith requires ACTION; therefore, you must put your faith to use. When we avoid taking action, we will find that our lives tend to become a little more complicated, especially when life is demanding more from us. In my opinion, our lives will become a lot easier if we take action with a plan in place before jumping into things blindly or unquestioningly. Of course, there are times when we must think on our feet, but when it comes down to *The Lady's Code: As It Pleases God*, we must have a Plan of Action, a System, or a Strategy in place, or it may not yield the GREATNESS that we rightly deserve.

With *The Lady's Code*, we will always have something to work on or work at; therefore, we should not become so hard on ourselves when we fall short. Please pick up the pieces, dust yourself off, look for the good, focus on the positive, and keep it moving in the Spirit of Excellence. Trust me, that piece that did not work will work when it is in the right groove of your Life Puzzle.

Life Puzzles are designed to create a Picture-Perfect life if we allow the positive aspects of our lives to supersede the negative. In addition, if we focus on bringing forth *The Lady's Code: As It Pleases God*, we will find that it will become our NAVIGATIONAL TOOL to Greatness. According to the Heavenly of Heavens, regardless of whether you understand your life's puzzle or not, you already have what you need inside of you. Believe it and take action, *As It Pleases Him*, and it will come forth as pure GOLD...I am living proof.

Now that you have an understanding of a few things, it is safe to move on to other things you may be tiptoeing around. In *The Lady's Code*, just as the *Wall of Prophecy* begins with faith, your faith begins with the way you THINK.

Wall of Thinking

The Art of Thinking is just as important as the Art of Breathing, and most often, we will not realize their value until we have to fight for every rational thought and breath we take. When we take the process of thinking for granted, we will find that the guard over our mouths will become a gateway to negativity, depriving us of our Spiritual Rights to *The Lady's Code*.

On the other hand, if we guard our thoughts and redirect them to the positive, we can better control what comes out of our mouths, giving us better control over our lives by default. In my opinion, it is hard to embarrass ourselves if we are following *The Lady's Code: As It Pleases God*. If we follow our emotions without consulting our Inner Guide, we will subject ourselves to the atrocities of not being able to mastermind our unique perspectives.

As life would have it, on the *Wall of Thinking*, we are all searching for meaning in some way, shape, or form. We all have a hidden desire to be something, and we all have a desire to have access to the desires of our hearts.

Writing On The Wall

What do we do when we find ourselves searching for the meaning of life? Do we doubt ourselves, or do we go for it? For one, in *The Lady's Code*, there is no room for doubt. Secondly, when going for it, we must know what we are going for and the reasons why. If not, we will find ourselves jumping from one thing or one person to the next, leaving us with an even bigger void.

In my opinion, we must slow down and think through the meaning process while conducting a self-analysis, a thought analysis, an emotional analysis, a character analysis, as well as a behavioral analysis. If not, the trial-and-error process could lead us on a journey that could become detrimental to what we are actually searching for. Better yet, it may lead us away from our mission in life. The search may be different for each of us, but the Life Principles, the Biblical Precepts, and the Spiritual Laws do not change. In other words, when it comes down to accessing *The Lady's Code*, there are Spiritual Rules that we must follow and particular character traits we must possess.

The emptiness we may experience is often kept secret from those around us, yet they experience the unnecessary wrath of our inner longings. Is this fair? Absolutely not! At the same time, we cannot really blame ourselves if we do not understand what is taking place, right? Absolutely not, as long as we are attempting to help ourselves! It is our responsibility to understand what is taking place and the reasons why. Nonetheless, if we carry on with our lives, ignoring the emptiness from within while allowing negativity to permeate our lives, as well as the lives of others, then we have a real problem.

For example, let us take a look at King Solomon, the son of King David, in Ecclesiastes 1:1-11. He explains how everything in life can feel meaningless when we have everything that our heart desires and we steer away from our purpose. Trust me, when depression hits a WISE MAN, it is indeed a blow to the ego!

Solomon was honest with his feelings to give us a better understanding of how we are not immune to feeling this way and how to recognize when we get to this point in life. I have always heard, 'Be wary of someone who has nothing to lose because they will be quick to draw others into the web of deceit.'

Writing On The Wall

In *The Lady's Code*, we do not have to become a victim in such a manner. We can avoid getting to this point in life or getting caught up by simply acknowledging where we are and being willing to do something about it.

We are who we are, right? Absolutely! In being who we are, we do not get a free pass on things we ignore or when we capitalize on our negative characteristics. Nevertheless, it is also a matter of perspective. We must make a conscious attempt to become positively better at being who we are. If not, we will fill our inner void with power, money, sex, status, relationships, having a good time, or worldliness. Clearly, there is nothing wrong with these things, but they must be put into their proper perspective without filling a void.

Furthermore, we cannot use them as a distraction to keep us from following the Will of God. Proverbs 3:13 tells us, "*Happy is the man that finds wisdom and the man that gets an understanding.*" Therefore, in order to become truly happy in life, we must seek an understanding, *As It Pleases God*, to gain WISDOM!

How do we know if we have a void? The most common way to know if we have a void is to check our thoughts. Is it that simple? Absolutely! Negative thoughts and unhinged mental chatter are an automatic indication of some sort of void within the psyche. Here are a few other indications, but not limited to such:

- ☐ When we focus on the problem, not the solution.
- ☐ When we become extra sensitive about others' opinions.
- ☐ When our perception shifts to the negative.
- ☐ When we reject someone who is actually trying to help.
- ☐ When we reject the WISDOM of others.
- ☐ When we make a mountain out of a molehill.
- ☐ When we are out of control, Mentally or Emotionally.
- ☐ When we are quick to blame others, who are NOT at fault.
- ☐ When we are quick to point out others' mistakes.
- ☐ When we refuse to put ourselves in the shoes of others.
- ☐ When we think we are better or superior to others.
- ☐ When we are a control freak or enjoy running the show.
- ☐ When we constantly bring up the past as leverage.

Writing On The Wall

- ☐ When we are constantly judging or degrading others.
- ☐ When we are not able to give or accept compliments.
- ☐ When we are unable to apologize.
- ☐ When we are unable to say 'Please' or 'Thank you.'
- ☐ When we go from relationship to relationship.
- ☐ When we are always in the middle of chaotic confusion.
- ☐ When we cannot control our tempers.
- ☐ When we cannot hold our tongues.
- ☐ When we are always on edge.
- ☐ When we use a medical condition to excuse misbehavior.
- ☐ When we are exhausting others with our behaviors.
- ☐ When we constantly engage in complaining or folly.
- ☐ When we are always on the defensive and doubting others.
- ☐ When we think everyone is a liar.
- ☐ When we are outright rude.
- ☐ When we are stressed over things that we cannot change.
- ☐ When we are holding on to life's baggage or the past.
- ☐ When we are battling with depression.
- ☐ When we have a hard time being alone or sitting in silence.
- ☐ When we close ourselves off to those who want to be a part of our lives.

We can sugarcoat or cover up whatever we need to conceal all we want! A negative charge is a minus sign or a zero for a reason! If we do not become aware of this one factor, we will zap our own energy without realizing what is taking place. For this reason, we must make a conscious attempt to stay on the positive side of the spectrum.

If one is not accustomed to being positive, it will feel weird. However, when it comes down to *The Lady's Code*, it requires a positive current. We must become conscious of our negative state of mind while replacing it immediately with a positive thought or affirmation. Now, here are a few other things we can do to stay positive, but not limited to such:

Writing On The Wall

- [ ] We must remember that we choose to be and remain positive.
- [ ] We must understand we are in control of our thoughts, emotions, and words.
- [ ] We must exhibit gratitude; saying 'Please' and 'Thank you' will do the trick.
- [ ] We must exhibit the Fruits of the Spirit.
- [ ] We must refuse to complain. Simply state the concern, find the solution, and move on.
- [ ] We must know and understand our triggers to ensure that we are able to maintain our self-control at all times.
- [ ] We must know and understand what is positive and what is considered negative, according to scripture.
- [ ] Do not use the past as leverage against someone.
- [ ] We must set a guard over our mouths. We must think before we speak.
- [ ] Do not gossip. It is a thin line in the gossip factor; however, when spreading the tea, exercise extreme caution. If it does not concern us or the person we are speaking with, then it is our reasonable service to stop the conversation with fact-finding questions. It is never a good thing to slander others intentionally!
- [ ] We must exhibit mercy and compassion to others.
- [ ] We must forgive ourselves and others with no strings attached.
- [ ] We must love our neighbors as ourselves.
- [ ] We must be willing to help others when it is in our power to do so.
- [ ] We must make it our business to laugh and smile; it is medicine for the soul.
- [ ] We must refuse to pass judgment, especially without putting ourselves in the person's shoes.
- [ ] We must be supportive.
- [ ] We must find a quick exit when dealing with troublemakers or toxic people.
- [ ] We must be willing to understand and listen without providing a solution. There are times when we only need

to be heard. Remember, all the answers to our life's dilemmas are already within.
- ☐ We must remain calm at all times. We can exude our authority without acting ugly!
- ☐ We must always cast down jealousy and envy.
- ☐ We must make it our business not to take things personally. We never know what a person is secretly going through or where they came from. Therefore, we must create a positive shield to ensure that their energy does not penetrate us.
- ☐ We must eat healthily and take care of ourselves.
- ☐ We must understand that everything in life has a lesson or a BLESSING attached to it.
- ☐ We must understand that we are our best brand, and people are watching and emulating us.
- ☐ We must understand and track our negative thought patterns.
- ☐ We must be willing to walk away from a negative situation, circumstance, or event.
- ☐ We must set a guard over our egos.

Of course, there are more; however, this gives us an understanding of what we need to do for ourselves in order to protect our sanity and *The Lady's Code: As It Pleases God*.

According to the Heavenly of Heavens, we are all here to learn, grow, and share. The moment we cease to do so, we will find our lives will begin to become chaotic. If one does not believe it, simply pay attention to the days when we are selfish as opposed to the days when we are sharing. There is a big difference in the way we feel!

From experience, the most selfish people are indeed the most secretly depressed. Thus, we must pay attention to this overlooked primitive characteristic of selfishness; it is one of our greatest hidden downfalls that goes unrecognized by most.

I have consulted with great, well-to-do individuals who could not understand why they were not getting their breakthroughs.

Writing On The Wall

During my analysis, I recognized they were outright selfish, Mentally, Emotionally, Physically, and Spiritually. I advise that when it comes down to *The Lady's Code*, life is not about us; it is about purpose, Divine Purpose, to be exact.

We are the Vessels that God uses to reach those who are in need. If we are consumed with the Spirit of Selfishness, it leads to other negative attributes. He cannot and will not use us until we deal with our inner issues, and most often, the emptiness or pressure we are feeling is usually CHASTISEMENT. *"For whom the Lord loves he corrects; even as a father, the son in whom he delights."* Proverbs 3:12. Unfortunately, this is precisely why we find ourselves repeating lessons we have the opportunity to get right the first time around.

In the pursuit of meaning, we must understand, according to Genesis 1:26, that we are created in the image of God, and we have the authority to rule over ourselves, as well as the things around us. But, more importantly, according to Psalms 8:5, we are created a little lower than Angels. This means God has a strategic order set for us, as well as our Divine Mission. If we follow the passion from within, we will be crowned with glory and honor. However, on the flip side of the coin, if we think we are exempt from the reason why we are here, think again.

If we allow a negative self-image to blind us from our true Divine Purpose, we often suffer an inner struggle from within, along with major confusion or chaos. Before I move on, here are a few things we should understand, but not limited to such:

- ☐ On the *Wall of Thinking*, we are relational by design. According to Genesis 2:18, *"The Lord said, it is not good for the man to be alone. I will make a helper suitable for him."* Keep in mind that not everyone we meet is designed to be in a relationship with us. We cannot pick up anyone or anything and expect the relationship to work. We must bring God into the equation to help us in our choices.

- ☐ On the *Wall of Thinking*, we are designed to work for a specific purpose, to nurture or take care of something or someone. According to Genesis 2:15, it says, *"The Lord God took the man and put him in the Garden of Eden to work it and take care of it."* Now, whatever our 'it' is, it is our responsibility to find it, work on it, or work toward it.

- On the *Wall of Thinking*, we are designed to communicate with each other. *"Let us consider one another in order to stir up love and good works, not forsaking the assembling of ourselves together."* Hebrews 10:24-25. Most people associate this with going to church; in my opinion, this is so far from the truth.

  It is the church folks who are quick to avoid us, especially if they feel as if we have a problem, we are cursed, or we are indulging in sinful behavior. Is it not the church that is keeping us divided into denominations? Is it not the church that crucifies us when we are in dire need of help? I am just saying! We have to do better than this! Nevertheless, this is all about communicating with each other and building relationships of substance, as we *"Let our speech always be gracious, seasoned with salt, so that we may know how we ought to answer each person."* Colossians 4:6.

  If we are always in the church and we cannot communicate effectively, then what do we really have? Chaos in the House of God. We must master our ability to communicate with others inside and outside the Walls of God.

- On the *Wall of Thinking*, we are designed to avoid specific conversations or intentionally inflicting wounds with what is coming out of our mouths. According to 2 Timothy 2:16, *"Avoid irreverent babble, for it will lead people into more and more ungodliness."* When we are rude, degrading, or negative, it is possible to lead the innocent into destruction based on the bullying tactic of control.

Writing On The Wall

☐ On the *Wall of Thinking*, we are designed to worship God. According to Psalm 37:4, we must *"delight ourselves in the Lord, and He will give us the desires of our heart."* However, when we worship Him, we must *"worship Him in SPIRIT and TRUTH."* John 4:24. We cannot fake the funk when it comes down to worship; God knows our hearts better than we do.

☐ On the *Wall of Thinking*, we are required to love one another. According to 1 Peter 4:8, *"Above all, keep loving one another earnestly, since love covers a multitude of sins."* Hate divides us, whereas love brings us together. If, for some reason, we are having a battle with our fears, it is a possibility our Elements of Love are off balance.

What does love have to do with fear? According to scripture, they are definitely related. It says in 1 John 4:18, *"There is no fear in love, but perfect love casts out fear. For fear has to do with punishment, and whoever fears has not been perfected in love."* In my opinion, this is a great way to pinpoint our fears, as well as our inability to give and receive love effectively, or the fear of loving others without conditions.

☐ On the *Wall of Thinking*, we function best when we are at peace with ourselves. Without it, we will find ourselves all over the place, doing things we should not be doing.

On this note, with the *Wall of Thinking*, I totally understand that no one is 100% positive all the time. What I also understand is that we can use the 80/20 rule of being positive 80% of the time while working on the 20% of the negative. This process will ensure we are not beating ourselves up about perfection. Once we become stronger in this area, our ratio will become 90/10, 95/5, and then 99/1.

Why can we not have 100% positive thoughts? Unrealistic expectations create disappointment, confusion, failure, and delusional impulses. We must keep in mind that we are humans with human emotions, human thoughts, and human nature, living in a world of good and evil! With this being said, we have choices; it is also the reason we need to repent, forgive, pray, and fast on occasion.

If, for some reason, we are feeling discouraged, distracted, or confused about our purpose in life, we must regraft our character flaws. If not, it will make us feel as if we are not good enough, strong enough, educated enough, smart enough, wise enough, rich enough, and the list goes on. However, according to *The Lady's Code*, they are all lies...everything we need is already within.

For me, my Divine Purpose would not allow me to throw in the towel. It shook my life upside down until I yielded to the calling. Once I yielded, I spent many years in Spiritual Training—I mean serious training!

As a matter of fact, I thought my intense training process would never end. As God would have it, here we are with the *As It Pleases God®* Movement. Above all, it provided a platform for me to understand that we are all a work-in-progress on a moment-by-moment basis. More importantly, as the Kingdom of Heaven is on my side, I came out of my trials, training, and traumas with this book, *The Lady's Code: As It Pleases God*, with the information to transform lives for the Greater Good from the least to the greatest.

Wall of a Proper Perspective

In *The Lady's Code: As It Pleases God*, we all want to live in a perfect world, but we all know it is impossible to do so. However, we do have the power to protect, fine-tune, and govern our neck of the woods or our inner circle. This circle is not designed to discriminate; it is designed to protect *The Lady's Code*. There is no need to be unkind, rude, or abrasive with others if they do not fit in or disrupt our Spirit. As *Women of Stature*, we should always exercise kindness and humility while finding an exit before it zaps our positive energy or power. With this being said, we can tiptoe around *The Lady's Code* or our Inner Circle all we want. But when

Writing On The Wall

it comes down to protecting our sanity, we must cast down negativity and chaos while ushering in positivity and peace.

Our lessons will be hurled at us when we least expect them, and we need to be ready, willing, and able to glean Divine Wisdom. If not, we may never get a second chance at that particular fleeting moment of Divine Wisdom. For this reason, in *The Lady's Code*, we must always have pen and paper ready to capture unique thoughts, ideas, and concepts, even if they do not make sense at the time.

Why must we document, especially if we do not understand something? There are things we may not be able to understand until we are unveiled in three ways:

- ☐ Unveiling our **Spiritual Eyes** to see what our physical eyes cannot see.
- ☐ Unveiling our **Spiritual Ears** to hear what our physical ears cannot hear.
- ☐ Unveiling our **Spiritual Tongue** to speak what our physical tongue cannot speak.

Is this real? Absolutely! However, as *Women of Stature*, our Spiritual Eyes, Ears, and Tongue must be trained to see, hear, and speak correctly, *As It Pleases God*! If one is not trained in this area, they could create problems or unintentional curses.

In *The Lady's Code: As It Pleases God*, there are Spiritual Rules, Concepts, Laws, and Precepts guarding our Divine Wisdom on the *Wall of a Proper Perspective*. For example, if one is mistreating people, do we think God will empower this person to feed or mislead His sheep? Maybe or maybe not, depending upon the purpose; we do not know who or what God may use. If God allows it, He may use it as a testimony or a lesson to others. There are times when God will drive us out of the camp to teach us a lesson, as he did with Mariam, Moses' sister, in Numbers 12:15. This is where she was shut out of the camp for seven days due to leprosy, as well as her disrespectfulness.

If one is violating Spiritual Laws, they must still account for it. Yes, we do have grace and mercy to fall back on, but it does not exempt us from the Spiritual Laws pertaining to what God hates. Before I move on with *The Lady's Code*, I need to advise on the seven things that will get us in serious trouble with God. It is located in Proverbs 6:16-19.

- ☐ Arrogance.
- ☐ Lying tongue.
- ☐ Hands that shed innocent blood.
- ☐ A heart that devises wicked schemes.
- ☐ Feet that are swift to do evil.
- ☐ Bearing false witness.
- ☐ A person who stirs up strife among brethren.

If we think what we are doing today does not matter, then think again. Our invisible dots of today connect to the dots of tomorrow. The invisible dots of our tomorrows are all interconnected with our Predestined Blueprint.

When our perspective is foggy, it has a way of preventing us from clearly envisioning the desires of our hearts. In so many words, we may become confused or doubtful regarding our wants, needs, or expectations in life. When or if this happens, it will cause us to settle for temporary comfort, ending in the appearance of a setback, failure, affair, broken relationship, or divorce.

As simple as it may seem, it is tough for others to understand and relate to us when we do not know how to relate to ourselves effectively. Often enough, it is in our nature to want people to understand our wants, needs, and desires as if they are mind readers. In all seriousness, if we LACK the understanding of who we are from the inside out while NOT being able to articulate it accordingly, then we set ourselves up for disappointment or shattered expectations.

Relationally speaking, your best bet is to know and understand yourself first. Then, you need to pinpoint what you want, need, and desire in and out of a relationship, leaving little or no room for doubt or false expectations to have their way in your life. Doing so will ensure that you can please yourself while satisfying those with you are with as well.

When you can change your perspective on your life, you are then able to shift your vision at the drop of a dime or remain devoted without being moved negatively. By doing so, it helps to create a more desirable result rather than having history repeat itself constantly, wasting precious time.

If you do not shift your perspective, *As It Pleases God*, your life will continue in the same cycle, with different scenes, characters, etc. According to *The Lady's Code*, if the same thing keeps happening, there is a lesson that you are not learning. When embarking upon a relationship of genuine quality, you are REQUIRED to shift your perspective to get a different result than what you have been receiving. Trust me, regardless of how you feel, rationalize, or point the finger, it is not them, it is not it, it is YOU!

The key to any successful relationship is to assume responsibility for your role without falling for the blaming game, even if it is not your fault. Why should we take the blame for someone's folly? If it has provoked any form of reaction within you, then that is the AREA you need to deal with, not ignore it! If there were no issues within you, it would not have provoked an adverse reaction in the first place. So, it would be best if you targeted the negative Mental or Emotional TRIGGER to create a win-win.

I must say this before I move on: You are the EXPERT in your own life. No one has more INSIGHT regarding your inner truth besides you. All the answers to every problem, situation, or circumstance reside from within. However, it is hard to find the solution when you are in denial, when you are too busy to pay attention, when you have too many distractions, when you are too emotional, when you are stuck on the negative, or when your mind is clouded with thoughts of too many things at once.

Wall of Busyness

Busy, busy, busy...Are you too busy to pay attention? Do you feel overwhelmed by the busyness of life? Has your hustle gotten you in a bit of a bustle? Well, at the moment, the busyness of life has us in an uproar, not knowing which way to turn, causing us to break *The Lady's Code*. When in the Eye of God, He wants us to turn our busyness into BUSINESS. Be it doing business or developing a business mindset, it is good enough for *Women of Stature*. Why must we focus on doing business? The Virtuous Woman in the Book of Proverbs was all about doing business, and so should we.

The *Writing on the Wall* precepts apply to every area of our lives, including how we manage our time or how we view the *Wall of Busyness*. What does time have to do with anything? Fortunately, time has everything to do with relationships or the lack thereof. Trust that a constant following of ineffectiveness, mismanaged time, or failure will cause the best of us to reevaluate our attitudes, actions, and reactions to that particular area. Plus, when the results are right in front of us, do we ignore them, allowing the same negative cycles to continue, or do we do something about them?

When we misappropriate our time, we will experience a higher level of stress, extreme fatigue, disrupted time with our family, strained relationships, or a constant bout with failure. If someone is continuously screwing up things, there is a bigger problem at hand, and one must decide if that is what they would like to deal with continually. If it is not, one must avoid cleaning up the mess of a grown person.

The *Writing on the Wall* admits that time is of the essence; it must be managed in order to become maximized, or we will not get anything done. For me, I simply determine the when, where, how, whom, and why of what is important by making a physical or mental list. Then, I decide in advance what needs to get done first and what gets dropped.

The goal is to train our minds in advance to deal with distractions within a time limit. By doing so, we are better able to deal with the biggest time-wasters, such as chatting on the phone, gossiping, texting, watching too much television, gaming, Facebooking, TikToking, and Instagramming. When we are busy accomplishing NOTHING, it is a big slap in the face, especially if

Writing On The Wall

we have nothing to show for it. Properly managed time creates that take-home and come back for more relational magic!

What is the comeback for more analogies all about? *The Lady's Code* is all about putting your unique spin on things, leaving no stone unturned. For example, I was excluded from several projects many years ago because I did not appear to fit the mold. After the projects went belly up, a new team was formed that included yours truly. Lo and behold, guess who had the creative spin on that multi-million dollar project? I did. This example is clearly a prime example of overlooked creativity or ideas, which causes a company or an individual to lose out simply because of favoritism, envy, or discrimination.

From this point on, we do not leave any stones unturned. All ideas are welcomed...most great ideas will never appear as such at first. Most often, we look down on others due to their pay grade; however, it does not make those who are beneath us less qualified.

There will always be that diamond in the rough on staff, at every company, in every household, or with every friend. As *Women of Stature*, it is our responsibility to find it! How do we find hidden creativity? I have found the easiest way to pinpoint creativity is to ask for it.

What is the best way to ask for creativity? The best way to draw the diamond out is with contests asking for ideas or feedback on specific projects. Here is a secret: People love winning, but a diamond in the rough loves award-winning ideas or challenges. They will also participate not just to win but to SHINE because it is grafted into their DNA. How is it grafted into their DNA when we are human, and a diamond is a gem? A diamond is pure carbon formed under pressure, and we are made of about 18% carbon! We definitely have a commonality with diamonds that most do not talk about. What is that? We can shine under pressure as well.

We all have different perspectives regarding certain things; it is our different views that give us vision. In my opinion, a person or organization with tunnel vision becomes locked into limitations. Limits are good on some things, but when it comes down to our vision or doing business, we cannot become limited to those who are just on our teams, with the family, or in our circles.

Writing On The Wall

We can all learn from everything and everyone if we learn how to ask the right questions to get others to speak about their point of view. There are times when it may take an outsider's perspective to shed light on the inside.

People are looking for innovative ideas, products, services, and solutions. If one has not noticed by now, we are subconsciously driven by progression. The new cars, houses, phones, gadgets, etc., capitalize on our desire for newness. If we want to stay ahead of the game, we need to continue to develop and grow, turning our *Wall of Busyness* into a *Wall of Business*.

Most people think success is a one-time occasion, but it is indeed a continuous process. Frankly, this is how the one-time wonders become dismayed by success. We must continue with the pursuit of accomplishments.

The best way to continue on the Path of Success is to follow a mission, desire, or goal while building a MIND MAP and a PLAN OF ACTION for each one. It is conducive to planning about five to ten years out. Why must we plan so far out? If we do not plan, it will become so easy to get lost, distracted, or discouraged. With this type of projection, we are able to track our progress accordingly, while making the necessary adjustments with confidence. Regardless of where we are in life, we want to be:

- ☐ Interesting.
- ☐ Innovative.
- ☐ Inspiring.
- ☐ Stimulating.
- ☐ Thought-provoking.
- ☐ Understanding.
- ☐ Revolutionizing.

There is an art and science to everything we do. How is this possible when we do not feel like an artist, and we are definitely not a scientist? Let me explain...it does not matter what our occupation is or is not; we are all creative. In addition, the Laws of the Universe are the science we take for granted, which stands

Writing On The Wall

with or without our permission. Simply put, we are involved in our lives more than we care to imagine; therefore, we must understand them in order to maximize them.

There are times when we think we do not need help and we have it all together. The moment we are asked to think outside the box, we become subconsciously blocked. Although we may not talk about it much, it happens more than we care to think, especially to writers.

In order to master the creative self, we must understand the logistics of science, which will teach us WHAT to do with proper protocol. Our creativity will give us insight into how, when, where, and why of the WHAT. In short, this is the formal breakdown most people overlook because they are looking all around for the light bulb to go off or the aha moment. When, in fact, the light bulb and the aha are already within us, provoked by the right questions, as well as with the proper understanding and respect for our creative side.

When we are creating a marketable product, service, or mindset, we must understand a few things, but not limited to such:

- ☐ Likes. What are we going to do differently to brand our creativity with this product or service to make it likable?
- ☐ Dislikes. What are the common dislikes about this competitive product or service?
- ☐ Wants. What strategy are we going to use to inspire people to want to purchase our product with a sense of urgency?
- ☐ Desires. What is the ultimate desire we would like conveyed?
- ☐ Objectives. What is the mission?
- ☐ Nature of. What is the reason for the product or service?
- ☐ Differences. What are we going to do differently to bring about repeat customers or brand loyalty?
- ☐ Niche. What strategy do we need to use to brand this product in the hearts of potential prospects?
- ☐ The Takeaway. What positive impact is someone able to walk away with?

Writing On The Wall

- ☐ Reciprocity. What are we willing to give back or pay forward in exchange for the success of this product?

When turning our *Wall of Busyness* into a *Wall of Business* as *Women of Stature*, these are a few ways to brainstorm or get us into the habit of asking the right questions to provoke the Creative Giant from within. We must keep using our creative minds to release unique ideas, concepts, and precepts because we never know which idea will hit the jackpot.

It is a great idea to get a little creative on how to ask for referrals. It is by far an excellent way of building our brands with loyal supporters, especially when moving in the Spirit of Excellence with *The Lady's Code* in hand. Therefore, it is good to be nice, make a great impression, respect others, and treat everyone with kindness. Listen, quality service sells! People will remember how we treat them, and they will definitely remember how we made them feel.

The Lady's Code of brand savvy is wired into a diamond's DNA on any level of living. So, we cannot discount our Creative Greatness because we all have it. We just may not know how to use it. Some like their greatness packaged up, and some like theirs unpackaged; regardless of how we like it, it is there! How do we bring our greatness forth? For the *Women of Stature*, listed below are a few ways, but not limited to such:

- ☐ Recognize and own the fact that it is there.
- ☐ Place God first, *As It Pleases Him*, Spirit to Spirit.
- ☐ Become ONE with the Holy Spirit.
- ☐ Cover yourself with the Blood of Jesus.
- ☐ Receive inspiration from the Bible, quotes, books, etc.
- ☐ Get coaching or mentoring to receive feedback.
- ☐ Actively document, share, and use the Fruits of the Spirit.

It does not matter which way works for you as long as you release the Creative Power that has been hidden or bottled up for years. If you take a moment to think back to your childhood, did you lack creativity then? More than likely, the answer is no...as a child, your creativity was automatic. Whereas now, you must get it back to the stage where it comes forth when it is called upon, turning our *Wall of Busyness* into a *Wall of Business* as *Women of Stature*.

Wall of Creativity

Unbeknown to most, when dealing with our Creative Power in the Eye of God, it has a profound impact on our relationship with Him, ourselves, and others. What does our creativity have to do with anything, especially as Believers? Regardless of whether we are Believers or not, our creativity is one of the fundamental aspects of being human, hidden within the DNA of everyone. However, it is our responsibility to connect to it without limitations, judgment, suppression, or fear.

Nevertheless, with all due respect, it is in the church settings that we tend to downplay the creativity that does not revolve around its functions. For example, if a child is scientifically creative, the church environment may not support their dreams because it does not align with their agenda. As a result, this child may be shunned or forced to participate in something else, such as playing the drums, ushering, or whatever. This atrocity, in my opinion, should never be the case because we understand Spiritual Principles, Tools, Gifts, Creativity, and Talents better than anyone. Still, we do less with the manifestation and multiplying efforts.

Whereas worldly individuals do more with their creativity with less knowledge, going on instinct alone. As a result, the Kingdom Wealth is residing outside of the church when it should be inside of it. And then, we have the nerve to judge those who faithfully use their creativity in a worldly system when we have not taken the time to use ours in the Kingdom. For this reason, we will find a lot of Believers abandoning their faith because they cannot find help with the Creative Force lying within.

All creativity should be respected and nurtured. In the Eye of God, for everything, there is a way to enhance the creativity of a child, even if we do not understand it. There is always a way, and it is our responsibility as Believers to find it, help them, and nurture their creativity. What makes this so important? As we grow older, we tend to bottle up our creativity, allowing it to fade into the background of our busy lives, affecting our overall well-being and relationships.

Blocked creativity is one of the culprits plaguing our relationships today; unfortunately, this is why social media has taken over like there is no tomorrow, allowing people to dream, even if it is fake or a parroting session, squashing their real creativity.

The bottom line is that *The Wall of Creativity* is about thinking outside the box, problem-solving, and approaching life with a fresh perspective without falling for the illusional okey doke. Whether our creativity lies in drawing, music, writing, painting, poetry, dancing, cooking, or whatever, it is imperative to designate time to engage in doing so without fear, judgment, or restrictions.

Unlocking your hidden Creative Power is less about the specific method and more about the willingness to engage in doing something consistently to release the creativity bottled up within. Unbeknown to most, if we do not release our bottled-up creativity, it will have an impact on our relations with people, especially behind closed doors. Why does this happen? Lost dreams, hopes, and desires take a toll on the human psyche, negatively. In *The Lady's Code*, the only way to reverse this effect is to get our creative juices to flow, *As It Pleases God*.

CHAPTER 3

UPFRONT AND HONEST

Do you practice being straightforward and truthful with God, others, and yourself? Are you aware of the advantages that come with being *Upfront and Honest* in the Eye of God? On the other hand, have you ever found yourself struggling to be *Upfront and Honest* about your genuine thoughts and feelings? Perhaps your perception has hindered your ability to be transparent and candid about what you are going through and why. In this chapter, *The Lady's Code* of being *Upfront and Honest* requires us to deal with the power of perception.

As *Women of Stature*, to gain *Territorial Control* and partake of the *Streets of God* according to the Heavenly of Heavens, we must approach people, places, and things with our *Eyes Wide Open* to glean from *The Secrets of the Garden*.

What is the big deal about perception, according to *The Lady's Code*? In the simplicity of it all, our perception gives our eyes the ability to see what we are looking for, our ears the ability to hear what we want to hear, and our mouths the ability to speak the desires of the heart. In so many words, we all have perceptions! We will see the positive or the negative; we will see the right or the wrong; we will see the just or the unjust, etc. The same applies to our hearing; we will tend to hear what we want to hear first unless we train our ears to hear correctly. Now, when it comes

Upfront and Honest

down to the mouth, anything can come out of its gateway unless we set a guard over it.

Our perceptional reality, or our personal drive to become more than we are, can become contaminated by ungoverned thoughts. Ungoverned thoughts? Yes, indeed...the thoughts of the secret envy, jealousy, and coveting we cannot tell anyone about. Oh, by the way, that secret competitiveness we keep hidden, what about that?

Most often, we would not admit we are plagued with envy or jealousy because it is a hidden emotion until we take action. However, it does affect our perceptions, contributing to negative or unproductive thoughts and behaviors, which could hinder our Spiritual Walk or break *The Lady's Code: As It Pleases God*.

If we want to tiptoe around our perceptions, we can. In my opinion, tiptoeing will create a great disservice when all we need to do is utilize the Fruits of the Spirit. While simultaneously turning our negative thoughts into positive ones before acknowledging, revealing, or confirming our perceptions, thoughts, or beliefs. I know it may seem like a lot to do when one has to make a quick emotional turnaround or respond swiftly. The first few times, it may become a little tedious. But, with use, I promise it will become very quick once we master *The Lady's Code: As It Pleases God*.

How do we apply being *Upfront and Honest* in a personal, professional, or Spiritual Relationship? In the Eye of God, we must use wisdom when approaching anything relational. The fill-in-the-blank relational mentality leaves room for too many heads running a relationship. Once this happens, it becomes challenging to be *Upfront and Honest*. Why would this become a problem as Believers? The attitude, waywardness, sabotage, and hostile cliques will eventually become non-conducive to the overall vision of the relational common goal. If the goal is not set in a relationship, then time is more than likely misappropriated, which leaves room for too many people to put in their two cents.

In *The Lady's Code*, the *Writing on the Wall* advises that it is always best to have systems, strategies, concepts, plans, structure, kindness, and integrity in place to build our households. Doing so

Upfront and Honest

helps us to mentor the up-and-coming greatness within ourselves and others. If one has never had a taste of an orderly lifestyle, it is genuinely like Heaven on Earth.

How can we change our mindsets toward being *Upfront and Honest* in a relationship? I am so glad to answer this question! I have found the best way to manage being *Upfront and Honest* is to relax in it. If we find peace in the midst of our communicative efforts, it will grant us the ability to think clearly, set priorities, and provide a way to manage our reactions or actions when we have a disruption.

Most often, when we make others feel as if we are too busy, lying to them, or standing them up, they subconsciously pull away, eventually causing a disconnect in the relationship. Even if we are busy, we must find a way to take a moment to give those we love our undivided attention. It only takes a fraction of a second to show an individual that they are more important than what really has our attention.

The mismanagement of time has caused more broken relationships than we would care to imagine. The truth is, if social media is getting more time than our families or if social media is getting more time than the ones that truly have our backs, then we must reevaluate the management of our time. Trust me, if there is something that we want to really do or someone that we really want to see, we will make time for it or them by any means necessary.

Excuses about not having enough time are just that, AN EXCUSE! If something or someone is not a part of our to-dos, own it! And, be so kind as to put it on the To-Do not list.

According to the Heavenly of Heavens, you do not have to make an excuse for wasting time on people, places, and things that are not conducive to where you are going or what you want to do, *As It Pleases God*. Once you master this, *The Lady's Code* says you will be granted a form of creative goodness that will be unexplainable to mankind, which is well-needed in keeping the spark in your relationships.

When building effective relationships, negotiating with an ulterior motive is a quick way to put a ripple effect on our

Upfront and Honest

integrity, regardless of whether we value it or not. From my experience, when we are *Upfront and Honest* about our intentions, we can earn more respect from those who are easily scorned.

According to *The Lady's Code*, the moment we know and understand who we are, what we want, and why we want it, we are better able to make the necessary adjustments in our lives. More importantly, by being *In the know* about ourselves, we are better able to accommodate the situations or circumstances at hand without beguiling anyone or anything to get what we want.

In my opinion, to preserve our sanity, we need to avoid those who are always trying to get us into bed. If people are always trying to get us into the bedroom, it does not take long to figure out what the relationship is based on. *The Lady's Code* advises that a relationship is doomed if it is confined solely to the bedroom. Why is this the case? In the Eye of God, a successful foundation is built on communication, trust, relatability, and companionship with mental and emotional depth before intimacy.

Suppose we are *Upfront and Honest* with ourselves and others about our intimate encounters, once we do the do, then what? Every time we do it, this question must be asked. Painstakingly, the psyche will answer, and most often, we may disagree with the answer, but it will not lie unless we tell it to do so! If we place intimacy before God and anything else to feed our lusts, we are asking for trouble, especially when the newness and thrill wear off and the Spiritual Transfers occur or are fully complete. It is only wise to establish our relational connections outside of the bedroom to withstand the tests of time. If not, regret will come knocking sooner or later.

Paul's Writing on the Wall is a prime example of this: Paul was infatuated with pretty women; all he wanted was one thing, and he did not make it a secret. His whole conversation is always about sex, so it did not take a rocket scientist to figure out what he was all about.

Paul went out to a social gathering where he met Erica, who was out looking for Mr. Right. Paul did not waste any time approaching Erica because she was quite stunning. He handed her his business card and went on his way, scoping out other women

Upfront and Honest

and giving out at least 20 business cards that night. Instead of him getting to know a woman, he would hand out business cards to rope them in, because he understood that most women are caught up in titles, status, and money. It was all a game to him, so he used it as leverage to cover up his insecurities before they found out that he was not what he appeared to be. He firmly believed in the 80/20 rule: 80% of the women he handed his card to would never call, and 20% would call back. Lo and behold, Erica became one of 20% who made the follow-up phone call, as she really believed that he was interested in her.

As Paul and Erica got to know each other, he made her think that he was such a wonderful man and that all he needed was a good woman. He ran the game down on Erica to get her goodies, and she gave in; sad to say, she fell for it! However, Erica soon realized that his method of operation was to play one woman against the other, making them jealous, confused, and needy. He knew that once a woman felt as if she was competing, she would give up all the goods in her candy store without them having a clue that he did not want them.

Paul and his friends would sit around talking about the women who gave up their goodies, hoping they would be the one. They figured every woman wanted a man with a 6-figure income, and they would do anything to get him, but Paul realized that there was something different about Erica.

Erica protected her candy like it was gold; she did not care how much money he made. She was not willing to give out her treats to be tricked in the end, especially after her first mistake with him.

Paul was so bold and arrogant that he would tell Erica about all the women who were emotionally entangled or wounded because he decided to move on. Although Erica let him speak about his rendezvous, it turned her off, causing her to put locks and chains on her candy store for good. She felt as if Paul had no value in her because if he did, he would never tell her about another woman.

After many moons of listening to his escapades, Erica began to feel sorry for his victims. In refusing to be a victim herself, she

Upfront and Honest

knew that she had to preserve whatever she had for her Mr. Right. One day, as God Promised, he came along. She had no clue her Mr. Right would lavish her with the candy of his love, attention, and adoration. Michael immediately recognized that Erica was a Queen, and He had the utmost respect for her.

Erica could not ask for a better man; he told her that he was going to plant a tree of love representing his love for her. He promised her that he would water that tree every day while believing that God would allow that tree to grow.

Several months later, Michael called Erica to let her know that their tree of love had broken ground and that their love would never die. It seemed too good to be true, as Erica wanted to doubt his love, but Michael refused to allow her to do so. He had hope in their relationship, and he would not do anything to destroy what they had worked so hard to build. So, Erica decided that he was the one for her and then opened her candy store of love as well. They were a match made in heaven, and he would do anything to empower her, and she would do anything to empower him.

Michael decided they were going to get married and have a baby to solidify their Divine Union before God Almighty. All of which were built on the terrain of honesty, trust, transparency, clarity, mutual understanding, and relational equality. Erica agreed with this Triple-Braided Cord Agreement on one condition: Their baby had to have his blue eyes. He came into a Binding Agreement with her as long as their baby had her beautiful hair.

Although Michael and Erica made a joke about their baby, he was indeed born with beautiful black hair like his mom and blue eyes like his dad. Their familial love blossomed like the tree planted in proxy at the onset of their relationship, becoming deeper, stronger, and more stable as time goes on. More importantly, they lead by example with God at the forefront of their lives, sharing their story with others, conveying the hope needed to continue becoming better, stronger, and wiser, *As It Pleases God.*

Now, Paul, the womanizer, eventually got married to a woman who played him for a fool, causing him to go bankrupt trying to win her love and keep her as a self-proclaimed trophy. At first

Upfront and Honest

glance, this man appeared to have found the love of his life. He was drawn in by charm, intrigue, and allure, blissfully unaware of the world hidden beneath the surface. Little did he know there was more to her story and the BBL he paid for. The woman he had chosen to marry had a career that thrived on lustful manipulation, using her looks, cheeks, and appeal to control men for monetary gain, like she did with him.

Paul landed himself in a marriage with a part-time stripper who manipulates men as an occupation. The moment of truth struck when financial strain began to encroach upon their lifestyle. The bills began to pile up, and she had to pick up the slack and pay his bills. And, guess what? He found himself helplessly dependent on her, trapped in a cycle where the 80/20 power dynamics had shifted dramatically. To his ultimate chagrin, his world turned upside down, and he could not say a mumbling word about her occupation or her way of handing out her business cards, similar to his method of operation back in the day. Nor was he willing to sacrifice his lifestyle due to the societal pressures and stigmas he had established for himself! Sadly, Paul had to suck it up!

Unfortunately, behind closed doors, the frustration, hurt, inner turmoil, and betrayal left Paul disenfranchised. After having to swallow his pride in such a manner, it caused him to kick himself for missing out on Erica for playing one game too many. The question is: 'Did Paul get what he deserved?' Or, 'Did he get what he wanted?' Who knows, besides Paul himself, but rest assured, having his wife swinging from a pole was the ultimate blow to his ego.

To say the least, Paul's life takes a tumultuous turn as he cannot escape the subtle side-eyed glances, the barrage of negative judgment, and the raised eyebrows that seem to whisper side-bar innuendos about their relationship. As Paul and his wife navigate their path together, they find strength in their bond, hoping one day she will pack up her candy store and climb off that pole for good.

Erica was smart enough to read the *Writing on the Wall*, and she sent a message to everyone: 'Protect your candy, because if you share it with everyone, what will you have left when you meet the

Upfront and Honest

right person?' Besides, you do not want to take that type of emotional baggage into another relationship. When all you need to do is pay attention and keep your legs closed to avoid negative Spiritual Transfers designed to drive you crazy.

A person who places value in their relationship takes pride in themselves, their home, their family, their career, their friends, setting priorities, helping those in need, and their Spiritual Connections. The *Writing on the Wall* says that a person of this caliber wears many hats, and they do not mind effectively balancing the people, places, and things valuable to them while exhibiting great character to all they come in contact with. If we would like to possess the characteristics of this type of individual, we must start with our perceptions first, attitudes second, and integrity third. Why must we begin in this order? Believe it or not, they are the deal-breakers in building effective relationships and influential circles.

The *Writing on the Wall* prides itself on building effective relationships with *The Lady's Code* Principles, giving us facts about human relations in a way that is conducive to the Inner Spirit of man. Of course, there is an exception to every rule, and there is a particular perception in every *Writing on the Wall* depending upon our mindsets; thus, it has zero tolerance for bad behavior.

For me, I do not proclaim to be perfect, nor is anyone perfect, but when a person proclaims to be a good person, I check to see how they treat their spouse, children, relatives, friends, coworkers, and then others, in this order. Trust me, it is a dead giveaway on the level of integrity one possesses from within. If someone treats people on the outside who are not related to them better than they treat their spouse, children, and family, some deep-rooted issues need to be resolved.

Your attitude, thoughts, and actions will be the determining factors in whether you build, destroy, or pick up debris. However, if you want lasting success in relationships, you must continue to build yourself and the lives of others without expecting anything in return. If not, one will find a long trail of irreconcilably broken, chaotic relationships. These types of relationships are a very touchy subject; however, I am going to give one the information needed to overcome these types of obstacles.

When an individual seems to attract chaos in their life, it could be due to various factors such as conditioning, their environment, or internal pain or trauma that they are struggling to cope with. It is essential to understand that being a chaotic person does not necessarily make someone a bad person; it simply means they may be hurting and are using chaos as a sedative to distract, cope, or deflect.

On the other hand, when faced with chaos, it can be helpful to remain quiet and avoid becoming a burden on someone else who may be struggling with their unresolved issues. Additionally, you may need to think creatively about how to navigate the situation or communicate with the person involved without compromising your values.

According to *The Lady's Code*, in times of chaos, staying composed and not adding to others' burdens can be a great help and inspire them. It may require us to think outside the box and communicate in a way that aligns with our values, *As It Pleases God*. But it is doable. As *Women of Stature*, we have the power to navigate any situation with GRACE and STRENGTH because we have paid the price to be who we are.

Territorial Control

People will place us in a box if we allow them to do so. Now, if one has a desire to adhere to *The Lady's Code: As It Pleases God*, they must think inside, outside, around, over, under, and through the box of life, leaving no stone unturned. We must evaluate or inspect every area of our lives to ensure that we do not have any hidden kryptonite that is zapping our Personal Power.

Once we understand that there is a time and place for everything, we will be able to let go and let God. Until then, we will find ourselves trying to control everything. According to Ecclesiastes 3:1-8, *"There is a time for everything, and a season for every activity under the heavens: a time to be born and a time to die, a time to plant*

Upfront and Honest

and a time to uproot, a time to kill and a time to heal, a time to tear down and a time to build, a time to weep and a time to laugh, a time to mourn and a time to dance, a time to scatter stones and a time to gather them, a time to embrace and a time to refrain from embracing, a time to search and a time to give up, a time to keep and a time to throw away, a time to tear and a time to mend, a time to be silent and a time to speak, a time to love and a time to hate, a time for war and a time for peace."

Regardless of whether it is our time or not, or whether it is our season or not, we all deserve fair treatment regardless of our creed, deed, or breed. In and out of season, I pay attention to everything, especially how people will treat us when they feel as if we need them or if they can capitalize on us.

As we tiptoe around the essential areas of life, we cannot negate the fact that we are our best Navigational Tool. When embarking upon the great unknown, fear can become debilitating. Then again, we can flip the switch, allowing it to become our fuel. As *Women of Stature*, we do not have to feel bad about fear because we all have it! All we need to do is learn how to rechannel, refocus, or redirect our energy with positive actions, affirmations, words, and thoughts.

When I speak about affirmations, I am not referring to the worldly ones. Keep in mind that material things lose their value quickly after they are purchased or the newness wears off, especially if our inner value is not determined beyond a shadow of a doubt. The affirmations I am referring to are the ones that are structural, inspirational, and scriptural, promoting inner growth and stimulation. It may take some getting accustomed to, but it is doable.

If conflicting emotions or thoughts try to invade our Navigational Zone, we must take a step back to understand the underlying reason before proceeding. If we ignore the WHY, then the what, when, where, and how become the distracting forces that will get us off track. Remember, the WHY of the SEED helps us to deal with every other aspect of the emotional or mental invasions.

Upfront and Honest

When fighting for our Territorial Rights and *The Lady's Code: As It Pleases God*, we are able to master our problem-solving skills when we understand, listen, and learn that all we need is already within us.

As *Women of Stature* in the Eye of God, whatever information, lesson, or training we need will find its way to us. Still, we must take our Spiritual Blinders off while unplugging the deafness in our Spiritual Ears, casting down emotional or mental bondage.

We are already the Empire of Greatness that we desire. All we need to do is align with the Spiritual Side of our being. Once we understand that we were Spiritual before we were human, we will then be able to cultivate Spiritual Power from the Heavenly of Heavens. Why do we need Spiritual Power? It is needed to put our fleshly desires under the subjection of the Holy Spirit to maximize *The Lady's Code: As It Pleases God*.

As humans, we tend to become relatively inflexible and set in our ways when it comes to certain things, primarily when dealing with *Territorial Control*. But even though we all have elements of selfishness, it does not necessarily mean that our way is always right or wrong. Instead, the love of God with *The Lady's Code: As It Pleases Him*, can serve as a gentle nudge, guiding us toward dealing with our selfish tendencies. It also helps us navigate interactions with people who may have different perspectives or who are dead set on having their way.

According to the Heavenly of Heavens, we are the source of our stifled innovations in the Eye of God. Once we overcome, learn, and master our challenges to create a win-win situation without breaking *The Lady's Code*, we are then able to invoke our Spiritual Innovations, *As It Pleases Him*. In my opinion, this is definitely needed in order to soar beyond our wildest dreams to embrace our *Streets of Gold*.

So, as *Women of Stature*, take your time and think through your decisions and the reasons why before you open your mouth. This will definitely help you to think on your feet while giving positive, effective, and valuable feedback. Nevertheless, if you make a

Upfront and Honest

mistake, apologize immediately while openly correcting it and keep it moving in the Spirit of Excellence.

Why must we self-correct according to *The Lady's Code*? Instantaneous self-correcting will teach your mind that you are not playing around with negative, unfruitful, or unproductive frailties. Will it work? The psyche will obey when it knows you are serious about Kingdom Etiquette, *As It Pleases God*.

The Streets of Gold Revelation

As we tiptoe around life about Kingdom Etiquette, or when being *Upfront and Honest* with ourselves and others, there is a scripture stating, "*The twelve gates were twelve pearls: each individual gate was of one pearl. And the street of the city was pure gold, like transparent glass.*" Revelation 21:21. For most, we interpret this as being the Holy City of Jerusalem or the Pearly Streets of Heaven while overlooking the elements of PURITY and TRANSPARENCY.

Although we are all entitled to our own opinions and free will, it does not mean that we must remain dingy, tainted, toxic, cloudy, or irresponsible. For this reason, and being that I am not like most people, nor do I think like them, it is only fair for me to put a Spiritual Spin on this matter, especially when dealing with the *Streets of Gold* and *The Lady's Code*.

What is the purpose of putting a Spiritual Spin on the *Streets of Gold*? As a *Woman of Kingdom Stature*, I am required to think, understand, interpret, and speak differently than most because I am held to a HIGHER accountability. So, my question is, 'Why do we have to wait on the *Streets of Gold*?' 'Why should we put off what can be done today?' 'Why are we waiting on the *Streets of Gold* when God is assessing our every thought, word, action, and even our hidden motives right now in real-time?' Wait, wait, wait; do not answer those questions yet. I have one more question, 'Why should we be for the streets, especially when the *Streets of Gold* are already within us as Believers?' Blasphemy, right? Wrong!

I could not make this stuff up if I tried...so, let us take it to the Word of God. The very next statement, Spiritually Sealing

Upfront and Honest

Revelation 21:21, says: *"But I saw no temple in it, for the Lord God Almighty and the Lamb are its temple. The city had no need of the sun or of the moon to shine in it, for the glory of God illuminated it. The Lamb is its light. And the nations of those who are saved shall walk in its light, and the kings of the earth bring their glory and honor into it."* Revelation 21:22-24.

Is this not Divine Instructions hidden in plain sight, telling us exactly what to do? The short answer would be, 'yes.' But the long answer would be that when we are walking with night vision in a state of disobedience, rebellion, pompousness, or selfishness, we will become Spiritually Veiled to the *Streets of Gold* in our Heaven on Earth Experiences, even if we pretend to have it going on. Is this not judging? No, it is called Spiritually Unveiling or getting a Spiritual Understanding!

For example, when someone presents themselves as if they have it going on, I pay attention to how they behave when no one is looking. I take note of how they treat people they do not seemingly need. I evaluate how they manipulate others into debauchery, waywardness, or out of the Will of God for their benefit. What is the purpose of paying attention to these things? It unveils their fruits without me having to say one word or test the Spirit.

Should we always test the Spirit? We only need to test what is not obvious. When dealing with the *Streets of Gold* from the Heavenly of Heavens, there is no need to waste energy on what God has made obvious or what the Holy Spirit has proactively vetted. For example, you do not need to test your foot every time you get ready to walk. Nor do you need to test your eyes to see, primarily when all you need to do is open them.

Remember, Spirit knows Spirit, and we do not need to reinvent the wheel, especially when God places certain things on a silver platter. Now, if our conscience is keeled, and we cannot instantly understand what is placed before us, it is best to test our very own Spirit to ensure our Spiritual Faculties are functioning properly.

Why must we test our Spirit first before testing the Spirit of another? When dealing with *The Lady's Code* or our Divinely Blueprinted Purpose for our *Streets of Gold*, they are Spiritually Protected and Governed. All this means is that when we are

Upfront and Honest

Spiritually Aligned, *As It Pleases God*, some of the legwork is already done for us. We only need to use our Spiritual Discernment Faculties and the Fruits of the Spirit to know what is what and who is whom, or to read the *Writing on the Wall*. Is this Biblical? Of course, *"Therefore by their fruits you will know them."* Matthew 7:20.

Advantageously, in the *Streets of Gold*, by your fruits, you will also know yourself! So, when testing the Spirit, it is wise to begin with your fruits first. What is the purpose of starting with our own fruits? The Fruits of the Spirit do not lie. *"For a good tree does not bear bad fruit, nor does a bad tree bear good fruit. For every tree is known by its own fruit."* Luke 6:43-44.

Keep in mind that God DOES NOT make mistakes; we do! He is NOT mistake-prone; we are! Above all, He PROTECTS what truly belongs to Him, especially when we are in Purpose on purpose. What is the big deal about being open to Divine Purpose when embarking upon the *Streets of Gold*? The best answer to this question comes from Colossians 1:10: *"That you may walk worthy of the Lord, fully pleasing Him, being fruitful in every good work and increasing in the knowledge of God."*

Picturesquely, when dealing with Divine Purpose, we do not need to wait for it to appear. Are we not advised to wait on God? Yes, we are advised to wait on Him according to Lamentations 3:25: *"The Lord is good to those who wait for Him, to the soul who seeks Him."* Still, with all due respect, we often miss the action word SEEK, which means something is required of us. And, it is our responsibility to seek God, *Spirit to Spirit*, to understand what is required for the Divine Unveiling of the *Streets of Gold*.

In addition, the very next verse says, *"It is good that one should hope and wait quietly for the salvation of the Lord."* In all simplicity, amid waiting, we must TAKE ACTION using the Spiritual Elements hidden within our hope because our Divine Purpose or Blueprint is ALREADY.

What are the Spiritual Elements of Divine Purpose hidden within our hope? Spiritually Speaking, hope is comprised of faith, trust, courage, anticipation, confidence, optimism, perseverance, gratitude, and expectation, fostering a positive outlook, mindset,

Upfront and Honest

and heart posture. For this reason, Psalm 27:14 advises us to: *"Wait on the Lord; be of good courage, and He shall strengthen your heart; wait, I say, on the Lord!"*

Without hope or patience, we will naturally gravitate to the negative side of thinking, behaving, speaking, and enduring. At the same time, we will also find ourselves twiddling our thumbs, capitalizing on victimization, using others to do what we are not willing to do for ourselves, or pimping God and lying on the Holy Spirit. Is all of this comprised of the lack of hope? Absolutely!

According to the Heavenly of Heavens, to make hope work in our favor, *As It Pleases God*, we must first avoid using it as a passive emotion. In *The Lady's Code*, we must use it as a Spiritual Tool or Catalyst of ACTION, seeking Divine Instructions, Lessons, or Information with proper documentation. What can this do for us? For instance, someone hopeful about overcoming personal issues, challenges, or struggles is more likely to seek help, pursue education, set goals, or adopt healthier habits without developing a woe-unto-me mentality.

Secondly, we must prepare for the Divine Unveiling through the transformational process of learning, growing, sowing, doing, tilling, regrafting, and sharing with a call-to-action mindset. Conversely, if we choose to do none of them, our Divine Purpose or Blueprint is withheld until we are ready. In my opinion, this is similar to the Children of Israel wandering in the desert for 40 years until they were prepared to enter the Promised Land, *As It Pleased God*.

What if the Promised Land Experience does not apply to us? Unfortunately, this is how we deceive ourselves. Here is the deal: According to the Heavenly of Heavens, we, as human beings, cannot enter the Earthly Realm without one. We may not remember the Spiritual Terms or Conditions, but no one enters the Earthly Realm for no apparent Reason, Purpose, or Season. In my opinion, this is similar to having roads or paths leading us to our destination. Without a road, a roadmap, GPS, or some form of guidance, we will get lost easily, causing us to settle where we do not belong.

Upfront and Honest

When being *Upfront and Honest* with yourself, if you do not know what your Promise is or is not, then it is time to get in the Face of God, *Spirit to Spirit*, to experience the transformative power hidden on your street called the Tablet of the Heart.

What is the purpose of knowing what is on the Tablet of the Heart, especially as a Believer? You have a Divine Right to be here to work toward your Predestined Blueprint as long as the Breath of Life flows through your body. Suppose you do not know this, *As It Pleases God*. In this case, pleasing yourself will become your portion while subjecting yourself to the consequences of complacency that will zap your Divinity until you awaken from your slumber. *"And do this, knowing the time, that now it is high time to awake out of sleep; for now our salvation is nearer than when we first believed."* Romans 13:11.

In order to keep *The Lady's Code* intact and on its toes, we must understand a few things before we move on: *"For the Spirit searcheth all things, yea, the deep things of God."* 1 Corinthians 2:10. What does this mean? As *Women of Stature*, if we want to become DEEP, really, really DEEP, we must incorporate the Spirit of God. Simple enough, right? Then why are we not doing it? Better yet, why are we doing it our way? Fortunately, once again, we are all entitled to this one thing called free will.

By embracing this Divine Awareness, it propels us to make choices that honor our Divine Purpose and contribute positively for the Greater Good, *As It Pleases God*. Furthermore, it challenges us to live fully in the moment, actively engaging in everyday life while being mindful of the legacy we are building.

In addition, Matthew 6:10 in the Lord's Prayer says, *"Thy Kingdom come. Thy will be done in earth, as it is in Heaven."* Was this written by accident? No, because it is prefaced with, *"After this manner therefore pay ye: Our Father which art in Heaven, Hallowed be thy name."* Matthew 6:9. These are specific instructions given by Jesus to assist us in living a fulfilled, purposeful life.

I know this sounds a little far-fetched, so let me line up what I am saying with scripture. In Psalm 8:5, He says, *"For thou hast made him a little lower than the angels, and has crowned him with glory and honor."*

Upfront and Honest

Based on this scripture alone, do we not already have our CROWNS? The answer is yes. All we need to do is learn how to own it, *As It Pleases God*, without breaking *The Lady's Code*!

It is amazing how we worship the crowns of others yet do not realize that we have our own crowns. Nor do we take the time to nurture the crown that we already possess while breaking *The Lady's Code* from the left, right, and center. Is it for a crown that we do not realize we already have? Then again, is it out of jealousy, envy, pride, greed, coveting, or competitiveness? Come on...we have to do better than this!

Now, the question is, "How do we obtain our crowns?" The answer is, *"When I consider thy heavens, the work of thy fingers, the moon and the stars, which thou has ordained."* Psalms 8:3. In so many words, we must maximize our gifts, skills, or talents.

When we align ourselves with our Divine Purpose, *As It Pleases God*, the Heavens must yield to assist. If one does not know this, one will depend upon oneself or someone else to fulfill one's heart's desire, mainly when it is not about us at all. Most often, we look to form an allegiance with man when our allegiance should be with our Heavenly Father first, then with self, and then with others in this order, according to *The Lady's Code*. If we deviate from this order, it throws us, our purpose, our cycle, and basically, everything out of balance. As a result, it will cause us to have to work harder to attain what should come naturally or effortlessly.

Revelations 21 wants to get the *Women of Stature* into the mindset of a new way of thinking, a new way of building our house with new walls, a new solid and secure foundation, a new way of exhibiting the Fruits of the Spirit, and a new chapter for our up-and-coming legacy of the New Heaven. *"Now I saw a new heaven and a new earth, for the first heaven and the first earth had passed away. Also there was no more sea."* Revelation 21:1.

As life has it, I am not here to interpret scriptures; I am here to bring life to them. I am here to bring our minds out of the lackadaisical, negative phase of conditioning and cohesion. Furthermore, I am also here to bring forth *The Lady's Code: As It Pleases God* while making it as TRANSPARENT as GLASS.

Upfront and Honest

We can speak on the Pearly Gates and Streets of Gold all we want, but if we are living our lives in total discord, falsehood, abusiveness, or negativity, we may miss the mark anyway. So, let us get an understanding of a few things because we do not want to unintentionally cause harm to ourselves and others by not allowing God to purify us on a moment-by-moment basis.

Of course, we all love God, but most often, our actions, reactions, words, beliefs, habits, or thoughts do not represent the Elements of Godliness. I am not here to point the finger because we are all guilty at some point in the game of life. Nonetheless, in the midst of it, we must understand, learn, pray, repent, forgive, and adjust accordingly.

Let us talk about GOLD for a minute...in its natural state, it looks nothing like what our mind perceives it as being or appearing. Our minds will revert to the finished product. But in order to get to the final stage, we must get rid of the layers of debris covering it. It has to be purified by fire, allowing the GOLD to rise to the top. Although life may put us through the pressures of daily living, the transparencies of what God has placed within us will come out if we allow it to do so. Let me say this: When going through the process, we must steer away from negativity, period!

Why should we avoid negative thoughts, words, actions, desires, and beliefs? It will bring contaminants that are not conducive to the ultimate goal or GOLD, so to speak.

What is our GOLD? From my perspective and according to *The Lady's Code*, it would be the Fruits of the Spirit! They are indeed the GIFT of the Ancient of Days.

Why are the Fruits of the Spirit a Gift to mankind? Fortunately, when used correctly, *As It Pleases God*, the liquid gold melts the human psyche. Blasphemy, right? Wrong! In the word GOLD, if we take the L, we get GOD. What is take the L? Take the loss of the L or lower the L, making us a little lower than the Angels. Once again, "*For thou hast made him a little lower than the angels, and hast crowned him with glory and honor.*" Psalm 8:5.

Is this not a play on words? Maybe or maybe not, but if it keeps your soul intact, breaks yokes, removes chokeholds, or frees you from bondage, *As It Pleases God*, what does it matter? It is no

Upfront and Honest

different from you playing yourself short or in a cycle of déjà vu, particularly when you have the same opportunity to use *The Lady's Code* to your advantage with proven results.

How do we make the Fruits of the Spirit our Gold? Simply put, there is no law against the Fruits of the Spirit. Really? Yes, really! *"But the fruit of the Spirit is love, joy, peace, longsuffering (Patience), kindness, goodness, faithfulness, gentleness, self-control. Against such there is no law."* Galatians 5:22-23. All this means is that living a life characterized by these qualities, which the Holy Spirit produces, is in line with God's Spiritual Laws and *The Lady's Code: As It Pleases Him*, and no greater or lesser law forbids them.

Why is there no greater or lesser law? The Fruits of the Spirit is our LIQUID GOLD or SPIRITUAL GLUE that is hidden in plain sight. And what do we do? We overlook them to capitalize on rotten fruits, leading us into the Pit.

Most often, we think the FAVOR and BLESSINGS of God reside in tangible items. In all truth, our GOLD lies in the things that we cannot see, feel, touch, hear, or taste. If one decides to wait on the Gold in Heaven, I have no qualms with that. Still, it is my responsibility to educate those who have an open ear to hear about the Treasures of the Spirit. To be clear about this matter, I am not saying that we are not going to need provisions to pay our bills, because Matthew 22:21 clearly says, *"Render therefore to Caesar the things that are Caesar's, and to God the things that are God's."* Nonetheless, with outright wisdom, we should not allow our bills to hinder our Spiritual Provisions, Predestined Blueprint, or Spiritual Process.

As the Law of the Land concurs, our Divinely Blueprinted Mission must provide for itself. If it does not, one must go back to the drawing board. For the record, when in this stage of growth, it is okay to revamp, retweak, regraft, readjust, restream, reposition, restructure, renew, reinvent, or resurrect.

What is the reason for having to redo things? In the Eye of God, Divine Purpose takes trial and error. It is improbable that we will get our Divine Purpose, Talents, Creativity, or Giftings right the first time around. If we do, exercise extreme caution because our self-induced purpose may be overriding our Divine Purpose. Is

Upfront and Honest

there a difference? Of course, the lowercase purpose is for you to please yourself or others. Whereas, Divine Purpose is from God, *As It Pleases Him*. Can we have both? Yes, but Divine Purpose and the Kingdom of God must come first.

According to the Heavenly of Heavens, instant anything should raise red flags when it comes to Destiny. It truly takes a classroom or a journey of lessons to draw out the *Woman of Stature* or the Excellence from within. For example, one cannot become a graduate without attending pre-kindergarten or kindergarten while progressing through the educational levels. As a matter of fact, gold is buried within the crevices of the earth, and it has to go through several phases of processing to get to its final stage, and so do you!

If we have a desire to stay on our toes in life, it is imperative that we know, understand, and walk according to our Predestined Blueprint. If, for some reason, we do not understand or know it, we will have a longing from within.

As a result of this longing, we will begin to fill it with people, places, and things that may lead us away from the Kingdom or break *The Lady's Code*. With this form of misleading, we may become abusers, or we will subject ourselves to abuse, Mentally, Physically, Emotionally, and Spiritually. It is not that we subconsciously try to become an abuser or an abusee; it is a default mechanism that comes into play when we lack a proper understanding of our Spiritual Design, *As It Pleases God*.

In life, it is vital to have a clear understanding of our ultimate goal before we start getting bogged down with trivial tasks. Whether it is creating a Mind Map, Goal Map, Journey Map, Success Map, or Life Map, the key is to know the WHAT first. Only once we have a clear understanding of what we want to achieve can we start filling in the gaps with an actionable strategy that includes the WHY, HOW, WHERE, and WHEN of the goal.

Today, be *Upfront and Honest* with yourself by putting a stop to the negative, repetitive stuff or the vicious cycle of déjà vu. And then, get the lessons on paper while asking yourself the right fact-finding questions, *As It Pleases God*. Doing so gives you more time and energy to focus on your life with your *Eyes Wide Open* without having to wing it or be for the streets.

Eyes Wide Open

For the record, with our *Eyes Wide Open* or closed shut, life continues with or without us. We are not here by chance; instead, it is by Divine Design. Despite any outward appearance, every single one of us serves a purpose. Even if we are unaware, have no comprehension, or are simply indifferent, we are all born with our *Eyes Wide Open*. In fact, we succeed simply by being born into this state of consciousness.

In *The Lady's Code: As It Pleases God*, we should not underestimate the potential for success or our ability to fulfill our true calling, according to our Predestined Blueprint. Nonetheless, we must see things for what they are while discerning and perceiving correctly without trying to justify or rationalize the red flags of our conscience. In *The Lady's Code*, we must know when to pursue, hold, fold, or walk away, governing our impulses, thoughts, reactions, and words accordingly. Why would *The Lady's Code* require this? In all simplicity, "*Sweetness of speech increases persuasiveness.*" Proverbs 16:21. And, "*Pleasant words are like a honeycomb, sweetness to the soul and health to the bones.*" Proverbs 16:24.

More importantly, as *Women of Stature*, we play to win. Above all, we do not play dirty because we are God's Chosen Elect...We play by Spiritual Rules to patiently gain Divine Leverage, Discernment, and Wisdom. "*And let us not grow weary while doing good, for in due season we shall reap if we do not lose heart.*" Galatians 6:9.

With our *Eyes Wide Open*, it is human nature to strive for success and growth. Even if someone pretends to be content with mediocrity or losing, deep down, they desire to achieve and improve. According to *The Lady's Code*, accepting failure without any benefits, learning, or attempts to become better can indicate a psychological or Spiritual block that needs to be addressed. Please allow me to align: "*For though by this time you ought to be teachers, you*

Upfront and Honest

need someone to teach you again the first principles of the oracles of God; and you have come to need milk and not solid food." Hebrews 5:12.

As *Women of Stature*, our Divine Mindset allows us to learn and grow from losses, but being complacent about losing is not a healthy mindset in the Eye of God. Why is complacency about loss unhealthy when exhibiting faith, faithfully? God has designed us to be multiplying winners by nature, not losers operating in Mental, Physical, Emotional, or Spiritual Deficits.

Here is the deal: We all have the potential to win and succeed in life, regardless of how it appears to the naked eye. Still, it is up to us to embrace that Divine Mindset and Potential while working towards achieving our goals, *As It Pleases God*. How do we make this make sense? Here is a scripture designed to give us Spiritual Leverage: *"But he who received seed on the good ground is he who hears the word and understands it, who indeed bears fruit and produces: some a hundredfold, some sixty, some thirty."* Matthew 13:23.

Most often, God will not place our TRUE BLESSINGS in what appears to be a blessing! He will wrap our blessings in something or someone that we, in our fleshly states, would reject unless the Spirit is AWAKENED to nudge us or intercede on our behalf. Frankly, this gives us the ability to see what most cannot see or hear what most cannot hear. It is for this reason that I am explaining the importance of casting down our earthly perceptions.

Actually, it behooves me how we worship people, engaging in outright idolatry, when we all have this element of Godliness within us. More importantly, it is God who allows the increase. Please allow me to align: *"I planted, Apollos watered, but God gave the increase. So then neither he who plants is anything, nor he who waters, but God who gives the increase."* 1 Corinthians 3:6-7. Simply, we have a role to play, and we should prepare ourselves to do what we were called to do instead of engaging in idolatry.

According to the Heavenly of Heavens, we must look from within to make sure that our heart matches what our mind thinks. If not, we must find out what is causing the CONFLICT and the reasons why while tending to our own business or staying in our

Upfront and Honest

lanes. Trust me, this will prevent unjustified, unwanted, and unproductive inner turmoil or breaking *The Lady's Code*. As a matter of fact, when we positively allow our conscience to become our guide, *As It Pleases God*, we are better able to save ourselves from making the wrong decisions or going down the wrong path.

With our *Eyes Wide Open*, if we use the Fruits of the Spirit and behave Christlike, it becomes a viable tool of GREATNESS, releasing the oxytocin needed to become and remain balanced and humble.

How can using the Fruits of the Spirit and behaving Christlike release oxytocin? According to the Heavenly of Heavens, our inner child suffers the most neglect known to man, yet it needs the most attention. As our way of escape, *As It Pleases God*, He provided a treasure trove of healing hidden in plain sight. He knows what the body needs better than us; therefore, He allows this social hormone to flow through RIGHTEOUSNESS, servanthood, or when engaging in our Divine Purpose, Passion, or Blueprint. The Fruits of the Spirit and behaving Christlike are a lifeline for the underprivileged, underdeveloped, unaware, abused, and misused, so NO ONE is left behind when used correctly.

What is the purpose of using corrective measures when releasing oxytocin? To maximize our full potential, *As It Pleases God*, we CANNOT have our bodies pumping negativity within us, our Bloodlines, or others; we must counteract it with positivity...POSITIVE ACTION, to be exact!

The release of this social chemical called oxytocin is what God used to bring us into this world by prompting the action of labor. As society continues to evolve, it is the same one connecting us to our reason for being. How do we make this make sense? Childbirth is a miraculous and transformative experience that has been a part of human existence. During childbirth, oxytocin is released from the pituitary gland in the brain. It helps to stimulate contractions in the uterus, which is necessary for the baby to be born. In addition, it is also considered a love hormone, but it is not limited to such. Unbeknown to most, oxytocin also helps to reduce stress and anxiety through the use of the Fruits of the Spirit.

Upfront and Honest

Why do we need oxytocin beyond childbirth? With our *Eyes Wide Open*, we often think we detach ourselves from childhood experiences when we grow up, but we do not often let go. Instead, we inadvertently focus on the negative, unproductive, unfruitful, and most traumatizing, or seek revenge, blocking the full manifestation of our Divine Blueprint. When in all actuality, our inner child is only pinpointing our Spiritual Errors or open wounds, hoping we would positively learn, grow, and sow back into the Kingdom of God, unveiling our magnetic PASSIONS.

According to the Heavenly of Heavens, our outward manifestations follow suit when our inner child heals with *The Lady's Code* enforced, *As It Pleases God*. More importantly, once we respect the psyche, it will begin to respect us without having negative back-and-forth chatter, stealing our ability to become a *Woman of Stature*. It also helps us understand the GRAVITATIONAL PULL of our Divine Blueprint, knowing what is for us and what is not, as a part of our Spiritual Alignment.

The struggles or the issues of life are real for everyone; simply keep it positive, stop judging, and do not give up. Besides, it is the struggle, overcoming, and giving back that build strength, wisdom, and endurance. We are our best miracle! With this in mind, keep your Eyes Wide Open and your ears to the ground Spiritually, as your strength of character becomes wrapped in your integrity. Lastly, you must know, understand, and appreciate this one fact to ensure you do not downplay or overlook the MIRACLE that is designed to BUILD or BLESS you.

The Secrets of the Garden

Everyone is looking for the Garden of Eden…when God has said it would never be found, and it is well guarded. Why would he say this? Because He has hidden the Garden of Eden in plain sight. God has given us the keys to the Garden, yet we are looking all over the place when He has placed it within each and every one of us. In this chapter, I will explain the elements of the Garden that will assist in guiding us to our rightful place in the Kingdom.

Upfront and Honest

The Rules, Concepts, Precepts, and Revelations of the Garden are hidden in plain sight. Do you remember when God clothed Adam and Eve in Genesis 3:21? Of course, we all know the story of God making a sacrifice on Adam and Eve's behalf in the Garden. After doing so, He clothed them on the outside, but more importantly, He clothed them with the Garden from Within before driving them out of the physical Garden.

From my perspective, they were carrying the Garden within them to ensure it was not easily exposed to the natural eye. Plus, if they wanted the Fruits of the Garden, they would have to work for the benefits they were entitled to. Could it be possible that the Fruits of the Garden are really the Fruits of the Spirit? Think about it! No pun intended; let us take this to the Word of God. *"The fruit of the righteous is a tree of life, And he who wins souls is wise."* Proverbs 11:30. *"A wholesome tongue is a tree of life, But perverseness in it breaks the spirit."* Proverbs 15:4.

If we bring this up to today's day and age, the Curse from the Garden is applicable to us as well. Here is the scripture, *"Because you have listened to the voice of your wife and have eaten of the tree from which I commanded you not to eat, cursed is the ground because of you; through toil you will eat of it all the days of your life. Both thorns and thistles it will yield for you, and you will eat the plants of the field. By the sweat of your face you shall eat bread, till you return to the ground, for out of it you were taken; for you are dust, and to dust you shall return."* Genesis 3:17-19. Yet, we do not have to become bound by the curse if we simply understand where God has hidden our solutions.

As life would have it, God has clothed us as well. How do I know? According to Isaiah 61:9-11, *"Their descendants will be known among the nations and their offspring among the peoples. All who see them will acknowledge that they are a people the LORD has blessed. I delight greatly in the LORD; my soul rejoices in my God. For he has clothed me with garments of salvation and arrayed me in a robe of his righteousness, as a bridegroom adorns his head like a priest, and as a bride adorns herself with her jewels. For as the soil makes the sprout come up and a garden causes seeds to grow, so the Sovereign LORD will make righteousness and praise spring up before all*

Upfront and Honest

nations." Need I go any further? It is written in black and white...so, no more pity parties!

As life is upon us, we must take the time to ask ourselves the right questions before we point the finger. Self-analysis and Self-Awareness are the key players in building our Cornerstone of Greatness. If not, they could become contributing factors to our downfall. It behooves us to think about things before passing judgment because, most often, we are guilty of the same things. Better yet, we have been exposed to the same things with a different label attached to them.

In my opinion, we must do a mirror check on ourselves often. In all simplicity, this means that we must keep up with our self-analysis on a consistent basis because there are times when we forget about our history and judge someone else's present situation. We are all subjected to this glitch in our system; thus, we must correct it immediately and consistently.

We all have secrets! It is for this reason that we need to forgive, have mercy, and offer compassion. We never want the things that we are passing judgment on to mirror or manifest themselves in our lives.

Before I move on, let me say this: There are times when we are passing judgment on someone when it is a Spiritual Matter, Spiritual Oppression, or Spiritual Entrapment. If we add to or feed into that negative energy, it becomes contagious. The bottom line is that the negative energy will transfer to us. Whatever that person is going through, we will begin to experience it as well. In order to avoid this, we need to remain positive, prayerful, and compassionate while exhibiting the Fruits of the Spirit. I speak about the Fruits of the Spirit quite often; it is indeed a Spiritual Covering or Protection from the negative atrocities of life.

Certain people can be Spiritually Sifted, and certain people cannot, due to the fact that God has them COVERED. Why does God cover them? Most often, it is due to a Specific Purpose, the contents of their heart, their character, or when we do the right things. Do not get me wrong; God loves us all; however, the Spiritual Favor or Supernatural Favor will be upon those who

Upfront and Honest

exhibit the Fruits of the Spirit while staying positive, prayerful, thankful, compassionate, and merciful.

Of course, no one is perfect. But trust me, we cannot go wrong with clean hands and a pure heart! Now, before we move on to *Avoiding Dullness*, here is what we must know: *"Blessed are those who do His commandments, that they may have the right to the tree of life, and may enter through the gates into the city."* Revelation 22:14.

Avoiding Dullness

According to *The Lady's Code*, a drought is nature's way of correcting itself to keep us universally balanced and harmonious, especially when we are not *Upfront and Honest* with God, ourselves, or others. Without a doubt, this principle applies to every aspect of life; therefore, a drought does not enter our lives to kill us. It comes to heal us in places where we are knowingly or unknowingly wounded, handicapped, or disobedient.

When we stop progressing toward Divine Purpose, *As It Pleases God*, or when we become codependent, we will find that we begin to thirst for something or someone that is not conducive to our well-being. Quenching our thirst for the wrong thing will keep us all over the place mentally and emotionally. Also, it will keep us running to and fro in our busyness, accomplishing nothing, or it will keep us wallowing in a bed of indecisiveness, delaying our bountiful harvest as it relates to our ability to love effectively.

The Lady's Code encourages you to take the time to master those dry, dull, or thirsty places in your life to ensure you do not defy the Purpose of your drought or your reason for loving God, yourself, and others.

In the Eye of God, if the mind is cloudy, it will inhibit our ability to see correctly, resulting in our FOCUS becoming distorted to our detriment. When the door of distractions is open, we will find that any and everything will begin to bombard us with foolishness. Can we control the foolery in our lives? Absolutely. We do not have to entertain distractions by staying calm, not responding at all, or responding positively, keeping our disposition neutral.

Upfront and Honest

How do we know if our disposition is a little off? Here is the deal: Take a look in the mirror, honestly analyzing your thoughts or your perception of yourself. *"As in water face reflects face, So a man's heart reveals the man."* Proverbs 27:19. If they are positive, fruitful, and upright, we have nothing to worry about; however, if our thoughts are negative, abusive, egotistical, or we have to fight off the feelings of disgust, then we have work to do.

Underneath our clouded thoughts, there is sunlight; we need to peel back the layers of the not-so-good to create a win-win to ensure we do not allow people to get into our heads, making us unwise.

How do we create a win-win in the midst of confusion, frustration, and chaos? Take out a sheet of paper, list the problem, and then list the solution positively several times. Personally, I would aim for 100, but if one is not an ELITE strategist, then 10 will do. Does it work? Absolutely.

When we force our minds to think rationally and positively, we have less time to entertain the hogwash of negativity. If we do not train our minds to think inside, outside, around, over, and through the box, we may not be able to think on our feet when turning a negative into a positive at a moment's notice. Besides, our minds will surprise us regarding their GENIUS abilities if we force them to do so.

You have the answers; you simply need to know that you do; therefore, I challenge you today to push your mind beyond your superficial limits while *Making Sense of It*. Here is a list of items that will cause our love to become dull or repulsive:

- ☐ Nagging.
- ☐ Whining.
- ☐ Complaining.
- ☐ Criticizing oneself and others.
- ☐ Indecisiveness or always wishy-washy.
- ☐ Negativity.
- ☐ Fakeness.
- ☐ Abrasiveness.
- ☐ Abusiveness.

Upfront and Honest

- ☐ Lack of responsibility.
- ☐ Lack of understanding.
- ☐ Intentionally hurting others.
- ☐ Yelling.
- ☐ Fighting.
- ☐ Addicted to chaos.
- ☐ Always giving ultimatums.
- ☐ Putting people in a box.
- ☐ Lack of initiative to become proactive.
- ☐ Hatefulness.
- ☐ Rudeness.
- ☐ Lying.
- ☐ Abrasiveness.
- ☐ Arrogance.
- ☐ Disobedience.
- ☐ Disrespectfulness.
- ☐ Unhelpfulness.
- ☐ Kicking people when they are down.
- ☐ Expecting more than we are willing to give.
- ☐ Contentiousness.

When we exhibit dull and repulsive behaviors, we will find that life will pull us into an unpleasant place, Mentally, Emotionally, Physically, and Spiritually.

According to the Heavenly of Heavens, being in a dry, dull place or when experiencing a drought in life is really a time of self-correction. If we do not self-correct, *As It Pleases God*, a Spiritual Chokehold or Yoke will remain.

What does self-correction have to do with anything, especially when having free will? In the Eye of God, self-correction is a crucial aspect of our Spiritual Growth, Divine Navigation, Predestined Blueprint, and maximizing the effects of Spiritual Dualism. More importantly, in *The Lady's Code*, without exhibiting personal accountability, it is impossible to become Spiritually Accountable, *As It Pleases God*.

Upfront and Honest

As *Women of Stature*, we must take responsibility for our actions, reactions, thoughts, beliefs, words, desires, and decisions to maintain our Divine Poshness. Clearly, self-correction is not merely about identifying our flaws, habits, patterns, or traumas only. Spiritually, it is more about introspection, honesty, transparency, and an acknowledgment that we are capable of mistakes with a work-in-progress mentality, *As It Pleases God*.

This mindset in *The Lady's Code* helps us become teachable, usable, understandable, relatable, and actionable, knowing what to do, when to do it, where to do it, why we are doing so, and with whom to do or not to do it.

In recognizing our imperfections and striving for improvement, *As It Pleases God*, we can overcome the challenges and uncertainties in life. With this approach, we become more adaptable and better equipped to handle future difficulties with a Divine Sharpness that will put our enemies to boot or crack open the Heavenly of Heavens at the drop of a dime.

What if we opt out of becoming teachable, usable, understandable, relatable, and actionable? The Baggage will remain, weighing us down with whips and chains of our own making.

Embracing Teachability

Embracing the Spirit of Teachability is not just about being open to learning. It is also about Spiritually Aligning ourselves with a Greater Purpose for a Greater Good with obedience, growth, and understanding, *As It Pleases God*.

When being *Upfront and Honest*, the willingness, receptiveness, and humility to learn from others, *As It Pleases God*, opens the door to Divine Greatness, allowing us to grow in wisdom and stature. In addition, as a bonus, it also assists in strengthening our relationships and helps us to face life's challenges with peace, grace, understanding, and tenacity.

On the other hand, disobedience, inflexibility, complaining, fussing, fighting, and pompousness get the Door of Wisdom closed

Upfront and Honest

in our faces, weakening our relational bonds as life does a number on us. Why would this happen? First, disobedience and complaining are a sore spot for God. Secondly, when we do not listen in our teachable moments, we will find ourselves between a rock and a hard place.

In the Eye of God, we are taught to teach, and teach to be taught, activating the Law of Reciprocity and Growth, while becoming our Acts of Service. What does this mean? In the Kingdom of God, it is our duty or reasonable service to evolve and transfer knowledge, wisdom, and understanding as a Sacred Exchange for our Heaven on Earth Experiences. With this mindset, we open ourselves up to Divine Wisdom and Kingdom Usability. It is often said, 'If God cannot get anything through us, it hinders His ability to get things to us because we will not recognize it.'

If we become unteachable, we cannot teach correctly and effectively; then again, we may teach with malicious intent, or we may teach with falsity, inflicting harm on the minds and hearts of our relational hearers. In addition, we will become stagnant and murky, erecting all types of walls and barriers with misconceptions or perpetuated biases, making it more important for the *Women of Stature* to read the *Writing on the Wall*.

Why must we read the *Writing on the Wall* with the unteachable? First, as *Women of Stature*, there is something to learn from everything and everyone, and just because they refuse to learn from us does not mean we cannot learn from them. Secondly, people will tell us who they are if we listen long enough. Here is what Proverbs 25:26 wants us to know about paying attention to the *Writing on the Wall*: "A righteous man who falters before the wicked is like a murky spring and a polluted well."

In essence, our willingness to learn, grow, and sow back into the Kingdom of God when called upon will Divinely Illuminate our paths toward Greatness. In *The Lady's Code*, without this capacity, our Predestined Blueprint will remain hidden from us until we open ourselves up to become humble, teachable, and serviceable. If not, *The Baggage* will remain.

Upfront and Honest

Unpacking our Divine Blueprint or Baggage, *As It Pleases God*, is not a daunting task as most would think, especially when we are *Upfront and Honest* with God, ourselves, and others. The moment we become genuinely, transparently, and readily willing to confront our past, weaknesses, traumas, scars, fears, regrets, and unresolved conflicts, they become the catalysts for Divine Transformation, Healing, and Growth.

As we embark upon the path of Divine Liberation, as *Women of Stature*, let us shine brightly and unpack *The Baggage* in the next chapter.

CHAPTER 4

THE BAGGAGE

Are you carrying unnecessary baggage? Have you inherited baggage from another? Are you becoming weighed down by the amount you are carrying? Are you ready to unpack or carry your own load? In this chapter of *The Lady's Code: As It Pleases God*, get ready to unpack what is draining your creative juices as a *Woman of Stature*.

In the Eye of God, emotional and mental baggage can deprive you of reaching your full potential, *As It Pleases Him*. Even if you appear to have it going on with or without Him, there is always more to your potentiality of Divine Greatness or your Predestined Blueprint.

Why are we deprived of our maximum potential as Believers when we are faithfully serving God? Just because we serve Him, our Heavenly Father, does not necessarily mean that we are obedient, forgiving, repentant, kind, or humble. Nor does it mean that we are on the correct Level of Spirituality using the MEAT of the Word of God, *As It Pleases Him*. Furthermore, as Believers, if we opt to remain in the milking or pretense stages of Spirituality, we can create a disservice to ourselves and others.

When we remain on Spiritual Milk, which is the first Level of Spirituality, unresolved issues within a traumatized psyche lead to

The Baggage

negative emotions, thoughts, beliefs, biases, behaviors, habits, and words. All of this leads to the spoiled milk of jealousy, unregulated envy, superfluous pride, excessive greed, unmanaged anger, elongated fear, unfettered hatefulness, hidden resentment, outright disobedience, limited beliefs, underlying coveting, secret competitiveness, longstanding rudeness, obvious dullness, hidden self-doubt, a history of lukewarmness, and a stiff neck.

Is it humanly possible to possess all of these negative characteristics? Unfortunately, it is humanly probable with a trail of rotten fruits that do not lie. Then again, in my opinion, the stench of rotten milk is not a pleasant smell either.

Meanwhile, when dealing with positive or negative characteristics in *The Lady's Code* with *The Baggage* you are carrying, you have two choices:

1. Carry *The Baggage*.
2. Unpack *The Baggage*.

Carrying *The Baggage* from a previous relationship into a new one weighs it down. Why would a relationship become weighed down in such a manner? It has a Competitive Spirit of Oppression attached to it.

In the Kingdom of God, having a Competitive Spirit means selfishly focusing more on oneself and trying to outdo others rather than working collaboratively for the common or greater good. With unresolved baggage, one tends to compare oneself to others, wanting to be better than them, and feeling envious when others achieve success. Unfortunately, this hinders personal growth and relationships with others, as it can lead to a lack of empathy and respect.

When one is comparing the old bags with the new, it could leave a bad taste in someone's mouth. There are some things that we may have to expose out of honesty. But there are some things that we are going to have to leave in the closet and vow never to expose.

Should we not be open and honest in a relationship? Of course, we should. Nevertheless, some things about previous relationships should be left alone.

The Baggage

For example, in your previous relationship, your mate was a better bed partner, making you climb the walls. Do you think it is wise to convey that to your new partner, especially if you are struggling to climb into bed with them? Out of respect, you should keep that information about your ex to yourself and convey what you like based on your current situation.

Why should we withhold this information from them? If your ex had you climbing the walls but could not keep you mentally, emotionally, or physically satisfied, then they have no place in your current situation. Would you not agree? Wait, wait, wait, before you agree, please allow me to make a statement: They are your ex for a reason; therefore, you should never allow their inability to keep you to interfere with your present situation.

Everyone has a past, but we should never allow our history to prevent us from embracing our future. If one is done with the old, we must put it away and enjoy the new with humility, kindness, respect, and selflessness, working together for the betterment of all.

In the Eye of God, comparing is one of the biggest time wasters known to man. While at the same time, measuring has proven to be one of the biggest time-maximizers. They are sort of the same but very different in their very own unique way, creating a thin line between the two.

What is the big deal about comparing, especially when dealing with *The Lady's Code: As It Pleases God*? Comparing is indeed a form of measurement, but the difference is the MOTIVE behind it. Typically, comparing is used to examine, justify, or rationalize based on an individual's perception, which usually creates limits.

Meanwhile, measuring is based more on facts that typically heighten the growth of an individual. Furthermore, measuring allows us to set reasonable boundaries to maximize our effectiveness, which will produce something positive and productive.

When setting goals, measuring is a prerequisite! With that being said, comparing ourselves with others is not an option; we must find a way to avoid this at all costs. *"For we dare not class*

The Baggage

ourselves or compare ourselves with those who commend themselves. But they, measuring themselves by themselves, and comparing themselves among themselves, are not wise." 2 Corinthians 10:12.

In or out of a relationship with *The Lady's Code: As It Pleases God*, you will not have to compete against anyone besides yourself. How is it possible to compete against ourselves? Competing against yourself to become better each day is a win-win; it only means you will have to get a little creative or strategic while challenging yourself, Mentally, Emotionally, Physically, and Spiritually. "*But let each one examine his own work, and then he will have rejoicing in himself alone, and not in another.*" Galatians 6:4.

As *Women of Stature*, when your game is tight, working on yourself, *As It Pleases God*, you do not have to compete with others against your own uniqueness. How can we develop this mentality? Repeat this: "*I can do all things through Christ who strengthens me.*" Philippians 4:13. While standing on this scripture: "*Trust in the Lord with all your heart, and lean not on your own understanding; in all your ways acknowledge Him, and He shall direct your paths.*" Proverbs 3:5-6.

The Lady's Code: As It Pleases God warns against player-hating or playing one person against another. Why should we exhibit caution? It indicates an instigator, a problem creator, or a troublemaker. So, exercise extreme caution with anyone who exhibits this type of charactorial behavior.

Unbeknown to most, a Competitive Spirit is an obvious sign or red flag of insecurity. "*For where envy and self-seeking exist, confusion and every evil thing are there.*" James 3:16. On the other hand, if you have someone all in your chops trying to steal your ideas to outdo you with your stuff, this is outright PIRACY! For this reason, it is imperative to deal with three walls:

- ☐ The Wall of Forgiveness.
- ☐ The Wall of the Breaking Process.
- ☐ The Wall of Letting Go.

The Baggage

What is the purpose of dealing with these three Walls? Regardless of the baggage we are dealing with and from whom, forgiveness, breaking, and letting go are required. If we hold on to baggage, we will eventually turn on ourselves.

As an Element of Wisdom and a *Woman of Divine Stature*, I use my ideas as a gauge to see who I can trust and who I cannot. I will also allow individuals to paint a superficial scenario without correcting their perception of who I am. Why would I allow them to develop a false perception? According to *The Lady's Code: As It Pleases God*, I must give them the free will option to ACCEPT or REJECT what God has designed to BLESS them.

But more importantly, I reveal my imperfections first before I reveal the Hidden Greatness. Why would I not put my best foot forward? I allow people to REJECT the not-so-good things about me before they can enjoy the Fruits of my Labor. In my opinion, if their judgmental, thwarted perception caused them to think I am not worthy of becoming a part of their life, they would remove themselves without me having to do the legwork.

With my personality, I am incredibly friendly and humble, but I also strategically appear weak to draw out the wolves in sheep's clothing. As my trump card, I will place half of the idea on the table, or I will give them just enough information to betray me in a relationship, friendship, or when doing business. Is it a game? The answer is NO. It is Kingdom BUSINESS!

I am required to TEST the Spirit. When doing business, you need to know who you are dealing with; if not, you will look very UNWISE going toe-to-toe with someone with your idea in its totality! I have been there before, and it is not enjoyable to be surpassed by those with your ideas. So, protect yourself.

How can we spot an insecure person? It is very simple, just look around. We are all insecure about something, and we are all a work-in-progress. However, an extremely insecure person can be spotted by their jealousy, envy, coveting, character, attitude, and behavior. In addition, they are also known by their fruits. Here is what to look for, but not limited to such:

- ☐ Their extreme ability to browbeat others.

The Baggage

- ☐ Their hatefulness and disobedience.
- ☐ Their loose lips.
- ☐ Their ability to criticize others about the same things they are guilty of.
- ☐ Their ability to gossip profusely about others.
- ☐ Their ability to use the past against others as leverage to get what they want.
- ☐ Their ability to be insensitive to the feelings or emotions of others.
- ☐ Their lack of consistency, peace, or patience.
- ☐ Their ability to abuse others without giving it a second thought.
- ☐ Their lack of self-control.
- ☐ They are rude and disrespectful.
- ☐ They lie a lot, and for no reason.

What is the significance of being conscious of such aspects? Insecurity can lead an individual to seek out flaws in others to conceal their own insecurities or struggles with forgiveness.

On the other hand, if you desire to attain a sense of security with *The Lady's Code: As It Pleases God*, try focusing on the positive aspects of people and situations with forgiveness at the forefront. You will be amazed at how this simple change in perspective can bring out the innate goodness within you and bring forth the *Woman of Stature* in the Eye of God.

Wall of Forgiveness

Are you forgiving? Are you aware of the benefits of forgiving? Do you feel better holding a grudge? Are you aware of the consequences of not forgiving yourself and others? Do you believe in self-forgiveness? *The Lady's Code: As It Pleases God* stakes its claim on REPENTANCE and FORGIVENESS. Without the two, we will make our lives more complex. Plus, it prevents us from becoming a *Woman of Stature* in the Eye of God. Even if we have

The Baggage

worldly or self-proclaimed stature, it does not equate to Heavenly Standards. Therefore, the *Wall of Forgiveness* has a viable message for those who are carrying *The Baggage* of unforgiveness.

Carrying *The Baggage* of unforgiveness can be a heavy burden that weighs us down, causing us to play pretend. When we hold grudges and refuse to forgive others, we are essentially allowing their actions to have power over us, regardless of how we rationalize or justify them.

How do we know if unforgiveness is controlling us? We become consumed with anger, hatefulness, revenge, resentment, and bitterness, which can negatively impact our mental and emotional well-being. Not only does unforgiveness damage us, but it also affects our relationships with others, like falling dominoes, and causes us to lash out at others who may be innocent.

Forgiveness is a powerful tool that can help us let go of the past and move forward in life with a sense of peace and freedom because mistakes are going to happen. The *Writing on the Wall* says that when we make a mistake, we will see it in two ways:

1. We will see it as MI-STAKE or MY-STAKE, where we have suffered some form of loss of what we may have had at stake.

2. We will see it as MIS-TAKE, where our perception of the situation, circumstance, or situation was inaccurate, basically taking something the wrong way that resulted in some form of REGRET.

As *The Lady's Code* concurs, mistake or not, we forgive for our sake or salvation, not theirs. Self-forgiveness is an essential aspect of personal growth, understanding, and healing. It involves acknowledging and accepting responsibility for one's actions or the lack thereof while also showing love, compassion, and consideration for oneself.

It is no secret that forgiveness is a process, and it may take time to fully work through our emotions, traumas, upsets, and resets.

The Baggage

And it is perfectly okay in the Eye of God because He knows it takes time to heal and process our feelings instead of blocking or suppressing them. However, we cannot leave Him out of the equation. *"If we confess our sins, He is faithful and just to forgive us our sins and to cleanse us from all unrighteousness."* 1 John 1:9.

What if we are not the culprits of sin? We have been sinned against, then what do we do? *"But if you do not forgive men their trespasses, neither will your Father forgive your trespasses."* Matthew 6:15.

As *Women of Stature*, living with no regrets requires forgiveness, period. However, in order to do so, we must begin to look at everything from a positive perspective, learn the lesson, share it, and move on to create a win-win situation in the Spirit of Excellence. What if it is not that easy? I understand all too well. So here are a few tips that may help you in the process of forgiveness, but not limited to such:

- ☐ Calm your mind and emotions by taking deep breaths.
- ☐ Develop a *Spirit to Spirit* Relationship with God.
- ☐ Pray, repent, and forgive.
- ☐ Give or release it to God.
- ☐ Release expecting an apology or reconciliation.
- ☐ Give thanks for the experience.
- ☐ Invite the presence of the Holy Spirit.
- ☐ Cover yourself with the Blood of Jesus as Spiritual Atonement.
- ☐ Practice meditation.
- ☐ Try to understand the person or situation that caused the hurt.
- ☐ Avoid holding grudges.
- ☐ Focus on moving forward.
- ☐ Put yourself in the other person's shoes.
- ☐ Let go of the need to be correct.
- ☐ Realize and accept that everyone makes mistakes.
- ☐ Practice self-forgiveness.
- ☐ Let go of any guilt or shame you may feel.
- ☐ Seek guidance or speak with a therapist or counselor.
- ☐ Write a letter expressing your feelings or journal them.

The Baggage

- ☐ Surround yourself with positive and supportive people.
- ☐ Practice patience and give yourself and others time to heal.
- ☐ Set healthy boundaries to prevent future hurt or resentment.
- ☐ Release negative energy.

Always remember, when it comes down to forgiveness, there are TWO sides to every coin, positive or negative, good or bad, successful or unsuccessful. But the funny thing is that we get to choose our side of the coin by our MINDSET and our willingness to put away dead things. If we cannot change it, then get over it! Each side of the coin takes the same amount of energy to cultivate freedom or bondage....so choose!

Wall of the Breaking Process

Have you been broken? Are you having a hard time healing? Is your heart oozing all over others? Better yet, the ultimate question is, 'How do we heal a broken heart?' Straight off the cuff, TIME heals all wounds when the Holy Trinity is involved. Really? Yes, really! On the other hand, self-healing without the Holy Trinity prolongs the process, with band-aid healings continuing to reopen when triggered.

With the *Wall of the Breaking Process*, it is always best to add God into the equation, allow the Holy Spirit in, and cover ourselves with the Blood of Jesus. Why do we need to add the Holy Trinity into the equation, especially when operating with free will? It is not mandatory; it is optional.

Here is the deal: Heartbreak is a common human experience that can be caused by a variety of circumstances, such as the end of a relationship, the loss of a loved one, betrayal from someone we trusted, or abusive trauma. Although it can be a harrowing experience, it is essential to remember that we are not alone in our pain, and there are ways to cope, heal, and grow GREAT.

According to the *Wall of the Breaking Process*, no one is exempt from being broken. Although we want to live in a perfect world,

The Baggage

as we all know, this is not the case. Here is what we must know: *"I returned and saw under the sun that—The race is not to the swift, Nor the battle to the strong, Nor bread to the wise, Nor riches to men of understanding, Nor favor to men of skill; But time and chance happen to them all."* Ecclesiastes 9:11.

In *The Lady's Code: As It Pleases God*, heartbreak is not the end of the world but rather an opportunity to grow, understand, and learn from the experience. How do I know? For *"The Spirit of the Lord God is upon me, because the Lord has anointed me to preach good tidings to the poor; He has sent me to heal the brokenhearted, to proclaim liberty to the captives, and the opening of the prison to those who are bound."* Isaiah 61:1.

Most often, we think being broken is a bad thing when it is not in the Eye of God. According to scripture, *"The sacrifices of God are a broken spirit, A broken and a contrite heart—These, O God, You will not despise."* Psalm 51:17.

Amid brokenness, it is best to avoid people who make excuses or blame others for their shortcomings. In any relationship, it is best to learn how to own our faults. If we make a mistake, own it; if we fall short, own it. Refusing to admit mistakes will contradict or compromise a person's ability to learn, adapt, and adjust to change, thrusting them into a cycle of déjà vu. In essence, this is the place we want to avoid.

Make no mistake about it: Just because a bad decision is made in climbing up the wrong tree does not necessarily mean that a wrong decision was made. It is possible to make the right decision to do the wrong thing! In doing so, it will do two things:

- ☐ BREAK YOU. *" 'Is not My word like a fire?' says the Lord, "And like a hammer that breaks the rock in pieces?"* Jeremiah 23:29.

- ☐ MAKE YOU. *"He heals the brokenhearted and binds up their wounds."* Psalm 147:3.

In so many words, God will break you out of your old habits or limitations and put you back together by transforming you into

The Baggage

a person of substance. Easier said than done, right? But it is doable! As a rule of thumb in *The Lady's Code: As It Pleases God*, you never want to bear fruit in the wrong tree, regardless of the appeal or desire.

Bearing fruit in the wrong tree could be devastating if you allow the bad or wrong fruit to take root in your heart. Better yet, start listening and allowing your conscience to become your guide as you wait for God to synchronize your heart and your mind. Here are a few ways to begin the healing process, but not limited to such:

- ☐ Acknowledge and accept your emotions or brokenness.
- ☐ Develop a *Spirit to Spirit* Relationship.
- ☐ Pray, forgive, repent, and meditate.
- ☐ Usher in the Holy Spirit over the broken area.
- ☐ Cover the brokenness with the Blood of Jesus.
- ☐ Reverse the negative into a positive and document the win-win.
- ☐ Give thanks in all things.
- ☐ Write in a journal to process your thoughts and feelings.
- ☐ Understand your WHY or CYCLE.
- ☐ Ask, 'What do I need to learn?' 'What do I need to understand?'
- ☐ Engage in creative outlets like art, writing, or music.
- ☐ Connect with nature and spend time outdoors.
- ☐ Set boundaries and say no to things that do not serve you.
- ☐ Focus on the positive aspects of your life.
- ☐ Challenge negative thought patterns.
- ☐ Reframe your mindset with the Word of God.
- ☐ Practice deep breathing exercises to calm your nerves.
- ☐ Seek out support groups.
- ☐ Engage in acts of kindness towards others.
- ☐ Prioritize sleep and establish a consistent sleep routine.

Although everyone's brokenness will be different, we do not have to feel lost. Once we develop a Spiritual System, *As It Pleases God*,

The Baggage

we are better able to learn, grow, and sow back into the Kingdom when called upon, especially if we read the *Wall of Letting Go* and do not break *The Lady's Code*.

Wall of Letting Go

Do you have a problem letting go? Is fear crippling you? Do you know how to let go? Are you holding on for dear life? With *The Lady's Code: As It Pleases God*, you should not throw away a great relationship because of one mistake. If your partner, spouse, or mate came clean and assumed responsibility for their infidelity or error, and you want to restore the relationship, then why not? If you decide to do so, to move on properly, you must repair the broken bonds of trust, vowing to forgive and forget.

Of course, it may take a little time to forgive or forget; however, you must never bring up the reason for the initial breakup again. Even though it may become tempting, do not live in the past, especially when you have chosen to move on with your relationship. Nonetheless, if you cannot forgive or forget, then you should let go of the relationship!

The *Writing on the Wall* says that when someone has their mind made up, it is our cue to deal with it or not to deal with it. We should never stress ourselves out with adults who are playing childish mind games to get what they want. Fundamental growth starts when we put away childishness! If one is going to forgive, then forgive! If one is going to love, then love! If one is going to behave, then behave! If one is going to do, then do! If one is going to leave, then leave! If one is going to win, then win! The bottom line is that it is either a deal or not a deal, period!

Why do we need to forgive someone who is constantly making a fool out of us? Forgiveness is a must in order for us to move on Mentally, Emotionally, and Spiritually. Once again, we do not forgive someone for their sake; we forgive them for our own! What if we feel like a fool for forgiving? In my opinion, what makes us more of a fool is when we give someone power over our lives by controlling us when we have the power to disengage.

The Baggage

Why would we want to torture ourselves when it is obvious the person we are holding a grudge against is living happily ever after or doing their own thing? And here we are, torturing ourselves with our own emotions or allowing them to get into our heads. Come on! It is not wise to cause ourselves to suffer when we have the option to live in freedom if we simply forgive and let go.

When we hit the RESET button on our emotions, choosing to forgive, we are better able to glean from the vestibule of grace and mercy when it is our turn to be forgiven. It is not a matter of IF we need forgiveness; it is a matter of WHEN.

In *The Lady's Code: As It Pleases God*, we are all a work-in-progress, regardless of how well we paint the picture. We must exercise our God-given right to forgive to ensure that when we fall short, grace and mercy become a shield to cover us, even when we cannot foresee the wiles of the enemy. I am not saying that we will not get angry, but "*Be angry, yet do not sin. Do not let the sun set while you are still angry,*" according to Ephesians 4:26. As *Women of Stature*, if we need to vent, go ahead and do so. By the time the sun sets in the west, so should our anger. And forgiveness should reside in our hearts before we go to bed to ensure that we are able to have peace while we are sleeping.

Unbeknown to most, unforgiveness is the main contributor to what we call insomnia! For this reason, we must cleanse our souls of this negative emotion as soon as possible.

Do I have my moments? Absolutely! There are times when I just want to stay mad, especially when my kindness is taken as a weakness. I have trained myself so well that I cannot stay mad for long, even if I tried. I will forget about being mad because my mind will automatically move on to a happy state, superseding my emotions.

Once the Spirit of Forgiveness and letting go becomes a part of who we are, grudges are less likely to be held against someone. Thus, it is easier to let go of people, places, and things unless there has been a severe psychological trauma, causing us to harbor unforgiveness temporarily. However, in order to move beyond any type of trauma, according to the *Wall of Letting Go*, forgiveness and repentance must take place, whether they are a part of our

The Baggage

character or not. In *The Lady's Code*, here are a few tips on letting go, but not limited to such:

- ☐ Know and understand WHAT you must let go.
- ☐ Understand WHY you are letting go.
- ☐ Write down your thoughts, qualms, and feelings.
- ☐ Ask for help from the Holy Spirit.
- ☐ Cover the issue with the Blood of Jesus.
- ☐ Visualize and release them to God.
- ☐ Embrace your healing.
- ☐ Practice deep breathing to help you calm down and relax.
- ☐ Learn to recognize negative thought patterns.
- ☐ Replace them with positive ones.
- ☐ Let go of toxic or triggering relationships.
- ☐ Surround yourself with positive and supportive people.
- ☐ Practice forgiveness towards yourself and others.
- ☐ Take responsibility for your thoughts, actions, and emotions.
- ☐ Practice acceptance of what you cannot change.
- ☐ Let go of false expectations.
- ☐ Learn to accept things as they are.
- ☐ Spend time in nature.
- ☐ Practice gratitude for all things.
- ☐ Let go of regrets.
- ☐ Focus on the lessons you have learned.
- ☐ Be kind to yourself.
- ☐ Share your Testimony with others, *As It Pleases God*.

The Heavenly of Heavens has blessed you with a wonderful gift—the ability to hit the reset button on your emotions, forgiveness, or favor anytime you need it. As a part of *The Lady's Code*, it is imperative to utilize this gift to free yourself from any emotional burdens and make peace with those who have wronged you or whom you have wronged. So, take advantage of this gift, *As It Pleases God*, and let go of any negativity that may be holding you back.

CHAPTER 5

THE LADY'S CODE

Are you standing up for other women? Can you stand up for each other in the face of discrimination, lies, or harassment? Can you overcome societal expectations and stereotypes that pit us against each other? Are you willing to work together to break down barriers and promote equality? In *The Lady's Code*, women need to have a unified voice when advocating for their rights, *As It Pleases God*. As *Women of Stature*, it is our responsibility to lead by example in the Spirit of Excellence, training the younger, immature, and misled regarding our personal, professional, and business relationships.

What is the big deal about relationships in *The Lady's Code*? Most of our issues surround relationships because we are not a one-pony rodeo. God created us as relational beings, and the moment we stop relating, *As It Pleases Him* to please ourselves instead, we will have issues. Here is what we must know regarding this matter: *"Two are better than one because they have a good reward for their labor. For if they fall, one will lift up his companion. But woe to him who is alone when he falls, For he has no one to help him up."* Ecclesiastes 4:9-10. On the other hand, *"A man who isolates himself seeks his own desire; He rages against all wise judgment."* Proverbs 18:1.

The Lady's Code

The Lady's Code deals with the *Writing on the Walls*, unveiling relational issues affecting the Mind, Body, Soul, and Spirit, contending with the vices of love. What does this mean? In the Eye of God, love is our kryptonite or most significant asset. In all simplicity, our biggest downfall surrounds love...the lack of it...too much of it...the desire for it...the longing not to lose it, and so on.

When going from the girl's code to *The Lady's Code* is not a faint feat. It takes work, diligence, self-control, and know-how, *As It Pleases God*, to put love in its proper perspective.

Love is not about being weak; it is about being humble. Yes, humility will take us places where a stone-cold heart can never keep us. Of course, this does not mean that one cannot exhibit tough love; it means that one can humbly love and exhibit positive strength at the same time. There is nothing weak about this type of individual; they are very polite and confident, know what they want, and do not have to abuse love to get it.

What is *The Lady's Code*? It is a Divine Code of Spiritual Ethics to govern ourselves *As It Pleases God.* The BINDING Spiritual Principle we adhere to is: *"Do not let your adornment be merely outward—arranging the hair, wearing gold, or putting on fine apparel—rather let it be the hidden person of the heart, with the incorruptible beauty of a gentle and quiet spirit, which is very precious in the sight of God."* 1 Peter 3:3-4. This position in the Eye of God is coveted by most and achieved by few. Why is this the case? Spiritual Laws govern us, separating the girls (Women of Games) from the Ladies (Women of Stature). For this reason, breaking *The Lady's Code* is highly frowned upon by the Heavenly of Heavens; therefore, we must always read the *Writing on the Wall*. Nonetheless, when *"She opens her mouth with wisdom, And on her tongue is the law of kindness."* Proverbs 31:26.

Am I being biased about *The Lady's Code*? Maybe or maybe not, depending on the mindset of the individual who is reading it. I am not preventing anyone from gleaning this information; however, the characteristics of a woman are different from those of a male. Nonetheless, when dealing with Lady Justice or Divine Wisdom from the Book of Proverbs, it is feminine in gender. So if we are gender biased, then Divine Wisdom would never abide within the one who judges her in such a manner.

Is the femininity of wisdom real? Absolutely. She demands respect! Blasphemy, right? Wrong! Here is what we must know regarding this matter: *"Get wisdom! Get understanding! Do not forget, nor turn away from the words of my mouth. Do not forsake her, and she will preserve you; Love her, and she will keep you. Wisdom is the principal thing; Therefore get wisdom. And in all your getting, get understanding. Exalt her, and she will promote you; She will bring you honor, when you embrace her. She will place on your head an ornament of grace; A crown of glory she will deliver to you."* Proverbs 4:5-9.

The love of a mother or mother figure is essential in a child's eyes, but more importantly, she is a mother for all. How do we make this make sense? According to scripture, if Eve is the mother of all things, then so are we as *Women of Stature*. Here is what we must know: *"And Adam called his wife's name Eve, because she was the mother of all living."* Genesis 3:20.

Understandably, we all have a birth mother, mom, mum, or ma, but the Proverbs 31 Woman of *The Lady's Code* takes motherhood to another level in the Eye of God. How so? A *Woman of Stature* operates in her Divine Blueprinted Purpose to Spiritually Seal her Bloodline for generations with intentionality, creativity, and preciseness, documenting her Spiritual Journey for the next in line.

Why do *Women of Stature* go to such extremes? She prepares her DNA to remain with determinational Fruits of the Spirit and character traits that are dependable and proven by the Word of God. What does this mean? She ensures her children can sustain, determine, and maintain the Bountiful Blessings associated with using their Gifts, Calling, Talents, and Creativity with Supernatural Discernment, according to their Divine Blueprint and *Spirit to Spirit* Relations with God.

Above all, *The Lady's Code: As It Pleases God* for the *Women of Stature* is derived from this scripture: *"The older women likewise, that they be reverent in behavior, not slanderers, not given to much wine, teachers of good things—that they admonish the young women to love their husbands, to love their children, to be discreet, chaste, homemakers, good, obedient to their own husbands, that the word of God may not be blasphemed."* Titus 2:3-5.

The nurturing of *The Lady's Code* in the Eye of God is a TEACHER to those she interacts with, leading by example. As a *Woman of Stature*, she is keen on not wasting her life experiences, as her alertness makes her attentive to the areas most overlooked. Although a *Woman of Stature* can go from 0 to 100 quickly, she has mastered a level of calmness and cautiousness to protect her family with boldness, letting everyone know what belongs to her without saying one word. Her eloquence is unmistakably exuded through her motherly confidence in caring for herself with loads to share with those in need.

The *Writing on the Wall* gets ignored time and time again based on our current emotions, mindsets, present situations, or experiences. I am sure this is not done intentionally; however, it is by default by those who do not understand how to read it, those who refuse to read it, or those who are blinded by their own reality. What commonly occurs is that we get into relationships while basing our new experiences entirely on the past. Then again, it could arise from mere tit-for-tat games while expecting the relationship to be perfect.

Not only are we unconscious of our behavior or character, but most often, we couldn't care less about the *Writing on the Wall*, as long as we are getting what we want or it is providing some sort of benefit. Even though this sort of behavior is very destructive, we must understand that most of our really bad habits are learned from our childhood experiences or traumas. More specifically, I am speaking about the common practice of selfishness, ungratefulness, conditional love, and unforgiveness toward ourselves and others. In my opinion, these are the biggest woes we have to deal with as being derivatives of our Mental, Physical, Emotional, and Spiritual Abuses.

Whether the *Writing on the Wall* is for us or someone else, these subtle, destructive behaviors must be dealt with in order to have great relationships. For this reason, we have three walls to deal with in this chapter:

The Lady's Code

- ☐ Wall of Divorce.
- ☐ Wall of Dead-Ends.
- ☐ Wall of Relational Assets.

What if we are not a *Woman of Stature* or fall short in these areas, knowing nothing about being a Proverbs 31 Woman? All women have a hidden desire to be a Proverbs 31 Woman or have motherly instincts. Still, we do not all know what it truly takes or the wisdom needed to become such a woman, *As It Pleases God*. At the same time, we appear to be the best of the best in our own eyes, doing our own or the wrong things to the best of our ability or level of conditioning.

Regardless of our feelings, our life provides the experience needed for the transformational process to occur through the Power of our Testimony. Really? Yes, Really! A Proverbs 31 Woman is a developed and evolved MINDSET, *As It Pleases God*, using the Holy Spirit to guide and the Blood of Jesus as a covering over her, her family, her home, her circle, and others.

A *Woman of Stature* is not perfect; she is humbly teachable, easily understood, intentionally calm, repents or forgives quickly, and knows how to align herself Spiritually, *As It Pleases God*. How does she do it with an active lifestyle? By using *The Lady's Code* and working on her thoughts, attitude, actions, biases, conditioning, character, and fruits daily through self-examination and self-analysis according to the Word of God.

How can we apply this to real life? In all simplicity, it is operating in the Spirit of Excellence with the Word of God in hand, faithfully reversing negatives into positives, and creating a win-win out of everything with enthusiasm, regardless of how it appears to the naked eye.

Regardless of whether we are in or out of a relationship, we still need to learn how to date and provide excitement, or life will get very dull. Why would dullness consume a Believer who is on fire for God? With boredom, infidelity comes looking for our attention...so, beware. As it relates to *The Lady's Code*, it behooves us to become experts on how to read the *Writing on the Wall* to ensure that the lame pickup lines or flimsy excuses do not become our worst nightmare, resulting in a brutal breakup or divorce.

Wall of Divorce

We have been conditioned to think that divorce is the solution to our differences, excuses, or cheating, which is so far from the truth. Divorce has a way of creating a wound that time will only heal. We do not like to talk about divorce; it is just something we are conditioned to do when one or both parties choose not to work something out. It has become an easy way out when we feel trapped, unsatisfied, or unhappy.

When we lose faith in our relationships or marriages, infidelity has a way of calling our names. Most often, we will not admit that we have lost faith in our relationships; however, it is established in our actions.

We are often taught to look down on cheaters, but why are so many people getting hurt by something we are taught to refrain from? Or, better yet, why are there so many Christians getting a divorce? Unfortunately, this happens when we set our own standards in a relationship. In so many words, we determine the needs of our spouses without asking them.

Christians are hiding behind the Bible and not taking care of their husbandly or wifely duties. They also use God as a tool to crucify or disrespect their mate for doing something Physically, which they may have been doing Emotionally, Mentally, or Spiritually.

I feel very strongly that, whether you are a Christian or not, relationship restoration or healing is imperative before moving on to another relationship. Regardless of whether you are the cheater or cheatee, instigator or instigatee, problem-solver or problem-maker, or whatever, you need to discuss and understand the reason behind the actions that are causing the divide.

People cheat for a reason, and cheating is one way that helps them deal with their inner frustrations or lack. Nevertheless, it is

The Lady's Code

your responsibility to find out what is lacking; if not, history may repeat itself.

The most common reason why people cheat is because of sex. Still, we overlook the other reasons, such as, but not limited to:

- ☐ The lack of appreciation.
- ☐ The lack of attention.
- ☐ The lack of listening.
- ☐ The lack of respect.
- ☐ The lack of kindness.
- ☐ The lack of emotional support.
- ☐ The lack of communication.
- ☐ The lack of security.
- ☐ The lack of money.
- ☐ The lack of power.
- ☐ The lack of sex appeal.
- ☐ Being judged.
- ☐ The nonstop nagging.

I could say taking out the trash, but that is only a cover-up for the underlying reason. Whatever it is, you must find it, understand it, and work on it if you cannot resolve it. If you need counseling, get it.

When something dies in a relationship or when you check out of it Mentally and Emotionally, it is only a matter of time before you check out Physically. If this happens, you will not be able to see eye-to-eye; you will always find something to justify pulling away from the relationship, and you will become attached to other people, places, and things. In short, when the thrill is gone, so will you! Despite the investment into the relationship, when one or both give up, there are times when it is best to part ways to preserve your sanity.

Regardless of what anyone says about divorce or a breakup, it is a traumatic experience, even if someone pretends to be happy about it. The truth of the matter is, when someone goes from being committed to a life of dealing with other people with all types of issues on top of their divorce, separation, or abandonment, it can become challenging or overwhelming.

Let's face it: After a divorce or any form of breakup, you need to heal before considering dating someone else, regardless of the reason for the split. If you have not done any soul-searching after the split, you need not take your baggage into the life of someone else. You must deal with your issues first, and if you say that you do not have issues after a divorce or some form of a breakup, it is quite apparent that you are not ready for someone else.

The first step to moving beyond the state of separation is to OWN your role in the relationship. Although no relationship is perfect, you must understand what took place and the reasons why to ensure history does not repeat itself. Not only this, but if you are seeking the fulfillment of others in a relationship to fill a void from within, or if you are looking for someone to replace or remind you of your spouse, you need to STOP right here and seek counseling. Why should we seek counseling? As you know, hurting people hurt others!

According to *The Lady's Code: As It Pleases God*, if you know you are not ready for a relationship, if you cannot stop talking about the divorce, breakup, or betrayal, or if the demons of your past relationship keep rehashing images that are causing regression in your state of being, you need to take a time-out. To say the least, it is by far safer this way for yourself, for others, and for the innocent victims, having nothing to do with what you have going on, with whom, what you may have missed out on, or what led you into a dead end with a brick wall staring you right in the face. So, let us talk about this matter a little more.

Wall of Dead Ends

When you are going through any form of breakup, it is never easy for anyone. No one likes losing, even when losing is the best option. The emotions that come along with a split can become challenging, especially if you love and care about the person you are breaking up with. Going through this phase of a relationship causes some to retreat back to a dead-end or lousy relationship to avoid being lonely or going back into the dating field.

Why would the fear of loneliness cause one to retreat back to abuse and unhappiness? Can the fear of loneliness have that much power over someone? The answer is yes! The emotional or mental trauma of being alone has outweighed the emotional or mental trauma of being subjected to abuse, cheating, betrayal, etc. Lowering our standards or selling ourselves short just to have someone has become a relationship epidemic! Yes, it is an epidemic that creates a domino effect of a generational curse, attracting horrible relationships out of the simple fear of being alone.

Some may like the breakup and makeup phase of a relationship. Still, if you do not resolve the issue of why you parted ways in the beginning, you may be doing yourself and your generational seed a great disservice. Believe it or not, some relationships thrive off this sort of behavior; however, it is not suitable for the human psyche. Why? It causes dysfunction, eventually breaking you down and leaving you Emotionally, Mentally, Physically, and Spiritually traumatized with a negative, abusive nature that you may take out on yourself or innocent victims.

In my opinion, it does not matter the reason for the breakup or who was at fault, but if you or your partner has not changed, then why go back to torture yourself? It does not make sense to go back and split up again if you cannot get over the past issues that caused the initial breakup in the first place. Plus, if you go back expecting to change them and not you...then, this is a double standard when, in fact, you can only change yourself!

However, you can fake it all you like, but in the end, you will only be playing yourself short. There are times when it is best **NOT** to return back to your own vomit, so to speak! As a matter of fact, do not take my word for it; let us Spiritually Align this grandiose vomiting matter, *As It Pleases God*. *"For it would have been better for them not to have known the way of righteousness, than having known it, to turn from the holy commandment delivered to them. But it has happened to them according to the true proverb: 'A dog returns to his own vomit,' and, 'a sow, having washed, to her wallowing in the mire.'"* 2 Peter 2:21-22.

The Lady's Code

Eighty percent of the time, it is always best to let go, work on yourself, and move on. Twenty percent of the time, there is a change within both participants in the relationship, and sometimes, it does make them a stronger couple. Nevertheless, it must be a MUTUAL AGREEMENT without rehashing or dragging each other through the dirt, hurt, or pain of the past.

Now, if you break up with someone because they do not want to commit to you or marry you, then you should not force them to commit by breaking up with them. In my opinion, you should have gotten the commitment before having sex with them. What does this mean? Simply put, it would be best if you were not giving up the goodies without some form of commitment first. If you did it in reverse order, giving up the goodies to lock in a commitment, then one should not be disappointed if the relationship has resulted in a dead-end. Suck it up and move on.

Is this not a little insensitive? Absolutely not! In *The Lady's Code*, the best way into a real man's heart is to keep your legs closed! Why is it so important for a *Woman of Stature* to keep her legs closed? It gets rid of the riffraff! Casually dating and sleeping around with multiple partners is dangerous, and it is a Spiritual Atrocity in the Eye of God. Consequently, you must be very careful with this sort of behavior because soul ties are involved.

Now, getting back on the topic, forcing someone to marry you or to be in a relationship with you should never become an issue. If someone does not naturally want and love you, you do not need that person in your life. *The Lady's Code* is a stickler about its number one rule: Never force someone into a relationship. It is imperative that you never, and I mean never, violate the free will of another person if they are not your child.

If someone does not give you an opportunity to love them, it is their loss, not yours...MOVE ON. However, do not settle for being the 2nd in a relationship or the side chick. Yes, you can give them the opportunity to choose before a commitment, but do not hang around, hoping they will drop a relationship to choose you.

Besides, if this person hurts someone else for you, what makes you think that they would not do the same thing to you? This type of rebound relationship may not be the most conducive one. Why

The Lady's Code

should we opt out of rebound relationships? The Law of Reciprocity, or Seedtime and Harvest, is all over this sort of behavior. The *Wall of Dead Ends* advises that you do not want to become a victim of a bad seed knowingly sown on your behalf.

When it comes down to vetting, panicking over life is not going to help us or change anything. It will only hinder or block our belief system, as well as our instincts. More importantly, it will create more stress than necessary, causing us to become Spiritually Blind, Deaf, or Mute. Once this happens, we will begin to misread or misunderstand the *Writing On The Wall*. Listed below are a few things that will help your belief system or clear your vision:

- ☐ KNOW YOUR PURPOSE!
- ☐ Know that everything works for your good.
- ☐ You are responsible for yourself.
- ☐ Remain teachable!
- ☐ You cannot blame anyone for your mishaps.
- ☐ Assume responsibility for your life.
- ☐ Use your shortcomings as hidden strengths.
- ☐ Look for the good in everything to create a win-win.
- ☐ Finish what you start.
- ☐ Take a time-out for yourself.
- ☐ Forgive and repent often.
- ☐ Pray and meditate every day.
- ☐ Never lose your sense of humor and smile.
- ☐ Face your problems, and never deny that they exist.
- ☐ Give yourself positive affirmations.
- ☐ Commit to working on the undeveloped areas of your life.
- ☐ Know that you are the best at what you do.
- ☐ Do everything in the Spirit of Excellence.
- ☐ Accept rejection without allowing your ego to become bruised.
- ☐ If you fall, get back up again.
- ☐ Refuse to have a pity party.
- ☐ Refuse to be a victim—you are a victor!
- ☐ Steer clear of toxic people.
- ☐ Never complicate things; keep life simple.

The Lady's Code

- ☐ Make sure everything is in writing; write out your vision, goals, etc.
- ☐ Keep track of your BLESSINGS.
- ☐ Read every day.
- ☐ Spend time on your goal(s) 6 out of 7 days a week.

As we develop our minds to become *Women of Stature*, we must ensure everyone feels superior or worthy of our kindness, regardless of whether we feel as if it is deserved or not. According to *The Lady's Code*, it is our responsibility to treat others the way we want to be treated.

Rest assured, if we provoke fear or insecurity in others, we will find that we bring those same attributes back to us, creating an imbalance or turning us upside down. Why should we avoid such negative behavior, especially in the Eye of God? To properly answer this question, it is only wise to take this one to the Word of God. *"Then He said to them, 'Take heed what you hear. With the same measure you use, it will be measured to you; and to you who hear, more will be given. For whoever has, to him more will be given; but whoever does not have, even what he has will be taken away from him.'"* Mark 4:24-25.

Wall of Relational Assets

Our goal in a relationship is to become an asset and not a liability. To become such as it relates to *The Lady's Code: As It Pleases God*, we must understand the value of who we are, why we are, how we are, where we are, when we are, and what we are. If we do not understand those essential *Writing on the Wall Principles* about ourselves, we will begin to become a liability to those who do not find value in who we are or what we have to offer.

This book, *The Lady's Code: As It Pleases God*, prepares us to understand a few things about having leverage. In a solid relationship, it is hard to get rid of an asset, but it is very easy to get rid of a liability. Therefore, we must provide some form of

The Lady's Code

substance that is irreplaceable in a relationship that is worth having, keeping, or pursuing.

I am going to share the *Writing on the Wall* from several points of view to show you how to forget, get through, or overcome the hurts, pains, and reservations you may have about love. *The Lady's Code: As It Pleases God* gives you the opportunity to have what truly belongs to you, and that is your right to be happy, your right to love, your right to have joy, your right to experience peace, your right to be patient, your right to be kind, your right to exhibit goodness, your right to embrace your faith, your right to be gentle, and your right to exercise self-control.

Once you understand your **RIGHTS** as an individual, you will no longer expect this from others; you will be able to achieve this for yourself and then freely share it outwardly with others. In essence, this creates value from within that is hard to replace once you have mastered it, and it will also open your eyes to clearly see what is *Written on the Wall* about you and others.

In *The Lady's Code*, once you learn how to recognize the types of people to avoid, you will begin to love, date, mate, or relate as if you have never been hurt before. Plus, you will find yourself healing beyond all human understanding as your good relationships begin to overflow with confidence. By far, this helps you to exhibit eloquent people skills, charming the pants off of anyone, guaranteed!

A lasting, positive impression is indeed a perfect impression, even if you are not perfect in all things. Your ability to positively relate to yourself and others creates solid yet valuable relationships on many different levels. Therefore, when you are able to leave a good impression on someone's heart, they will always love you, even if they are not in love with you or you are not in love with them. Remember, not everybody is for everyone. Therefore, if the groove does not fit, do not force it. You must learn how to love and let go with no regrets, with a smile on your face, while knowing that all things will work together for your good.

According to the Cycle of Change, if one has caught a bad break in life or a relationship, it is only a matter of time before the good appears. How do we make this make sense? According to the

The Lady's Code

Cycle of Life, there is good and evil, period. Nevertheless, the value encapsulated in the good must be recognized by us and for us. If not, the cloud of negativity will overshadow or fog our ability to see the good, even if it is right before our very eyes.

Why would we get a little foggy? Spiritual Blindness is a derivative of negativity or stinking thinking. We cannot think for a minute that we can speak ill of ourselves and not expect enmity to follow suit. Regardless of what type of Spiritual Platform we are on, enmity is designed to do what it does!

The Sense of Knowing and Understanding about the Seeds of Enmity resides within all of us; we have simply forgotten its impact from the Garden of Eden. Nevertheless, it is our responsibility to resurrect our understanding of how to take our authority back through the Power of Love, Communion, Positivity, and Goodwill to make a positive impact or difference.

We have everything we need for our God-Given Mission, or the love we so desire. And it has a lot to do with one's perception of reality, whether it is good, bad, or indifferent.

Listen, when we understand that positivity and negativity are wrapped in our ability to CHOOSE, and regardless of which one we choose, we will begin to train our Eyes to see, our Ears to hear, and our Mouths to say likewise. Nevertheless, if we stay on the positive side of the spectrum, we are better able to exhibit SELF-CONTROL in the areas we are tempted to lose control; plus, we are better able to regulate our Spiritual FRUITS to exhibit Christ-Like Character, *As It Pleases God*.

As the days come and go, *The Lady's Code* gets stronger by the day, whether it is to our liking or distaste. It does not matter if we feel loved or not; we cannot deny the fact that we are truly BLESSED beyond what we could have ever imagined. Although we have become accustomed to a particular lifestyle or way of doing things, we should never allow ourselves to become limited, ungrateful, or unresourceful, where we begin to withhold our ability to LOVE on Purpose.

From my perspective, when we are able to think outside, around, through, and over the box regarding ways to love ourselves and others, we will find nothing is as bad as it seems. We simply

The Lady's Code

need to remember that our seemingly bad can always become good if our perceptions are set on looking for the positive or how to create some form of win-win.

In *The Lady's Code: As It Pleases God*, there is a lesson, blessing, and testing hidden in every obstacle or setback to spark our CREATIVITY. If we can take the time out of our busy schedule to understand what God is trying to say to us, when being ever so KIND, we will find that He is only trying to navigate us in the direction of our Destiny.

The Lady's Code says the moment we begin to secretly fight against ourselves or overshadow our faults through materialism or showboating, we will sometimes block out the message. What is more, we may overlook the Teacher who has been predestined to open our MINDS to the Spiritual Elements needed to secure our Destiny-Enriched Provisions.

Regardless of how self-sufficient we are, we cannot do it alone; we need Divine Guidance. In the Eye of God, we have been designed this way since the Garden of Eden. If we do not come to ourselves to realize our Spiritual Interdependence, God will clothe us with the information, but He will not violate our will in the utilization process.

What do we need to do to maximize our Spiritual Edifices? Here is the breakdown:

- ☐ We must develop a *Spirit to Spirit* Relationship with the Holy Trinity.
- ☐ We need to pray, repent, forgive, and fast on occasion.
- ☐ Set some time aside to hear our minds think.
- ☐ Become loveably transparent without continuously lying to ourselves.
- ☐ Document what God is saying.
- ☐ Exhibit the Fruits of the Spirit consistently.

If we can do this for 40 days while saying 'THANK YOU' and 'SHOW ME,' our lives will begin to come into agreement with our Predestined Design of Greatness. But more importantly, we must

The Lady's Code

remember that God will test what belongs to Him. If we are not tested, we will not understand or recognize the true Power of FAITH and TRUST. So, cheer up...you got this!

Our Spiritual Awakening regarding *The Lady's Code* will usually arise through means that we would normally reject. For example, a rich person will decline to learn from a seemingly poor individual due to arrogance, or vice versa, due to envy and covetousness. An educated person develops mental roadblocks from learning from the uneducated, as if they have nothing to offer, or they will turn up their nose, creating a Mental or Emotional divide due to a piece of paper. The wise individual develops a deaf ear to the unwise as if they are not serving the same God. The Spiritual Elite will not allow the non-elites to take the lead in areas in which they are CREATIVELY ANOINTED. The biased individuals tend to downplay, reject, or traumatize the unbiased because they do not fit into their clique, and the list goes on. For this reason, I am here to DEBUNK this superficial myth.

When dealing with *The Lady's Code*, we must understand that we are all ONE. We need to learn from each other because we all have a Wealth of Knowledge that has the potential to become a Well of Wisdom or a Spring of Greatness. If we dare to stop judging where our lessons, tests, and blessings are derived, we can become a Powerhouse in the Kingdom. How do I know? I learn from everything and everyone, period! If there is a nugget of wisdom hidden, I am going to extract it to feed God's sheep.

The value of *The Lady's Code: As It Pleases God* is predicated on our desire to exhibit Love, Joy, Peace, Patience, Kindness, Goodness, Faithfulness, Gentleness, and Self-Control, which are the 9 Fruits of the Spirit. What would the Fruits of the Spirit have to do with anything? They keep us RATIONAL. 'Trial and error' is a part of life, but there are certain things we can avoid if we use them, *As It Pleases God*.

According to the Heavenly of Heavens, we should never allow what we are going through or our biased ways to prevent us from gleaning the wisdom needed to take us to the next level. Always keep in mind that we are able to learn from everything and everyone. We only need to humbly open our Spiritual Eyes to see

The Lady's Code

and Spiritual Ears to hear while availing our Spiritual Voice to speak on behalf of the Kingdom, as well as for the edification of those we come in contact with. Furthermore, if we have not noticed by now, God will take the least likely and make them likely; plus, He will also take the likely and make them unlikely. We cannot judge where God has hidden our answers, blessings, tests, or wisdom.

There may come a time in your life when you may be faced with a compromising situation, but always remember that there is hope, healing, and restoration in all things, even after a rebound. So today, with the Fruits of the Spirit in hand, leave no stone unturned because *The Lady's Code: As It Pleases God* has your back.

Why do we need backing as *Women of Stature*? To be clear, when it comes to *The Lady's Code*, there is a difference between normal backing and Spiritual Backing. If we do not understand the difference between the two, we can get confused about what is what and who is whom, from the worldly realm to the Kingdom of Heaven. Does it matter? Absolutely. When the Heavenly of Heavens backs us, *As It Pleases God*, no one or nothing can stop us but us! As Romans 8:31 concurs, *"What then shall we say to these things? If God is for us, who can be against us?"*

More importantly, when you are in Purpose on purpose, it comes with a built-in Spiritual Covering that you have the Divine Authority to ENFORCE to protect your *Relational Assets*, especially when dealing with *The Lady's Code*. Here is the Spiritual Seal: *" 'No weapon formed against you shall prosper, and every tongue which rises against you in judgment you shall condemn. This is the heritage of the servants of the Lord, and their righteousness is from Me,' says the Lord."*

On the other hand, if you are out of the Will of God, doing your own or the wrong things in a state of unrighteousness, debauchery, and rebellion, it is possible to cause your own tongue to rise against you without realizing it. James 1:22 advises Believers: *"But be doers of the word, and not hearers only, deceiving yourselves."*

Unfortunately, we deceive ourselves more than others deceive us. Why do we deceive ourselves in such a manner? For some odd reason, we avoid or neglect reading the *Writing on the Wall* for fear of it saying something we do not want to hear or do not agree with.

The bottom line is that in *The Lady's Code*, we all matter. When we lift our voices to our Heavenly Father together, *As It Pleases Him* to be fruitful and multiply, we get His attention. To build legacies, overcome barriers, empower the next generation, encourage collaboration for brighter futures, and drive economic growth, we unlock the full potential of our Divine Dominion for our Heaven on Earth Experiences with our *Relational Assets*.

According to the Heavenly of Heavens, here is one of the Spiritual Seals to use as Spiritual Ammunition when being about our Father's Business: *"Therefore do not cast away your confidence, which has great reward. For you have need of endurance, so that after you have done the will of God, you may receive the promise."* Hebrews 10:35-36.

Why do we need this Spiritual Seal? When dealing with Spiritual Dualism, we need to understand the values associated with dealing with equals and opposites to remain Spiritually Balanced, *As It Pleases God*. What if we do not know about this stuff? Do not worry; we will explore this matter in the next chapter. So, without further ado, let us move on to *Opposites Attract*.

CHAPTER 6

OPPOSITES ATTRACT

We all have heard that opposite attracts, right? As odd as it may seem, it is true. However, it may only be temporary, especially if they are unequally yoked and are not in agreement with each other. Once the newness is over, or the temporary void is filled, reality will begin to set in. When this happens, the attraction of the opposite may begin to become a repellent, causing us to legitimately question our actions, thoughts, decisions, and motives.

Money, flowers, a box of chocolates, gifts, a teddy bear, or a little smooth-talking will indeed sugar-coat this issue, but it will not fix it. Why would it not fix things, especially when this is what we like? If people offer us things to sell our souls or to outright compromise ourselves, then the question is, 'Is it really a fix?' Then again, we can also ask ourselves, 'Is it really a dig to get us uprooted in the Eye of God, sending us straight to the Pit?' I understand that most of us do not like talking about this issue, but I am not like most people...we need to discuss this issue, pulling the rug from under this matter and exposing it for what it is.

What is the purpose of recognizing when issues are being sugar-coated? The first reason is that most of the *Opposite Attract* relationships are on the REBOUND, even if we are lying to ourselves about getting over someone or something. The second reason is due to infatuation, lust, pride, or greed. Although there are a lot more, these are the top two that we will deal with in this chapter.

On the other hand, *Opposite Attracts* because they bring unique perspectives, experiences, and qualities that can complement each other. For example, someone who is outgoing and spontaneous may be attracted to someone more introverted and thoughtful, as they can balance each other out. If the *Opposite Attracts* leads to growth, learning, and exposing each other to new ideas and ways of thinking, then it may not be such a bad idea. Remember, shared values and goals are also significant factors in successful relationships. So, embrace your differences and learn from each other because together, you can achieve great things.

It is often said we become who we hang around with, and I have found this statement to be highly accurate. We have an inner circle and an outer circle of relationships, and we must understand the difference between the two. If not, we will have a constant flow of people in and out of our lives, providing little or no substance with an opposite agenda.

Everyone has a role to play in our lives, whether we like it or not. Therefore, we must learn how to create an inner circle where we allow people close to our hearts. Meanwhile, we also have an outer circle where they are not in our hearts...they are at arm's length, so to speak.

How do we build our circles without losing ourselves in the midst of change? The first step to building a circle is to understand that we are not able to control everything. We cannot control others, nor should we violate their free will. If we have not noticed by now, even God will not violate the free will of mankind. However, the moment we think we need to fix someone else, this is the moment we need to take a look from within to fix ourselves.

With *The Lady's Code*, we are not here to fix people; we are here to help, motivate, and encourage others. Fixing people is God's job, not ours! Why should we not try to fix people, especially when they are not our speck, or they are screwing up royally? Because we are all imperfect in some areas of our lives. We as a

Opposites Attract

people must recognize that we are a source of inspiration to someone, and it is through that failed expectation or disappointment that we unawaringly lead those who look up to us astray. Nevertheless, it is our responsibility as *Women of Stature* from the Most High to lead without intentionally causing dismay to those who are counting on us to lead them.

Opposite or not, every generation must become better than the previous one. If we are digressing in this formality, we must gain control over our lives to leave a legacy worth leaving behind. Our inner circle is for the LEGACY and BLUEPRINT building. Our outer circle should become a source of empowerment or inspiration, inwardly and outwardly. If it is not doing this, it is justification for reevaluation of someone who may need to be avoided.

In my opinion, as we mature, if our circle does not change, then something is wrong. Change is a part of the Cycle of Life, and if we have not expanded our circle, it is too **SMALL**. We have not gone through all of our challenges for nothing; we have not overcome insurmountable defeat to allow it to go in vain. It is time to gird up our loins, get back on track, and live the life God has predestined for us to live.

Everything we need is already within us. Every experience has provided a roadmap for us to follow, and all we need to do is become masters of our minds, instincts, and emotions to tap into the Divine Wisdom from within.

Although we may not be able to explain a lot of things about our lives, what is taking place, or the reasons why, if we can embrace or open ourselves up to the Wisdom of God, I promise He will redefine everything about our minds, our emotions, and our instincts; thus, giving us the ability to move into our faith and favor at the appropriate time.

Let me say this: faith and favor without God will render one's mind scattered, emotions all over the place, and our instincts ineffective. In my opinion, if this is what is happening, it is better to use the Spiritual Tools God has given us to gain our POWER back.

Opposites Attract

What are the Spiritual Tools in *Opposites Attract*? Whether we attract or repel, there are many Spiritual Tools. For *The Lady's Code: As It Pleases God*, we use the POWER of the Blood of Jesus to cover us and the presence of the Holy Spirit to guide us with prayer, repentance, forgiveness, fasting, gratefulness, and the Fruits of the Spirit to build Christlike Character. All of which helps us with the following walls:

- ☐ The Wall of Rebound.
- ☐ The Wall of Equally or Unequally Yoked.
- ☐ The Wall of Restoration.

What can these walls do for us? It is more like what they cannot do for us. Either way, they will all place us on a learning curve. And it will be left up to us to maximize them, *As It Pleases God*, or fall for the okey doke, pleasing ourselves and others.

Wall of Rebound

As relationships come and go, it does not matter how bad you want to be in a relationship; do not put yourself in a position to date while you are on the rebound, or date someone who is on the rebound. It would be best if you healed, or they must heal first. Rebound relationships are a recipe for disaster. Yes, you can provide emotional or mental support, but as far as dating, back up! As a *Woman of Stature*, I really mean back all the way up, period!

What is the big deal about backing up with a rebound relationship? According to the Heavenly of Heavens, TIME will heal all wounds, and without it, healing cannot occur properly, *As It Pleases God* due to the violation of the SEASONS and CYCLES of Life. Here is what Ecclesiastes 3:1 wants us to know: *"To everything there is a season, a time for every purpose under heaven."*

What does God have to do with our healing process? First, we cannot force the Hand of God with anything or anyone. Secondly, He has everything to do with it because He Divinely Created us in

Opposites Attract

His IMAGE while we are trapped in time. Thirdly, He cares for us, His prize possessions, even when we do not care about ourselves or when we keep lying and deceiving ourselves. As a matter of fact, Psalms 147:3 gives us Divine Leverage on this matter by letting us know: *"He heals the brokenhearted and binds up their wounds."*

In *The Lady's Code*, all we need to do is align ourselves, *As It Pleases Him*, while giving ourselves time and space to confess, pray, repent, fast, forgive, learn, and grow. Even James 5:16 says, *"Confess your trespasses to one another, and pray for one another, that you may be healed. The effective, fervent prayer of a righteous man avails much."*

On the other hand, if your time is in the middle of a rebound with God nowhere in the equation, it is fair for me to say, 'Your timing is OFF.' Take a step back, adding patience, faith, and understanding to your healing process or journey. Rest assured, if the person is meant for you, they will be there for you when you heal; if not, that relationship was not meant to be.

For the record, in or out of our Seasons and Cycles of Life, God does not make mistakes; we do! Here is the Divine Mindset Daniel 2:21 wants us to have: *"And He changes the times and the seasons; He removes kings and raises up kings; He gives wisdom to the wise and knowledge to those who have understanding."* Now, to get an understanding of the *Wall of Rebound*, let us go deeper.

When someone uses another relationship to get over a previous one, they bring all of the baggage along with them. Is this sort of behavior fair for those seeking a good, sound relationship? For some, it may or may not be, depending upon their motives or heart posture. According to the Ancient of Days, people break up and make up all the time as relational desires and preferences evolve. If you get caught up in this phase without the Divine Presence of the Holy Trinity, you may get egregiously hurt, severely wounded, or shakenly traumatized.

Why would we get hurt, especially when having free will to love whomever we see fit? Fighting for the heart of someone whose heart is with someone else is not wise. *"For where your treasure is, there your heart will be also."* Matthew 6:21. Unfortunately, it is only a matter of time before you get left out in the cold, especially if you caused the breakup in the first place or created havoc in their lives as a side piece. Is this not a little insensitive? Absolutely not! What is insensitive is forcing someone to love you by violating their free will or making their lives a living nightmare to satiate your unresolved desires or perception of love.

In my opinion, this is where a lot of Emotional and Mental trauma takes place, mainly when a person has fought hard to win the heart of the rebounder while making secret sacrifices to obtain or sustain the relationship. Once the rebounder has healed, or once they realize they cannot live without their ex, they leave. Regrettably, the relationship scapegoat gets kicked to the curb as if they did not matter.

Clearly, being kicked to the curb is indeed a slap in the face, and it is not a laughing matter. Still, this is nothing new. It happens every day, especially when someone's heart is not genuinely with us or is not aligned in SPIRIT, *As It Pleases God*. As *Women of Stature*, it is always best to take a wise approach to this rebounding issue while steering clear of any form of debauchery, confusion, or malice.

Once again, what is the big deal about being on the rebound? There is no big deal; it only gives us an indication of where we are in our relational status. In *The Lady's Code*, when a person enters into a relationship with someone who is wounded, broken, or hurt from a previous relationship, it is considered to be a rebound. Although most would not admit they are on the rebound, if you pay attention and listen closely, they will eventually tell you.

I have nothing against those who are on the rebound; however, I do know there is a grieving process one must go through when a breakup has occurred, especially if you claim to love the person that you just broke up with. For example, if you break up with someone today, and you are back to your old self tomorrow with zero emotions attached, it means that you did not love them. Then again, it could mean that you mentally or emotionally detached yourself a long time ago while waiting for the right moment to break it off.

Why do we mourn over lost relationships? In all simplicity, we are human. Nor should we lie about our condition. For this reason,

Opposites Attract

Matthew 5:4 says, "*Blessed are those who mourn, for they shall be comforted.*" Spiritually, we have the Divine Right to take this matter to God, *Spirit to Spirit*, admitting that we are mourning and we need to be comforted, regardless of who is at fault or our present-day flaws or qualms.

What is the purpose of admitting our state of being as Believers? Where real love exists, there is a grieving process with roller-coaster emotions of sadness, anger, fear, and despair. During this time, one must become aware of what they are feeling to balance out the emptiness they may experience. If one does not allow themselves to go through this grieving phase completely, then after the next breakup, the emotional impact will be X2 (double-impact).

Over a period of time, if their emotions are still left unchecked, then after the next breakup, it is X3 (triple-impact), and so on, until they deal with the underlying feelings of rejection. God forbid it gets to an X20, X30, or X40...this person is going to need intense emotional and mental healing. To avoid getting to the extreme phase of a rebounder, simply take the time to heal, understand your mistakes, and figure out what you want and DO NOT want in your next relationship.

How do you know when you are ready to date? When you are able to stop thinking or talking about how hurt you are. Although everyone is different, the moment you start to feel more confident is when you start to get your groove back and have an idea of what you want in life. If you start dating and the feelings rehash, then you are not ready! Take a little more time for yourself, but you will get there.

The goal is to have a fruitful relationship with the ultimate freedom of choice without indulging in a rebound, out-of-bounds, free throw, outright fouled, or sideline relationship. To keep the ball in our court, one must pride himself or herself on having a good, solid relationship without causing harm to anyone. Once we allow this mindset to become second nature, it will help keep our relationships inbound, *As It Pleases God*. Not only this, but it will also give us the ability to exhibit the willingness to communicate effectively, love freely, share generously, respect continuously, exude kindness to all, and allow free-flowing compassion to restore what the cankerworms tried to destroy.

Before moving on to the *Wall of Equally or Unequally Yoked*, I want to leave you with this Divine Instruction from the Heavenly of Heavens. *"Blessed be the God and Father of our Lord Jesus Christ, the Father of mercies and God of all comfort, who comforts us in all our tribulation, that we may be able to comfort those who are in any trouble."* 2 Corinthians 1:3-4.

When you heal, *As It Pleases God*, you must comfort others to keep the Spiritual Seal of Divine Healing active. As a picturesque view of how this works, you are HEALED to be a HEALING. You are BLESSED to be a BLESSING. You are LOVED to be LOVING. You were SAVED to SAVE another. Remember, the Law of Reciprocity does not lie, nor will it fail those who use it positively or negatively. So, keep all that you do, whatever you say, and whomever you become on the positive side of the spectrum in the Spirit of Excellence.

Wall of Being Equally or Unequally Yoked

In living real life, the Power of Love and Freedom can sometimes become very fearful if we have not mastered the yoking process, *As It Pleases God*. At the same time, *The Lady's Code* can become very empowering as well if we take the time to learn and understand the power of the Pre-Yoking Process without looking down on anyone.

Throughout my years of love and freedom, as well as the lack of it, what I have found is that in order to make love work for us, we must make a DECISION to do so. In addition, as *Women of Stature*, we must set limits, boundaries, and expectations in a relationship by following specific Spiritual Rules and Principles according to the Word of God and *As It Pleases Him*.

Why must we think and behave like a Woman of Stature, especially when dealing with the *Wall of Being Equally or Unequally Yoked*? If we do not operate in Divine Wisdom, *As It Pleases God*, we will become weak and vulnerable with the Spirit of Jezebel

Opposites Attract

breathing down our necks to snatch our poshness and virtue. If we become Spiritually Snatched in such a manner, first, we may not recognize it. Secondly, we will begin to engage in acts of manipulation, idolatry, intimidation, and rebellion against God. Thirdly, we will begin leaving rotten and mangled fruits behind with zero remorse or self-correction, while yoking ourselves to the core and blaming others for our issues, thoughts, beliefs, or desires.

In the Eye of God, our character matters. If we do not safeguard our souls, *As It Pleases Him*, we will fall for anything that gives us the appearance of what we want. And, falling for anything is NOT a Godly characteristic for those who are designed to soar like eagles or become *Women of Stature*. As we already know, the DO-IT-YOURSELF relationships only work temporarily without the Wisdom of God or the PreYoking Process. Therefore, we must learn how to incorporate Godly Spiritual Principles at the beginning of the relationship to ensure we do not have to backtrack, undo, or redo things we can get right the first time around.

According to the Heavenly of Heavens, love can very well mean something different for each of us due to our chosen mindsets, selected perceptions, adaptive conditioning, unresolved traumas, grafted beliefs, longing desires, and fearful reservations. But do not worry; we all will experience bouts of love, even if we pretend we do not need it or that everyone loves us.

In *The Lady's Code*, I am going to lay the groundwork to ensure we are equipped with the essential fundamental elements of love to ensure we do not fall by the wayside in the Eye of God. Even if we somehow get caught up in loving someone who does not love us back, the information will equip us for the right relationship if we follow instructions, *As It Pleases Him*.

As *Women of Stature*, why do we need to follow instructions in the Realm of the Spirit, especially when dealing with love? As *Women of the Most High God*, it helps us to Spiritually Discern our motives, actions, thoughts, beliefs, and desires with CLARITY before they make their way into reality. Secondly, it also helps us to pinpoint teachings that would cause us to stray from Biblical Truths.

Opposites Attract

Thirdly, it assists us in becoming accountable for what enters and exits our Eye Gates, Ear Gates, or Mouth Gates.

What is the purpose of becoming accountable for our Spiritual Gates? Often enough, when dealing with any form of gateway, we are dead set on Spiritually Discerning others without properly doing this for ourselves to determine the health, status, or integrity of our own psyche. As a result, we 'get got' by turning on ourselves without realizing it or crashing into a brick wall that we were privileged to see coming.

How is it possible to see and not see a brick wall at the same time? Spiritual Blindness, Deafness, and Muteness will do the trick every time, from the least to the greatest. Unfortunately, it is through disappointment, unresolved trauma, letting our guards down, or becoming unequally yoked that we will keep ourselves Spiritually Veiled. As a result, we unawaringly become led astray at the first sign of promise, be it good, bad, or indifferent. Then again, we may lead those who look up to us astray through infatuation, attraction, greed, materialism, and lust with blinders that shield our eyes from seeing the *Writing on the Wall* clearly.

As life would have it, in the initial stages of a relationship, differences can seem endearing, adding a layer of excitement and invigoration. Nonetheless, when *Opposites Attract*, as time passes and the newness wears off, the very attributes that were once cute and funny can morph into sources of frustration and dire pain, driving you stir-crazy.

The crux of the *Opposites Attract* methodology often lies in our unspoken and spoken, real or imagined expectations. The imbalance can lead to a feeling of being drained or overwhelmed, as one partner may feel they are giving too much of themselves without receiving enough reciprocation. When two individuals cannot grow together in a relationship, *As It Pleases God*, it may begin to take more than they can give. Moreover, once this occurs, they may check out of the relationship, Mentally, Physically, Emotionally, or Spiritually, with a veil of pretense.

As attitudes and feelings evolve, here are a few questions to ask yourself:

Opposites Attract

- How can someone opposite to you be perfect for you?
- What do you do when you have a relationship contradiction?
- What do you do when SETTLING has put a frown on your face?

Questions, questions, questions! Unfortunately, this is what we all do when we are perfectly unequally yoked, right? There must be some form of commonality in a relationship, or we will eventually bump heads due to a dire clash of character. Although no one is perfect, and we all have differences, we must become ever so conscious of the positive and negative character traits that create our FIRST FRUITS of the *Writing on the Wall*! If we become oblivious to the fruits without reading them, *As It Pleases God*, they could be rotten and mangled, appearing good on the outside and rotten to the core.

On this wall, here is my question: If one is a date, mate, or partner with ZERO Spiritual Power, *As It Pleases God*, how are they able to manage the woes of life or stave off the attacks of the enemy? Then again, will they buckle, run, or flip out under pressure? As *Women of Stature*, these are the questions we must ask when yoking up with someone. Whether we are the yoker or the yokee, equally or unequally yoked, it is our responsibility to read the *Writing on the Wall*.

For this reason, *The Lady's Code* says we need to be on one accord with specific characteristics. With the *Opposite Attracts*, we must view them as being the 4 Stages of being YOKED:

- PreYoked (Analyzation or Vetting Process Before Bonding).
- Unequally Yoked (Incompatible Soul Tie).
- Equally Yoked (Compatible Soul Mate).
- DeYoked (Breaking A Soul Tie).

Opposites Attract

Here is the deal: Being equally yoked in a relationship typically refers to two people who share similar beliefs, values, and goals. More importantly, they work together as a team, often with a shared vision for the future, and support each other in achieving their individual and joint ambitions without competing against each other.

On the other hand, being unequally yoked in a relationship means that two people have significant differences in their beliefs, values, or goals, which can lead to conflict, tension, distrust, competitiveness, and dissatisfaction. These differences could be related to religion, politics, lifestyles, career aspirations, or any other important aspect of life.

When two people are unequally yoked in a relationship, they may struggle to find common ground, bump heads, and cannot seem to work together towards their shared goals, leading to a breakdown in the relationship and unmet needs. In my opinion, this is similar to the right hand not knowing what the left hand is doing, leading to chaos, confusion, bullying, or abuse. Here is a story that opened my eyes to the *Writing on the Wall* of being Unequally Yoked.

The Warning - Silvia's Writing on the Wall

Silvia was from a quaint town situated between two bustling cities, and she found herself falling for a man who did not love her as she loved him. In my opinion, she was blinded by love to the point where she could not see the forest for the trees. But from her perspective, he filled the aching void, and she was willing to pay the price to have him in her life, regardless of the naysayers or player haters.

Nick was known by the women for his charm, wit, and the air of confidence that surrounded him. But beneath this facade, he was anti-God, and Silvia was an asset to him, as he was only in love with her mental capabilities. As a capitalist, Nick saw an opportunity to use her knowledge to build his dream while putting a few notches on his belt to feed his ego. Actually, his goal was to become a demigod to those who had less money than him

Opposites Attract

and cover up his weaknesses with showboating as a Big Catch or Big Dog.

Even though Silvia knew he was infatuated with her intelligence, she thought she could make him love her by having sex and covering up his hidden secrets about his inability to read or write. Of course, she did win temporarily, but as time progressed in the relationship, she started selling her soul to fill a lonely void while putting up with his gut-wrenching antics and debauchery.

Although Silvia was in denial about him using her, she still had a secret and lonely void buried deep within her heart. She was running—running from the shadows of her past and, more importantly, from God. From my perspective, her situation was similar to Jonah running from his calling, but in real-time.

As I was left scratching my head about Silvia's dilemma and how she avoided God, I could not believe this woman found herself justifying choosing a man over God Almighty. Unmistakably, as I questioned her further, I found that she was ashamed of God and the GIFTS that He had placed inside of her because people kept shaming her publicly and ostracizing her privately.

Consequently, as time progressed with this man, she willfully squandered her blessings with someone who couldn't care less about God or what He wanted her to do.

Most would ask, 'How can one be ashamed of God?' 'How can one be ashamed of the gifts from within?' Although I cannot answer this question for her, the fact of the matter is that Silvia was outright ashamed to be who God created her to be. Sadly, the truth is, this is not just Silvia's story; it is also ours as well. Most of us are dealing with this same issue under a different label, but do not have the guts to admit this ongoing struggle from within, only to bury it as if it does not exist.

For many, serving God can feel like a big task or stepping onto a stage where all eyes are watching, waiting for us to make a mistake or trip over ourselves. Unfortunately, this undue pressure can make individuals insecure or self-conscious about their faith, beliefs, expressions, or walking with God altogether. The feelings of being unworthy or imperfect weigh on the human psyche due to the underlying hypocrisy associated with the illusion of perfection. As a result, it detours a lot of people from developing a *Spirit to Spirit* Relationship with God.

For the record, and to debunk the elephant in the room, serving God is not about perfection. It is about intentions and heart postures with a WILLINGNESS to become a work-in-progress and use the Fruits of the Spirit, *As It Pleases Him*. So, there is no need to complicate our lives or fear judgment, especially if we desire to grow Spiritually and make a difference for the Greater Good.

Well, for the sake of Silvia's *Writing on the Wall*, let us get into the reason why I feel as if her story was similar to the Book of Jonah in the Bible. Now, the question is, 'Was Silvia really running from God, or was He setting her up to run toward Him?' I will allow you to be the judge as we crack this story wide open, getting into the handiwork of God Almighty.

As time progressed, every morning, a little red bird, presumably a cardinal, would come to her window, pecking on it as if he was trying to say something. By design, it created a sincere tugging in Silvia's heart because she knew it was a warning, but she did not want to give up this man. She also knew Nick was a bad influence on her and needed to make a decision, but she could not resist the temptation of living a fast lifestyle of glitz and glamour.

One day, during a thunderstorm, lightning pierced through the same window that the little red cardinal pecked on, hitting Silvia in the back of her leg. This woman became traumatized with disbelief, thinking this only happens in movies. In real-time, she was convinced her experience was not a movie scene because the pain left her leg felt like it was on fire while shaking out of control.

There she lay on the floor, praying to God Almighty while Nick, the man she claims to love, laughed hysterically as if this were a laughing matter. To add insult to injury, as she lay helpless, He DID NOT call for medical help or an ambulance. This woman probably suffered cardiac arrest, but he did not care...he had plans and did not want her to interfere with what he had going on. Instead, he gave her a pill to put her to sleep while she continued to scream for help. After she was knocked out, he left her alone for days while God became her comforter, protecting her.

Opposites Attract

As Silvia shared this story with me, I could not believe this man dared to leave her alone with no help whatsoever, as if he wanted her to die. What type of person is this? Does he not have a conscience? Was he not afraid of going to jail for not calling for medical help? Nevertheless, at that moment, Silvia was not ashamed to call on the Name of the Lord.

Although she survived being struck by lightning with Lichtenberg figures and neurological issues to prove her claim, the thought of Nick laughing and not taking her to the hospital did indeed shift her heart away from him. What type of person would laugh at someone being struck by lightning? That should have been her sign to walk away from him, but she was still blind.

Though the little red bird continued to peck on the window daily, she developed a deaf ear to God's will and His way. Her shame of devoting her life to God had somehow clouded her sense of good judgment.

One night, she was invited to a birthday party, and she decided that it was worth spending time with her so-called friends. As soon as she and Nick pulled up to the club, she heard a voice saying, 'This is your last night.' She played it off, saying, 'Okay, this is my last time going to a club.' Throughout the whole night, she kept on hearing, 'This is your last night, this is your last night.'

As a result, she became very uncomfortable, deciding to leave the club early. Of course, she did not express her concerns to Nick; she just pretended as if she was getting sleepy. For some reason, the late-night hunger pains began to kick in, so they made a pit stop at Waffle House. While there, they began to crack jokes about the two officers in the restaurant eating waffles instead of donuts. As they left the restaurant, they still chuckled at the officers.

As soon as they arrived home, when they walked in the house, something appeared unusual. Silvia just blew it off, but Nick took it seriously. He noticed things were out of place, so he secretly grabbed his gun to ensure Silvia did not panic. As soon as she walked into the bedroom with their take-out in hand, shots began to ring out. Silvia gets shot, and she then yells, 'MY GOD!' At that moment, everything from that point on went in slow motion. Her life flashed before her in a fraction of a second. All of her dreams, all of her goals, and everything she would ever do in life were placed before her at that moment.

As she walked through the tunnel leading up to the light, she stopped, turned around, and said, 'I am not finished. I cannot leave yet.' As soon as she made this statement, a presence beyond human understanding covered her. She began to feel her life coming back as she slumped down in a corner like a little rag doll.

After the shooting had ceased, they could hear that help was coming. The 1st officers on the scene were the same two officers they had laughed at a few minutes earlier at the Waffle House. They were grateful that those two officers chose waffles instead of donuts that night.

Nick was shot as well; he and Silvia survived, but one of the burglars was not so lucky. The media was all over the place; there were so many different stories about what happened, some lies, some truths, and some half-truths alike.

Silvia was ashamed of living for God. Now, the media really made her shame worth serving God. The media caused Silvia to lose her job, lose her friends, and lose her privacy. They camped out on her doorstep; actually, they made her life a living hell until she was glad to serve God.

After the investigation, one of the burglars turned out to be a friend of the guy who threw that spur-of-the-moment party, which happens to be Silvia's sister's boyfriend's friend, if that makes any type of sense. To add insult to injury, it was also the boyfriend of one of the women Silvia's boyfriend was sleeping with. The botched-up burglary was set up to teach Nick a lesson about sleeping with another man's woman. However, they did not expect Nick and Silvia to return home early to botch up their plans. You are talking about a party without a conscience!

By Divine Design, everything about this situation had gotten all twisted up over a woman, which almost cost Silvia, who knew nothing about this until after the fact, her life. Painstakingly, she also found out this was the same female that Nick had a date with, causing him to avoid taking her to the hospital when she was struck by lightning.

Opposites Attract

Silvia felt as if she was struck by lightning twice after the unveiling of Nick's underhanded debauchery. As Mark 4:22 concurs, *"For there is nothing hidden which will not be revealed, nor has anything been kept secret but that it should come to light."* Remember, our hidden actions, words, desires, and thoughts will eventually be brought into the open when we least expect them.

Now the question is, 'Was Silvia really an innocent victim?' Absolutely not! God warned her several times, but she was hell-bent on doing her own thing, shacking up, fornicating with a man who despised God, violating her conscience, and using her Spiritual Gifts for worldly purposes. In reinforcing the importance of integrity, truth, discernment, and valuing what is sacred, she was cooking up a recipe for disaster. So, she could not proclaim being an innocent victim, especially when God warned her to run for the hills, and she willfully chose to stay on the ground in that mess. At the same time, she knew what Matthew 7:6 said: "*Do not give what is holy to the dogs; nor cast your pearls before swine, lest they trample them under their feet, and turn and tear you in pieces.*"

Miraculously, Silvia rose to her feet out of the muck, shaken and filthy but alive. She realized that she had been given a second chance, a GIFT from the Heavens Above. And it was her responsibility to clean up her act.

The experience changed Silvia for the better as she transformed her life one step at a time with a work-in-progress mindset. She no longer sought thrill for the sake of thrill but instead sought purpose and connection, *As It Pleased God*. Her Jonah Experience made her choose to serve Him with no shame attached. And now, she does not give a rat's tail about what others think about her *Spirit to Spirit* Connection with her Heavenly Father.

But through it all, Silvia also stated there was a Spiritual Covering beyond human understanding, protecting her from bullets that were flying right by her head. She had to live through those few minutes of staring death right in its face while making a conscious choice to live, knowing she had been spared for a reason.

By truly experiencing the difference between the Earthly and Spiritual Realm or the Other Side, it changed her Spiritual Life forever, causing her to adhere to *The Lady's Code* without deviation. Above all, with every heartbeat and breath she takes, she is reminded of the miraculous intertwining of life, fate, hope, and faith, along with Divine Purpose, Passion, and Promise for the Greater Good.

The moral of Silvia's story of survival is to take nothing for granted while being grateful for everything! In addition, with every aspect of life, we must do our best to avoid people who do not have a conscience. Plus, we should never pretend as if we do not know who they are; we know! It does not take a rocket scientist to figure them out—check the FRUITS. As a Word to the Wise, if someone does not value human life or the Creator of it, find an exit quickly!

Even though we are *Women of Stature*, we are all a work-in-progress. And, we all have a Silvia in us, and there are certain things we must consider before violating our conscience or getting caught up with someone who is unequally yoked with us. For example:

- ☐ If we are loving people, we are unequally yoked with a person who cannot or who is unwilling to show love.
- ☐ If we are hateful people, we are unequally yoked with a truly kind person.
- ☐ If we are happy people, we are unequally yoked with a truly sad person.
- ☐ If we are giving people, we are unequally yoked with a stingy person.
- ☐ If we are positive people, we are unequally yoked with a negative, doomed, and gloomy person.
- ☐ If we are truly good people, we are unequally yoked with an outright evil person.
- ☐ If we are fun people, we are unequally yoked with a party pooper.
- ☐ If we are peaceful people, we are unequally yoked with a chaotic troublemaker.
- ☐ If we are patient people, we are unequally yoked with an impatient or reckless person.

Opposites Attract

- ☐ If we are a bonding people, we are unequally yoked with a person who creates bad blood between our brethren.
- ☐ If we are unfaithful, conniving, and scheming people, we are unequally yoked with faithful, trustworthy people.
- ☐ If we are gentle people, we are unequally yoked with a rough, abrasive, or abusive person.
- ☐ If we are caring people, we are unequally yoked with a rude, unapologetic person.
- ☐ If we are timely people, we are unequally yoked with a person who is late all the time.
- ☐ If we are hard-working people, we are unequally yoked with a lazy person.
- ☐ If we are people with great self-control, we are unequally yoked with a person who is easily swayed or manipulated.
- ☐ If we are people who think before speaking, we are unequally yoked with a person who has loose lips.
- ☐ If we are wise people, we are unequally yoked with a person who exhibits foolish behavior.
- ☐ If we are grateful people, we are unequally yoked with a complaining, ungrateful person.
- ☐ If we are people who build, we are unequally yoked with a person who tears down or causes destruction.
- ☐ If we are people who complete projects, we are unequally yoked with a person who never finishes anything.
- ☐ If we are polite, we are unequally yoked with a person with a mean, nasty, or rude attitude.
- ☐ If we are obsessive-compulsive tidy people, we are unequally yoked with an untidy, messy person.
- ☐ If we are respectful people, we are unequally yoked with a disrespectful person.
- ☐ If we are healthy people, we are unequally yoked with a person who has no interest in our well-being.
- ☐ If we are people who believe in God, we are unequally yoked with an atheist.

Opposites Attract

Although these items are not set in stone, if we use the 80/20 Rule, we will hit the nail on the head. What does this mean in layman's terms? If the qualities are 80% unequally yoked, leave them alone. On the other hand, if they have 20% unequally yoked qualities, then maybe...if you can live with it, and it is tolerable.

In all simplicity with *The Lady's Code*, do not be fooled by going against everything you believe; if it looks like a duck's egg, it is a duck's egg. Besides, you cannot make a duck's egg a chicken's egg, or vice versa, no matter how hard you try, no matter how hard you pray, and no matter how many ultimatums you give, a chicken is a chicken, and a duck is a duck! They can only produce after their own kind, according to their Divine Design. If we go outside of the Original Design, we create confusion among their GENES, creating rotten eggs.

Lo and behold, the same applies to us. According to *The Lady's Code*, we must become cautious about co-mingling with people, places, and things that break us down as opposed to building or taking us to the next level.

Relationships that lead to mating that contradict your character, violate your integrity, create Spiritual Blindness, violate Spiritual Laws, or create soul ties leading to irreconcilable generational dysfunction or genetic disorder—walk away! The *Wall of Opposites* says that if unequally yoked is NOT what you are looking for, do not waste your time—MOVE ON!

Once again, the Bible says, *"Do not give to the dogs what's holy, or cast your pearls among the swine."* Matthew 7:6. We must be mindful of who occupies our time. It is a proven fact that we become who we hang around with. Therefore, we must become ever so cognizant of the people with whom we are breaking bread.

Do you think for a minute that we can sit in the presence of fools all the time and expect wisdom to flow from our loins? We will never see Eagles on the ground with Chickens...the day we do, something is wrong! We will never see a Lion, the King of the Jungle, hanging out with Turtles; the day we do, something is wrong! Proverb 13:20 says, *"If we hang with the wise and we become wise, but we will suffer if we hang around fools."* We must select our

Opposites Attract

environment carefully because the wrong choice could become detrimental to our Mental, Physical, Emotional, and Spiritual well-being.

Before I proceed with the *Writing on the Wall*, I want to emphasize this: People can change, but it is important to recognize that the only person you can truly change is yourself. Additionally, you need to evaluate whether the potential risk is worth taking.

According to the Heavenly of Heavens, you must never settle for unequally yoked or inequality in a relationship because you are desperate, lonely, greedy, or deprived. It would be best if you were Mentally, Emotionally, Physically, and Spiritually sound when doing so. If you are not sound or you are confused, you must believe what the *Writing on the Wall* is saying, period!

Why is it not wise to settle for an unequally yoked relationship? In the Eye of God, it could become dangerous or traumatizing, especially if we are not properly trained or equipped to deal with it or them. An unequally yoked relationship deserves careful consideration, particularly in the context of love, romance, or partnership. With profound incompatibility, exuding differing values, beliefs, or life goals, taking us out of the Will of God is not a wise choice, regardless of how we justify our reasoning.

How does unequally yoked apply to us as Believers, especially when we are not animals, and we do not wear yokes? Please allow me to explain: The term 'unequally yoked' originates from agricultural societies, where pairs of oxen would be yoked together to plow fields. For the work to be effective, both animals needed to be of similar strength, size, and temperament.

When one ox is stronger or bigger than the other, the work becomes difficult and burdensome, leading to frustration, inefficiency, confusion, anger, conflict, and even injury. Similarly, in relationships, when one partner is significantly different in values, Spiritual Beliefs, or life visions, the partnership may face undue strain. For this reason, Apostle Paul emphasizes the importance of aligning values and beliefs in relationships by advising: *"Do not be unequally yoked together with unbelievers. For what fellowship has righteousness with lawlessness? And what communion has light with darkness?"* 2 Corinthians 6:14.

Opposites Attract

Experience is sometimes the best teacher, but there are times when we only need to exercise Spiritual Wisdom, self-reflection, and set boundaries proactively. How do we go about doing so, primarily when we are bombarded with the information highway of doing this and doing that? In the Eye of God, there is no cookie-cutter way of teachable experiences because the needs of each person may vary from person to person, mindset to mindset, perception to perception, trauma to trauma, and so on. Nevertheless, here is a list of a few things to do, but not limited to such:

- ☐ We must add God into the equation.
- ☐ We must remain humble.
- ☐ We must align ourselves with the Word of God.
- ☐ We must set standards, *As It Pleases God*.
- ☐ We must cover ourselves with the Blood of Jesus.
- ☐ We must invite the Holy Spirit into our situations.
- ☐ We must listen to and trust our instincts.
- ☐ We must be patient and understanding.
- ☐ We must communicate effectively.
- ☐ We must set a guard over our tongues.
- ☐ We must use the Fruits of the Spirit.
- ☐ We must behave Christlike at all times.

Why does it take all of this to understand the *Wall of Being Equally or Unequally Yoked*? We do not all think alike, and we all have different learning curves! As we navigate the complexities of relationships, if we do not know ourselves or set boundaries accordingly, we will 'get got' by the enemy's wiles.

Here is what happened to me by not setting limits and boundaries, and failing to discuss my beliefs, goals, and values early on to gauge compatibility. I entertained a relationship I was not too particularly interested in, but to kill time, in the meantime, I entertained it anyway. When this man found out that I was not serious about the relationship and he was not my speck, he broke into my house and robbed me of everything I had of value.

Opposites Attract

Due to my lack of clarity with this man about being unequally yoked with him, he shut my business down completely. I did not have any computers...All of my manuscripts, printers, business contacts, documents, connections, flash drives, etc., were gone. I cried like a little baby; the weight of my experiences came crashing down on me like a tidal wave, leaving me on my knees, gasping for air amid the havoc he caused.

The Empire that took ten years to build with my bare hands was torn down overnight for choosing NOT to love someone with the propensity to do something like this. Besides, it was not like I did not know he was capable of such...I knew! I just did not think he would do it to me. Amidst my ambitious pursuits, I overlooked the crucial truth about his character and rotten fruits, thinking I was exempt from becoming a bystander.

Why would he do such a thing? First, it was due to his insecurities. Secondly, he hoped I would lose everything and come running to him to build his business instead. Thirdly, he got a rise out of seeing me suffer.

As I climbed higher in my *Spirit to Spirit* Relationship with my Heavenly Father, I refused to help this man with anything. Is this being Godly or exhibiting Christlike Character? There are certain people we must leave alone, period! 1 Corinthians 15:33 says, "*Do not be deceived: 'Evil company corrupts good habits.'*"

The whole ordeal was an insult to me, my intelligence, and everything I stood for. A man steals my equipment, shutting my life down so I can build his business on the sly to lock me down. I tell you this: The devil is a liar!

Amid the grief, I found clarity. No matter what this man did to try to make me love him, it never worked. As painful as that experience was, it was a profound teacher, reminding me that my Empire is connected to my PASSION. If a person messes with me when I am being about my Father's Business, they mess with my Heart, my Blueprint, my Mission, and my Purpose in life. Thus, by Divine Authority from the Heavenly of Heavens, I will shut it or them down, period. It is a NO-GO for me; no matter how they take my kindness for weakness, they will see how kindness is my

Opposites Attract

GREATEST STRENGTH with Divine Leverage from the Most High God.

What is the purpose of completely severing ties with him? Once again, we were UNEQUALLY YOKED. For what I do, this is how I build the lives of others, asking for nothing in return from them—only from God. Why is a Spiritual Demand placed on God? It is my Covenant with Him, but more importantly, it is also my secret door to DIVINE WISDOM and INNER HEALING that money cannot buy.

By far, this COVENANTAL lifeline I have with God provides me with a SUPERNATURAL Covering beyond human comprehension, so I do not play around with it. Nor do I allow others to cause my MIND to jump the track with foolery. When a man crosses this line, he is cut off, period. No questions asked.

Why did God not prevent him from stealing from me? He allowed it because I knowingly had open doors in the enemy's territory while selfishly playing the field with cracks in my foundation, reducing me to rubble. Let me say this: I did glean the Divine Wisdom hidden within this ordeal, and the rebuilt ruins turned out better than what I lost!

One would ask, 'Did I forgive the thief?' Of course, I forgave him, exhibiting all the Fruits of the Spirit, but I also let go of him with a straight face. In *The Lady's Code*, when we walk away with our heads held high with a smile, the *Woman of Stature* branding becomes engraved on the tablet of our hearts. Plus, we can bounce back or make a comeback in ways that put the enemy to boot. Not so bad when this story made it into *The Lady's Code: As It Pleases God*.

For me, I am interested in *The Ride or Die Partner*, not the *Destroy and Steal Partner*. Even though I had to play his game for a minute to get myself together, I put my trust in God to restore that which the cankerworm had stolen, and He did. I am here to write this story today, and it has indeed made me a better woman to understand what types of people to avoid while exhibiting Christlike Character with a smile on my face.

We are not designed to stay where we do not belong, and if we are comfortable being out of Purpose, it means growth is not taking place in our lives. In the stillness of our brokenness, there

Opposites Attract

are times when God will allow events to happen to shake us up or break us down to the core to get our attention. Why would God operate in such a manner? Wherever there is a lack of growth, we will naturally become a sluggard in this particular area if left unchecked, creating a comfort zone that attracts people, places, and things contributing to that zone of choice.

Selfish love is not enough to put yourself or your seed in a relationship not designed for you. How do you know if you are unequally yoked? Trust me, you know! It is often ignored while being camouflaged with superficial or conditional love. Then again, it may fill a longing temporarily.

In essence, if a person is your missing rib, you will never question it...you will KNOW IT! Power, money, or sex cannot break this type of bond. As we navigate life's unpredictable terrain and distractions, this RIDE or DIE kind of love is hard to come by...but readily available once the Equally Yoked Prerequisites are met, *As It Pleases God!*

Moreover, once you are yoked with the right person with a deep connection and unity from the Heavenly of Heavens, an INSTINCTUAL and SACRED BOND will be recognized by both. Spiritually Speaking, this is similar to Genesis 2:23, where Adam proclaims: *"This is now bone of my bones and flesh of my flesh."*

What if it is just one party noticing the bond, and the other one does not? Unfortunately, that is NOT how Sacred Bonds work in the Kingdom of God. Remember, Spirit knows Spirit. Trust me, if our baby does not leap with the person we proclaim to be the one, more than likely, they are not the one; there is infatuation in the equation, or they are not readily prepared. So, my suggestion is to back up and take it to God in prayer. While doing so, make sure you take a serious look at the *Wall of Restoration* as you get into His face, *Spirit to Spirit.*

Wall of Restoration

On your Spiritual Journey toward restoration, have you ever taken a Spiritual Pause or Timeout to reflect on your heart posture?

Opposites Attract

Have you taken into account your mindset, thoughtset, behavioralset, wordset, beliefset, or traumaset? Do you feel like you need restoration? Do you have the courage to restore yourself, *As It Pleases God*? Then again, have you become complacent in the Will of God?'

Many of us, at some point in our lives, have found ourselves grappling with feelings of loss or discontent. If one has not, then live a little longer; life has a way of bringing the oil or wine out of us. For this reason, in *The Lady's Code: As It Pleases God*, it takes exceptional courage to move forward and become restored. It takes even more courage to move forward and to digress.

In the quest for restoration, when our relationships are in turmoil, it is common to look for a miracle to come from someone else outside of ourselves. As a *Woman of Stature*, I firmly believe our MIRACLES are within us, most often layered by something else. We often pray for God to send someone to help us on our terms, as opposed to praying for God to help us to help ourselves, *As It Pleases Him*.

According to the Heavenly of Heavens, Divine Restoration is not simply about healing or overcoming, though it may happen. It is more about the transformative process occurring, similar to the caterpillar to butterfly metamorphosis. Restoration without transformation is a recipe for disaster in the Eye of God, sometimes thrusting us into a cycle of déjà vu. For this reason, Romans 12:2 says, *"And do not be conformed to this world, but be transformed by the renewing of your mind, that you may prove what is that good and acceptable and perfect will of God."*

How do we know if we are not transforming properly? If one has to ask this question, then it is fair to say that there is residing doubt or disobedience occurring. For example, when we need to avoid someone, we know it within the depths of our souls, yet we ignore it. Only to become hurt, rejected, abused, or betrayed by the one that we knew that we should have exercised caution with anyway. Besides, we do not really kick ourselves because of what they did to us; we kick ourselves because we did not listen to the voice from within or the Voice of God.

Opposites Attract

Here is what Proverbs 1:24-27 shares with us about the consequences of ignoring Divine Wisdom and Wise Counsel: *"Because I have called and you refused, I have stretched out my hand and no one regarded, because you disdained all my counsel and would have none of my rebuke, I also will laugh at your calamity; I will mock when your terror comes, when your terror comes like a storm, and your destruction comes like a whirlwind, when distress and anguish come upon you."* Is this not a bit harsh? Maybe or maybe not, but when we do not listen to wise counsel, we inadvertently suffer dire consequences.

In a relationship, we have all been thrown under the bus at some point. I have definitely had my share of encounters. Out of willful disobedience, I have been dogged out, rejected, abused, cheated on, sold out...you name it...it has happened, but I have not allowed it to stop me, and nor should you. In reality, there are many different reasons why someone would throw us under the bus or why we would throw someone under the bus as well.

Still, as *Women of Stature*, we must understand this phenomenon of the colloquialism, 'Thrown under the bus.' It simply means to betray, blame, reject, or disown, which is based solely upon one's perception of the situation, circumstance, or event that may have led up to this FEELING of being thrown under the bus. However, it may or may not have been the intent or motive of the person who caused the atrocity. Nevertheless, it should give us enough willpower to weed through the types of people to avoid the next time around. The next time? Yes, the next time!

What is the deal with next time? Some people get an adrenaline rush by intentionally hurting others. Unfortunately, this type of person will create bad blood between the two of you. More than likely, they have a lot of enemies anyway. Once you encounter them, learn what you need to learn, exhibit the Fruits of the Spirit, and find an exit quickly because this is an emotionally and mentally abusive individual. Here are a few factors to adhere to in *The Lady's Code* for the next time, but not limited to such:

- ☐ We must get the facts first.
- ☐ Ask relevant fact-finding questions.

Opposites Attract

- ☐ Reverse a negative into a positive.
- ☐ Learn the lessons needed.
- ☐ Be quick to forgive.
- ☐ Extract the wisdom.
- ☐ Look for the win-win.
- ☐ Do not burn any bridges.
- ☐ Determine which Fruits of the Spirit are being used or the ones that were not used, personally, privately, professionally, or communally.
- ☐ Document the findings and align the associations with scriptures from the Book of Proverbs.

Why must we learn when thrown under the bus, primarily when we feel like blocking them out? First, it trains us to learn what types of people and characteristics to avoid. Secondly, it assists us in moving on in the Spirit of Excellence without feeling guilty, second-guessing ourselves, wasting time, or settling. Thirdly, it develops our people skills and self-control. Clearly, this is not a matter of being biased; it is a matter of being WISE and KNOWING when to walk away!

Now, if people are chirping in your ear about wrongdoings, walk away. If people are pressuring you to violate your conscience, walk away. If people are pressuring you for your secrets, walk away. Why must we walk away? Should we not face the issues? With the *Wall of Restoration*, you cannot entertain certain things, especially when dealing with someone with the potential to throw you under the bus.

In this situation, as long as you know and understand the truth about yourself, it does not mean you have to tell the whole world unless it is positive. If it is negative or condemning, put it away, and if you cannot bury it, then keep your innermost secrets or your most incriminating skeletons to yourself. You really do not know who is or is not envious of who you are, what you do, or what you may become. If they feel threatened in any way, they may use your past against you as leverage.

Opposites Attract

In *The Lady's Code*, we have the RIGHT to reject harmful or traumatizing fruits. It is written all over the Book of Proverbs regarding what types of people to associate ourselves with. Once we align the experience, *As It Pleases God*, and according to scripture, we develop our own *Wall of Restoration* and our personalized DIY Guide. If we do not have one, it is time to get started.

On the *Wall of Restoration*, if someone tells me they have never experienced failure, rejection, or defeat, I do not trust this person at all. Why is trust not extended to this person? It is very simple—we are not born walking and talking; therefore, in order to build strength to walk, we will fall down due to the Law of Gravity. As *Women of Stature*, we cannot defy the gravitational pull. As with babies, it is customary to crawl as they learn the value of balance before walking. And we are no different...with Divine Stature in the Eye of God comes real training. Without it, we become weak by default.

The same applies to talking as well...a baby will chop up words royally until they learn the proper etiquette of the language they are speaking. It is for this reason that when a grown person says they have never failed, it is a lie! Until we are able to own our mistakes and failures in life, we will continue to blame others for what we should be taking responsibility for.

What is the big deal about taking responsibility for the *Wall of Restoration*? In *The Lady's Code*, when we allow our minds to become led astray by our emotions, we will find that we will become extra sensitive about everything. We will think people are talking about us, we will think they are laughing at us, we will think they are judging us, we will think they do not like us, we will think everyone is out to get us, we will think someone is trying to take advantage of us, we will think everyone has an agenda, we will think, think, and think as the list goes on.

Unfortunately, this is how an ungoverned mind will set a trap for us so we can wallow in our unchecked negative emotions. If we do not strengthen ourselves mentally and emotionally, *As It Pleases God*, we will easily break physically. When this happens, it

Opposites Attract

is revealed through uncontrollable behaviors such as outbursts of anger, temper tantrums, yelling, screaming, fussing, nagging, fighting, attitude problems, the inability to control what comes out of our mouths, or exhibiting downright hatefulness.

Besides, when dealing with *The Lady's Code: As It Pleases God*, we have zero tolerance for excuses, ungoverned outbursts, loose lips, or the blaming game. In the restoration phase, the key is not to be afraid to ask for help. Before moving on, know this:

- ☐ We all need help from time to time.
- ☐ We all need encouragement from time to time.
- ☐ We all need comfort from time to time.

We all need a little inspiration to get our wheels turning in the right direction, and it is definitely okay to do so. In my opinion, opening ourselves up for help is our iron-sharpening-iron forum from within. Still, our Iron Sharpening Genius will not budge without having our Spiritual Instincts intact.

Why will our Iron Sharpening Genius not budge without having our Spiritual Instincts on full alert? According to the Heavenly of Heavens, first, it helps us discern what is what and who is whom properly. Secondly, when our Spiritual Instincts are on full alert, *As It Pleases God*, it prevents us from becoming Spiritually Reckless.

Contrarily, in a fast-paced world, if we are pleasing ourselves or in the pursuit of personal pleasures with our Spiritual Instincts switched off or silenced, we will become Spiritually Dull by default, which also equates to Spiritual Blindness, Deafness, or Muteness. When we become so engrossed in pleasing ourselves, our relationships will become negatively infected or influenced by our thoughts, behaviors, beliefs, biases, reactions, desires, and words.

In addition, when we sink into a cycle of self-indulgence, it invokes all types of relational plagues, providing temporary satisfaction and happiness with zero staying power, joy, or substance. Often enough, this leads to Mental, Physical,

Opposites Attract

Emotional, and Spiritual Malnourishment with a trail of rotten and mangled fruits.

In breaking free from any negative cycles, there must be intentional effort and reflection, *As It Pleases God*, while understanding two things:

- ☐ A relationship that falls apart can come back together if the two of you ACKNOWLEDGE and AGREE to work on it, *As It Pleases Him*.

- ☐ A relationship that is together can fall apart, especially if you DO NOT evaluate or agree on what you are or are not doing or contributing to the relationship.

Regardless of where you may have failed, you can succeed in your relationships without creating enemies. By applying the simple *Writing on the Wall Principles* and communicating effectively, you can rebuild and nurture connections that bring joy and unwavering fulfillment with a Triple-Braided Cord Connection. Here is what we must know about positive transformation: We all will face moments of failure, insecurity, miscommunication, and misunderstanding. However, we must know what to do when it happens and why we are doing what we do, allowing them to become stepping stones and a safe place. We definitely do not want these moments to become boulders or rock-throwing sessions.

What if our moments become rock-throwing sessions amid the *Wall of Restoration*? When we settle into a relationship or go against our conscience, we may experience intense feelings of self-blame and regret. Unfortunately, these emotions can also lead to bitterness, which can be particularly painful and can even trigger a desire for revenge. The bottom line is that airing out our dirty laundry or seeking revenge can ultimately compromise our integrity, making us lose sight of our values, leading us to behave in ways we never thought we would.

Opposites Attract

It is essential to remember that revenge is not worth sacrificing our integrity or making bad decisions. Rather than dwelling on negative thoughts and trying to harm others, we should focus on maintaining our own values and doing what is right. Even if we feel justified in our anger, it is never an excuse to engage in wrongdoing.

When we hold on to bitterness and resentment, we may experience mental anguish that keeps us trapped in the past. Frankly, this can also drain our energy, making us feel like a victim. Feeling victimized can slow down our restorative progress and prevent us from living an abundant life. To avoid this inner turmoil, it is essential to release the burden of carrying the exposed bites and bruises of the past. As *Women of Stature*, letting go of negative emotions can help us move forward and lead a more fulfilling life, *As It Pleases God*.

The *Wall of Restoration* emphasizes the importance of resting to overcome any obstacle. Resting is crucial for restoration. While daily renewal is beneficial, it is essential to find inner peace through rest to maintain healthy relationships. Without seeking peace from within, distractions and infatuations with external factors can impact our ability to rest and lead to seeking temporary solace in people, places, and things.

Plus, we do not want to rest our heads in the wrong places or on the wrong laps. For example, in Judges, Chapters 13-16, Delilah is a woman with whom Samson falls in love, but she is also working with the Philistines to try to capture him. In one instance, Samson fell asleep with his head in Delilah's lap, and she used the opportunity to cut off his hair, which was the source of his strength. This act ultimately led to Samson's capture and downfall.

In *The Lady's Code*, we do not want this to happen to any *Woman of Stature*; thus, we must remain diligent to avoid allowing our weaknesses to zap our strengths. Just in case you are having a hard time pinpointing them, here is a list of people that you may want to avoid:

Opposites Attract

- ☐ Avoid People Who Are Unequally Yoked With You.
- ☐ Avoid People Who Live By A Double Standard.
- ☐ Avoid People Who Do Not Love You.
- ☐ Avoid People Who Reject You.
- ☐ Avoid People Who Victimize You.
- ☐ Avoid People Who Are Selfish.
- ☐ Avoid People Who Are Hateful.
- ☐ Avoid People Who Are Abusive.
- ☐ Avoid People Who Judge You or Put You Down.
- ☐ Avoid People That Violate Your Conscience.
- ☐ Avoid People That Are Phony.
- ☐ Avoid People That Kick You When You Are Down.
- ☐ Avoid People That Pry.
- ☐ Avoid People Who Are Control Freaks.
- ☐ Avoid People That Are Ungrateful.
- ☐ Avoid People That Do Not Have A Conscience.
- ☐ Avoid People Who Steal From You.
- ☐ Avoid People That Are Arrogant.
- ☐ Avoid People Who Lack Self-Control.
- ☐ Avoid People Who Cannot Be Honest.
- ☐ Avoid People Who Nag.
- ☐ Avoid People Who Are Stuck On Negative.
- ☐ Avoid People Who Are Hypocrites.
- ☐ Avoid People Who Kill The Dreams Of Others.
- ☐ Avoid People With Anger Problems.
- ☐ Avoid People Who Refuse To Deal With Their Insecurities.
- ☐ Avoid People Who Constantly Relive Their Past.
- ☐ Avoid People Who Are Insensitive or Rude.
- ☐ Avoid People Who Are Constantly Looking For Your Faults.
- ☐ Avoid People Who Are Very Impatient With You.

Opposites Attract

- ☐ Avoid People Who Talk About You.
- ☐ Avoid People Who Are Not Compassionate.
- ☐ Avoid People Who Are Very Confrontational.
- ☐ Avoid People Who Do Not Listen.
- ☐ Avoid People Who Doubt Everything About You.
- ☐ Avoid People Who Are Ineffective.
- ☐ Avoid People Who Block Your Creativity.
- ☐ Avoid People Who Put You In A Box.
- ☐ Avoid People Who Have An Ulterior Motive.
- ☐ Avoid People Who Do Not Appreciate You.
- ☐ Avoid People Who Are Not Committed.
- ☐ Avoid People Who Give Up On You.
- ☐ Avoid People Who Are Bitter.
- ☐ Avoid People Who Are Unforgiving.
- ☐ Avoid People Who Bully You.
- ☐ Avoid People Who Lack Integrity.
- ☐ Avoid People Who Try To Block You.
- ☐ Avoid People Who Do Not Believe In You.
- ☐ Avoid People Who Are Deceptive.
- ☐ Avoid People Who Try To Sidetrack You.
- ☐ Avoid People Who Try To Get In Your Head.
- ☐ Avoid People Who Wage Spiritual Warfare Against You.
- ☐ Avoid People Who Deprive You Emotionally.
- ☐ Avoid People Who Deprive You Sexually To Control You.
- ☐ Avoid People Who Exhibit Foolish Behavior.
- ☐ Avoid People Who Are Envious or Jealous Of You.
- ☐ Avoid People Who Are Unaccountable To Change.
- ☐ Avoid People Who Are Not Generous.
- ☐ Avoid People Who Will Divorce You Over Anything.
- ☐ Avoid People Who Will Not Admit Mistakes.
- ☐ Avoid People Who Make a Fool Out of You.

Opposites Attract

- ☐ Avoid People Who Set You Back.
- ☐ Avoid People Who Procrastinate.
- ☐ Avoid People Who Do Not Prepare.
- ☐ Avoid The Sugar Daddies and Sugar Mamas.
- ☐ Avoid People Who Want The Benefits Without A Commitment.
- ☐ Avoid People Who Take You For Granted.
- ☐ Avoid People Who Are Lazy.
- ☐ Avoid People Who Will Not Fight The Temptation Of The Flesh.
- ☐ Avoid People Who Compare You With Others.
- ☐ Avoid People Who Rush All The Time.
- ☐ Avoid People Who Try To Oppress You.
- ☐ Avoid People Who Try To Steal Your Joy or Happiness.
- ☐ Avoid People Who Try To Keep You From Living The Good Life.
- ☐ Avoid People Who Are Emotionally Exhausting.
- ☐ Avoid People Who Are Undisciplined.
- ☐ Avoid People Who Do Not Embrace Opportunity.
- ☐ Avoid People Who Despitefully Use You.
- ☐ Avoid People Who Are Copycats.
- ☐ Avoid People Who Criticize You.
- ☐ Avoid People Who Do Not Communicate.
- ☐ Avoid People Who Take Your Kindness For A Weakness.
- ☐ Avoid People Who Embarrass You In Public.
- ☐ Avoid People Who Avoid You.
- ☐ Avoid People Who Laugh At You Mockingly.
- ☐ Avoid People Who Pretend Like They Know Everything.
- ☐ Avoid People Who Overlook You on Purpose.
- ☐ Avoid People Who Cringe When You Show Up.
- ☐ Avoid People Who Play Games.

Opposites Attract

- ☐ Avoid People Who Secretly Wish For Your Demise.
- ☐ Avoid People Who Secretly or Openly Contend Against You.
- ☐ Avoid People Who Treat You Like A Doormat.
- ☐ Avoid People Who Vex Your Spirit.
- ☐ Avoid People Who Will Not Help You.
- ☐ Avoid People Who Refuse To Mentor Others.
- ☐ Avoid People Who Prevent You From Doing The Right Thing.
- ☐ Avoid People Who Stalk You.
- ☐ Avoid People Who Refuse To Deal With Their Addictions.
- ☐ Avoid People Who Are Evil.
- ☐ Avoid People Who Prevent You From Praying or Developing a Relationship With God.

Once again, we all have issues, and this list is not designed for you to cut off everyone. In *The Lady's Code*, this is where you apply the 80/20 rule, pinpointing what you can live with intensified three times (3X), what you cannot live with, and what is in your zero-tolerance category. What does this mean? In a relationship, friendship, or whatever is decided, when the mask comes off, can you live with what made it to the AVOID LIST? As *Women of Stature*, if we cannot live with it, then politely excuse yourself with a smile while keeping it moving in the Spirit of Excellence.

On the other hand, in *The Lady's Code*, if you possess some of these characteristics, then you have work to do. How do we begin this process? Begin by using the Fruits of the Spirit to self-correct and the Book of Proverbs as a Spiritual Mirror to reflect or become self-aware, *As It Pleases God*.

Does using the Fruits of the Spirit really work? Absolutely. I am living proof, and *The Lady's Code: As It Pleases God* speaks for itself! The Spiritual Concept of the Fruits of the Spirit, derived from

Opposites Attract

Galatians 5:22-23 in the Bible, provides a dynamic framework for our lives and relations on any level, from the least to the greatest.

Our personal growth and interpersonal harmony are encapsulated in using the attributes of Love, Joy, Peace, Patience, Kindness, Goodness, Faithfulness, Gentleness, and Self-Control. According to the Heavenly of Heavens, everything we need for character building, transformation, or restoration is hidden within the Fruits of the Spirit. Frankly, all we need to do is use them, *As It Pleases God*.

As a Word to the Wise, the Fruits of the Spirit have natural Spiritual Default Mechanisms engrafted within them, releasing chemical compounds within the body, similar to a plant releasing pollen. More importantly, they are foolproof, doing what they were created to do.

What are the Spiritual Default Mechanisms prewired within the Fruits of the Spirit? They are not set in stone until we use them, *As It Pleases God*. Then the Spiritual Components kick in, filling in the gaps of what is needed, and being that there is NO LAW against the Fruits of the Spirit, we cannot limit them. If we as humans attempt to limit them, they will inadvertently work against us. Here is what I mean: John 15:5 says, *"I am the vine, you are the branches. He who abides in Me, and I in him, bears much fruit; for without Me you can do nothing."*

From the Ancient of Days, the counterbalancing system hidden within the Fruits of the Spirit is designed to CLEANSE the mindset, conscience, psyche, and senses of mankind by incorporating the benefits of use. Proverbs 11:30 advises us about what to do when using this clean sweep, *As It Pleases God*: *"The fruit of the righteous is a tree of life, and he who wins souls is wise."*

How do we make the benefits of the Fruit of Righteousness make sense, especially when applying it to real life? We must know the Fruits of the Spirit are not just for our consumption, use, or benefit. They are designed to develop our charactorial people skills into a Christlike heart and mind posture for personal, private, professional, or communal usage, leading us toward Divine Oneness in the State of Righteousness. Being that we are not in a state of Oneness, *As It Pleases God*, as of yet, it is only wise to work on our multiple fruits, one by one, until we perfect them in the Spirit of Oneness. Why one by one? Due to Spiritual Duality, it is best to understand both sides of a fruit, seed, or root to multiply them, *As It Pleases God*.

If we do not learn, understand, and till them to know the difference, we can become Bible experts, trying to correct those who know what they are talking about. Yet, we walk around without possessing the Divine Power to move mountains, as we become Spiritually Unpalatable. For instance, Leviticus 19:23 paints the ideal picture for us: "*When you come into the land, and have planted all kinds of trees for food, then you shall count their fruit as uncircumcised. Three years it shall be uncircumcised to you; it shall not be eaten.*"

Suddenly, everyone wants to be an expert on the Fruit or Fruits of the Spirit, debating its single or plural usage, while knowing absolutely nothing about Spiritual Duality, Spiritual Multiplying, or Spiritual Oneness. Nor are they experts on how to break them down for Kingdom Usage and Spiritual Training to make their baby leap from within. Nor do they possess the understanding or know-how to make someone else's baby leap from within to become the BEST or the Crème de la Crème in Earthen Vessels.

On the Wall of Restoration, here is what Genesis 43:11 wants us to know about the Gift to Joseph and the Spiritual Principle that was activated: "*And their father Israel said to them, 'If it must be so, then do this: Take some of the best fruits of the land in your vessels and carry down a present for the man-a little balm and a little honey, spices and myrrh, pistachio nuts and almonds.'*" When coming with the Divine Goods, we must become prepared with the BEST of the BEST, without half-stepping.

Above all, as *Women of Stature*, when we are coming correct with the *Wall of Restoration* due to any state of offense, and *As It Pleases God*, we must come with DOUBLE PORTIONS. Really? Yes, really! Here is what Genesis 43:12 advises: "*Take double money in your hand, and take back in your hand the money that was returned in the mouth of your sacks; perhaps it was an oversight. Take your brother also, and arise, go*

Opposites Attract

back to the man. And may God Almighty give you mercy before the man, that he may release your other brother and Benjamin. If I am bereaved, I am bereaved!" Double money, double seeds, double fruits, double whatever, can assist with the *Wall of Restoration* on our behalf or that of another. So, please do not get the multiplying factors twisted with the firstfruits of our actions, thoughts, beliefs, words, desires, or labors that are being sown in or out of our fields.

For example, when practicing love and kindness, *As It Pleases God*, it will naturally foster compassion and understanding by default. Then again, when we approach our conflicts with patience and gentleness, *As It Pleases Him*, we are more likely to seek resolutions with humility instead of escalating, broadcasting our issues, or outing each other out of fear or a desire for freedom.

The TRANSFORMATION and BLESSINGS resulting from living a life dedicated to God, *As It Pleases Him*, will provide a *Wall of Restoration* for the righteous partakers, walking worthy. For the record, regardless of where we are in life or how we got there, when we live in a manner that honors and PLEASES Him, we will become more sensitive to His Divine Guidance, Nudges, and Discernment.

Once again, using the Fruits of the Spirit and behaving Christlike works wonders on the psyche of mankind, developing our Spiritual Maturity. Colossians 1:10 states why we must do this: *"So that you may walk worthy of the Lord, fully pleasing Him, being fruitful in every good work and increasing in the knowledge of God."* As we deepen our understanding of God and Divine Restoration, we will gain the potential and know-how to overcome obstacles hindering our Spiritual Growth. In addition, we will also gain an understanding of what would cause us to stray away from our Predestined Blueprint.

To perfect the art of giving the first and best of one's harvest, whether it is our time, skills, talents, character traits, or finances to God, we must honor Him. Here is what we must do according to Proverbs 3:9-10: *"Honor the LORD with your possessions, And with the firstfruits of all your increase; So your barns will be filled with plenty, And your vats will overflow with new wine."*

Opposites Attract

Unbeknown to most, it is through our Spiritual Compass, already preset on the Fruit of Holiness from within, that provides the Divine Navigation needed to get us to where we need to be. But, when dealing with the *Wall of Restoration*, it needs an AGREEMENT from us to do what needs to be done, *As It Pleases God*. Here is what Romans 6:22 says about this Spiritual Seal: *"But now, having been set free from sin, and having become slaves of God, you have your fruit to holiness, and the end, everlasting life."*

In *The Lady's Code*, as *Women of Stature*, by daring to confront our past while reading *The Writing On The Wall*, we can emerge stronger, profoundly wiser, courageously equipped, and more resilient, all in the Spirit of Excellence. As we confidently step into our future, renewed and restored, *Opposites will only Attract* Divine Wisdom toward us to positively influence, inspire, and achieve for the Greater Good. Above all, with our Spiritual Understanding that we are Divinely Designed for GREATNESS, let us now extract the POWER hidden in *Fear and Freedom*.

CHAPTER 7

FEAR OR FREEDOM

In every corner of life, from the least to the greatest, we all will encounter both known and unknown forms of bondage, yokes, or soul ties. Whether it is the weight of past experiences, societal expectations, toxic relationships, social constraints, self-imposed limitations, systemic barriers, or environmental conditions, it does not eliminate the elements of fear or the desire for freedom.

According to the Heavenly of Heavens, when we are in known or unknown bondage, we have to fight for our rights to become free. When our past shackles us, we have to fight for our rights to live in the now. When we are faced with roadblocks, both expected and unforeseen, we have to fight for our rights to overcome or break down our obstacles. We cannot sit back and let life happen as if God has not equipped us with the Spiritual Voice or Tools needed to survive in the real world. Nor did He make a mistake with the tools, methods, or Spiritual Classroom used to TRAIN us for our Heaven on Earth Experiences.

As a part of *The Lady's Code: As It Pleases God*, we must pick up our CROSS and walk as *Women of Stature*. And, if we have to engage in Spiritual Warfare to get what belongs to us, then so be it, without putting our paws on anyone.

Fear or Freedom

Many of us are accustomed to fighting with our words or deeds; nevertheless, I am going to take it to the next level to engage in combat with the Word of God instead. In order to build our Spiritual Muscles with *The Lady's Code*, here are a few basic steps we must master in the building and molding of ourselves as *Women of Stature*, but not limited to such:

- ☐ We must know and understand that we have the POWER to change, choose, and govern our perceptions.
- ☐ We must acknowledge the problems or obstacles.
- ☐ We must identify the root causes.
- ☐ We must accept responsibility.
- ☐ We must understand the WHY.
- ☐ We must design a mind map of the solution or the regrafting process.
- ☐ We must align the solution or regrafting process with Biblical Scriptures with a Plan of Action.
- ☐ We must become proactive in using the Fruits of the Spirit.
- ☐ We must do a checkup from the neck up continuously to maintain a Positive Mental Attitude.

Once we get these items in order, then develop a *Spirit to Spirit* Relationship with our Heavenly Father, usher in the Holy Spirit, and cover ourselves with the Blood of Jesus at a set destination and time. If we are hardheaded or become resistant to the leading of the Holy Spirit, we will miss the mark. As a result, it throws us into the cycle of déjà vu to repeat the lesson, possibly with different characters. Nonetheless, in *The Lady's Code: As It Pleases God*, this is not the goal of this book; I am here to get those who are willing on point and on cue with the leading of the Spirit.

In the midst of mastering *The Lady's Code*, we must connect with people, and they must connect to us without resistance on our behalf. If we lack this ability, we will find ourselves in the midst of negativity, chaos, and confusion. Why would negativity erupt? Once again, we are relational beings, and our Divine Blueprint will also be a compilation of filling or serving the wants and needs of

Fear or Freedom

others by solving problems, bringing about social reformation, inspiring unity, or bringing forth revelation. For this reason, people will not always agree with us, or they may be unwilling to change for the better.

As *Women of Stature*, there is no need to manipulate, connive, or scheme to get what belongs to us. In the Eye of God, we need only to position ourselves to take ownership with the 3-P Heart Posture of Peace, Patience, and Perseverance, *As It Pleases Him*. What can the 3-P Heart Posture do for us? It leads us to the 3-P Mind Posture of Proactive Peace, Purpose, and Passion, transforming our pain into power and our obstacles into stepping stones.

By leaning into our Spiritual Resources, we can actively participate in the life we desire with the 3-P Heart and Mind Posture. Amid *Fear or Freedom* in *The Lady's Code*, we are all in search of meaning, and we all have some sort of positive or negative yearning from within the psyche, even if we are in denial. As the unveiling of our Divine Blueprint gets closer, the ability to query and extract the hidden wisdom from within is of the utmost essence. By doing so, it is designed to liberate our soulish nature out of the shadows into the LIGHT, *As It Pleases God*.

Peace, Purpose, and Passion

Are you peaceful? Are you in Purpose on purpose? Are you passionate about what you do, what you say, and what you already are? Wait, wait, wait, do not answer these questions yet; let us talk for a moment, *Spirit to Spirit*.

Unbeknown to most, our 3-P Mind Posture is directly linked to our *Peace, Purpose, and Passion*, the Spiritual Power Drivers for our Heaven on Earth Experiences. Though we do not think about our Mind Postures much, for a time such as this, posterity is crucial in the Eye of God. Here is what Jeremiah 17:10 wants us to know: *"I, the Lord, search the heart, I test the minds, even to give every man according to his ways, according to the fruit of his doings."*

There are indeed times when we feel as if we do not need the Divine Illumination of God because we have it all together, and we are on top of our game. However, from my perspective, this is the moment we need Divine Illumination the most to fuel our actions, govern our thoughts, influence our choices, and shape our identities according to our Predestined Blueprint, the core aspect of our existence.

Why do we need Divine Illumination, especially when everything is already? Just because we are prepackaged with our Divine Blueprint does not mean we are ready or palatable. For instance, when you buy a box of cake mix, the cake is essentially ready to be made. However, you still need to add specific ingredients, mix them properly, and bake them at the right temperature as instructed on the box. If you neglect to follow these steps, the cake remains a cake, but it may turn out to be unappetizing, unpalatable, or unattractive.

At the heart of anything we engage in lies the concept of *Peace, Purpose, and Passion*, even if we are not formally aware of them. In my opinion, this is our Spiritual Cake Mix with dualistic options to:

- ☐ Transform the dullish mundane into the extraordinary with enthusiasm, creativity, and a sense of purpose to inspire, heal, and motivate.

- ☐ Make the dullish mundane or extraordinary painstakingly rancid by the lack of enthusiasm, creativity, and a sense of purpose, who harm, manipulate, oppress, and discourage.

How do we make this make sense, primarily when we have it all together, operating in resilience? In the Eye of God, we are all a work-in-progress! If we had somehow ARRIVED, there would be no need for us here for the Heaven on Earth Experience. More importantly, if one does not honestly know their reason for being, if one is not at peace with oneself from within, or if one does not exude passion out of their loins, then one has work to do, *As It Pleases God!*

Fear or Freedom

Why would we have more work to do as Believers to become Divinely Unveiled, *As It Pleases God*? Simply put, Spiritual Cluelessness leads to Spiritual Recklessness, especially when we have nothing to gain or lose in the Kingdom. The moment someone says to me that they have it all together, I already know they do not. When dealing with *Peace, Purpose, and Passion*, we must remain on a Spiritual Learning Curve and be ready to step into the Spiritual Classroom at the drop of a dime.

When we have somehow developed a deaf ear or Spiritual Blinders, possibly out of selfishness or pompousness, Divine Illumination from the Heavenly of Heavens will VEIL those who think they are the best thing since sliced bread, who lack outright humility. Although GREATNESS resides within all of us, humility is still what keeps it thriving and alive for others to enjoy. Is this Biblical? I would have it no other way. Proverbs 22:4 says, "*By humility and the fear of the Lord are riches and honor and life.*"

Not only that, James 4:10 reminds us about who really does the lifting: "*Humble yourselves in the sight of the Lord, and He will lift you up.*" Above all, here is the Spiritual Instruction we can Divinely Enforce when residing in a humble state, *As It Pleases Him*: "*Let nothing be done through selfish ambition or conceit, but in lowliness of mind let each esteem others better than himself.*" Philippians 2:3.

How can we use Philippians 2:3 as Divine Leverage with *Peace, Purpose, and Passion*? In all simplicity, we need to quote the scriptures back to God in our own words, including the Spiritual Principles that PLEASE Him. Is this not engaging in a play on words? Absolutely not! It is called holding God accountable to His Divine Word, Promises, Truth, and Faithfulness. Isaiah 55:11 says, "*So shall My word be that goes forth from My mouth; it shall not return to Me void, but it shall accomplish what I please, and it shall prosper in the thing for which I sent it.*" As a *Woman of Stature*, I believe this, and so should you!

For example, here is how I would get this Spiritual Party started in my *Spirit to Spirit* alone time with my Heavenly Father. I would say: Lord, as I humbly and gratefully come before You, in the Name of Jesus, I give THANKS. I remove all selfishness or negative

Fear or Freedom

ambitions from the equation using the Fruits of the Spirit, as I remain in a selfless and usable posture. While behaving Christlike according to Your Word, I invoke the Presence of the Holy Spirit to guide and provide for me, *As It Pleases You* and according to my Predestined Blueprint. By Divine Decree, Lord, as I come into AGREEMENT with You and Your Word, BLESS me to be a BLESSING, confounding human reasoning to enrich Your precious sheep. As You freely give to me, I activate the Law of Reciprocity, giving back to the Kingdom. In Jesus' Name. Amen.

Can anyone use this prayer? Of course. As a matter of fact, if you pray this one prayer for 30 days and document what God is unveiling to you, it will change the trajectory of your life, guaranteed. How can a guarantee be extended with a prayer? Once again, I aligned this prayer with the Word of God and the Spiritual Principles that work. However, you can try it your way, or you can follow a proven way provided to you on a silver platter.

The Lady's Code is contingent on our ability to hone in on *Peace, Purpose, and Passion* by acknowledging our unique strengths, weaknesses, flaws, traumas, and experiences to create a win-win. Unbeknown to most, *Peace, Purpose, and Passion* are the driving forces of the psyche. If we dare to dig deep, this is the secret yearning that causes us to get caught up, yoked, and oppressed because we do not know how to obtain them, *As It Pleases God.* As a result, we patchwork our lives with all types of unequally yoked relationships for the appearance of having them. And then have the nerve to LIE about it.

As *Women of Stature*, we do not play around with the lies, nor do we feed them to the psyche, which keeps us grounded with the ability to push beyond our self-imposed limitations or the desire to give up. Even when the pressures of life are upon us, we can overcome obstacles in ways beyond human comprehension.

For me, I pride myself on staying calm, relaxed, and focused on my *Peace, Purpose, and Passion* at all times. I consider this my CENTER; it is indeed my reason to live, giving me the desire and willpower to push beyond any ailment designed to snuff me out. Listen to me, and listen to me well; everything I do, say, and

Fear or Freedom

become will reflect back to these three attributes, which give me the authority to invoke the Holy Veil to protect me on my Spiritual Journey and to bring forth *The Lady's Code: As It Pleases God*.

In addition, my *Peace, Purpose, and Passion* help me to become content with who I am from the inside out, especially when people attempt to bombard me with the negative rudiments of being better, stronger, and wiser than I am. Now, for the record, I do not compete...I EMPOWER. If I do not EMPOWER *Women of Stature* to become better, stronger, and wiser than I am, it means I am not doing my job. But that is not going to happen because I am going to do what I am called to do, period. I am not willing to lose one of God's precious sheep on my watch over jealousy, envy, pride, greed, coveting, or competitiveness...either you want it, or you do not!

Also, the 3-P Mind Posture aids me in avoiding any distractions designed to beset me as I cast down the plots of the enemy designed to derail my Divine Destiny. Above all, this will work for anyone who has the desire to put away their selfishness, pride, waywardness, and materialism.

In the frailties of life, we do not want to become overwhelmed with issues. Why must we avoid becoming overwhelmed? In short, it has a way of distorting our values and visions, as if we do not need God and that He has nothing to do with our Divine Blueprint or reason for being. In my opinion, it is unwise to think we can obtain *Peace, Purpose, and Passion* without God!

Even Jesus was baptized before the Holy Spirit descended upon Him, permitting Him to step into the fullness of His Calling in Matthew 3:16 and Luke 3:22. Now, do we think for a moment that we can have *Peace, Purpose, and Passion* without the Holy Spirit? The answer is no! When it comes down to *The Lady's Code*, we need the Holy Spirit and the Blood of Jesus, period. Just so we are clear, perfection is not mandatory: *"For all have sinned and fallen short of the glory of God."* Romans 3:23. However, the assistance of the Holy Spirit is required.

What if we are in a state of chaos? According to *The Lady's Code*, we should be practicing, learning, growing, preparing, and sowing using the Fruits of the Spirit faithfully until the Holy Spirit releases us into *Peace, Purpose, and Passion* with our Predestined Blueprinted Instructions, *As It Pleases God*. If we step in too soon or come out prematurely with rotten or mangled fruits and flawed character, we will not be equipped to withstand the wiles of the enemy. Sadly, this is the reason why we have God-fearing Believers beaten down by their enemies, unequally yoked, or outright oppressed.

Here again, we have Believers doing the right things at the wrong time without being commissioned or properly equipped, *As It Pleases God* to do what they are trying to do.

We cannot take over the world for God or become Spiritually Used by Him, doing our own thing without being Spiritually Equipped or placing Him first. For the sake of our souls, to protect our Bloodlines, as well as to safeguard our sanity, we must put on the Whole Armor of God to withstand the wiles of the enemy. If not, we can become sifted as wheat or bound by public humiliation in some way or some area of our lives. We must add God to our equational efforts, regardless of how insignificant it may seem.

Why must we add God into the equation of our lives, especially when having free will as Believers? It is the simple things that we overlook that will cause us to 'get got' by the enemy's antics and lies, making us *Spiritually Impoverished* while appearing right in our own eyes. Unfortunately, this is one of the reasons why Believers are being mocked by those who appear to be better, stronger, richer, or wiser than they are. But know this: "*Do not be deceived, God is not mocked; for whatever a man sows, that he will also reap.*" Galatians 6:7.

Spiritually Impoverished

In today's fast-paced society of instant everything, where material wealth and success often take center stage, we tend to forget that we are Spiritual Beings having a human experience. As a result, we become *Spiritually Impoverished* without knowing it or masking it with busyness, feelings of importance, or judgment of those appearing to have less compared to our more.

Fear or Freedom

Then again, we may know we are *Spiritually Impoverished* but do not care about our Spiritual Status in the Kingdom of God, especially when we are seemingly getting what we want and appear happy and successful on the surface.

According to the Heavenly of Heavens, while settling for an illusional appearance, we begin bargaining and overlooking what we need, *As It Pleases God.* Unwisely, when opting for the feelings of being unfulfilled, unsatisfied, and disconnected from ourselves, others, and our Divine Purpose, we will encounter Mental, Physical, Emotional, and Spiritual Roadblocks. Yet, once this happens from within and behind closed doors, we will find ourselves struggling with feelings of emptiness, loneliness, numbness, anxiety, fear, anger, unforgiveness, hatefulness, confusion, or dissatisfaction.

In the hustle and bustle of life, I have found those who take the Mission of God for granted, and I have also found those who mean well. Still, they are lost in the shuffle of life or totally confused about it, hiding behind work, social media, social engagements, and having fun, neglecting the well-being of the Mind, Body, Soul, and Spirit. The moment we become *Spiritually Impoverished* in such a manner, we will experience some form of inner defeat or humiliation, secretly or openly.

For the world in which we live, some of us do not give a rat's tail about our Predestined Blueprint or Divine Mission because we are living the good life, not realizing it will come to an end one day. The reality in which we live will meet up with us in some way, shape, or form; therefore, we must become conscious about what we are doing, as well as the reasons why. If not, the psyche will exude an unquenchable thirst, eventually driving us to our knees.

Unfortunately, in this unquenching state, this is where some people become *Spiritually Impoverished.* As a coping mechanism, they turn to harmful habits or addictions, and this is also where some people turn to God. Remember, He will never force us to choose Him; He will allow the Vicissitudes, Cycles, and Issues of Life to drive us to Him or away from Him. In this phase, we often develop the desires of *Fear or Freedom.*

Fear or Freedom

According to the Heavenly of Heavens, when the psyche is in the *Fear or Freedom* mode, either we are all in or we check completely out. For this reason, the word relationship brings about fear into the hearts of the strongest, most intelligent, and most courageous people because:

- ☐ They do not like disappointment.
- ☐ They do not like making mistakes.
- ☐ They do not like to be wrong.
- ☐ They do not like to be deceived.
- ☐ They do not like to be used or duped.
- ☐ They do not like feeling desperate.
- ☐ They do not like to be played as fools.

As a part of the do not like, they tend to opt out of the dating scene to focus on controllable things, such as work, career moves, and hobbies that involve creating, doing, implementing, and becoming more so than dating or mating. Most often, the hassle and the disappointment in dating or mating cause most of us to want to skip this part of the relationship, which, in my opinion, is the most important.

Now, before we move to the next section of *Relational Dating or Mating*, please allow me to share how to break *Spiritual Impoverishment*, but not limited to such:

- ☐ We need to become self-aware.
- ☐ We must acknowledge the need for Spiritual Nourishment.
- ☐ We must make a conscious choice to connect to God, *Spirit to Spirit*.
- ☐ We must pray, repent, forgive, fast, and meditate.
- ☐ We must cover ourselves with the Blood of Jesus.
- ☐ We must usher in the Holy Spirit.
- ☐ We must align ourselves with the Word of God.
- ☐ We must use the Fruits of the Spirit.
- ☐ We must behave Christlike.

Fear or Freedom

- ☐ We must counteract negative thoughts, words, desires, beliefs, and actions with positive ones.
- ☐ We must become a servant of the Kingdom of God.
- ☐ We must develop our people skills.

Remember, in the Kingdom, inner wealth and Spiritual Richness are more important than material gain. As a Word to the Wise, and with all due respect, if your legacy dies with you, then there is a problem with your workable efforts. It is time to revamp, *As It Pleases God*. Here is what Matthew 6:19-21 says, "*Do not lay up for yourselves treasures on earth, where moth and rust destroy and where thieves break in and steal; but lay up for yourselves treasures in heaven, where neither moth nor rust destroys and where thieves do not break in and steal. For where your treasure is, there your heart will be also.*"

Relational Dating or Mating

As everyone would agree, the dating phase of a relationship is the most entertaining, the most loving, and the most memorable. Most often, it is filled with laughter, excitement, flirtation, vulnerability, and the joy of discovering someone new. Whereas, in the Eye of God, the significance of this phase goes far beyond mere enjoyment or building emotional bonds; it is more about getting a true understanding of each other, *As It Pleases Him*.

This initial getting-to-know-you or exploration phase allows us to assess compatibility and determine if there is a potential for a deeper connection or whether we are equally or unequally yoked. By recognizing these signs early on, we can make informed decisions about the viability of the *Relational Dating or Mating* potentiality.

In the newness of it all, skipping the *Relational Dating or Mating* aspect of life may make life far simpler. Still, we would miss out on vital information, queries, red flags, wisdom, mismatched priorities, differing life goals, conflicting communication styles, and opportunities for personal growth. In addition, it also prevents us from meeting diverse individuals, determining our specks, experiencing different perspectives, and building our emotional intelligence, *As It Pleases God*.

In order to effectively read the *Writing on the Wall*, human connection and growth are a must. On your journey of love and self-discovery, you need to know the tastes, likes, dislikes, specks, quirks, and propensities of yourself, those who are in your circle, as well as the person you are dating or mating with. In the discovery phase, there is no better time to ask meaningful questions, engage in various activities, and share personal stories. By doing so, each person can better understand the other's values, thoughts, beliefs, lifestyles, desires, and relationship goals.

While marriages and partnerships are frequently depicted as unions founded on love, understanding, trust, respect, and mutual consideration, the alarming divorce rate of over 80% suggests that we are missing the essence of what truly matters, *As It Pleases God*. As my ear has been to the ground, and upon closer examination, many couples have significant gaps in personal and intimate knowledge of each other. The undisclosed or unexplored areas are astounding and heart-wrenching at the same time, unveiling the breakdown in our communication efforts while assuming we know everything about our spouses, partners, mates, or dates.

As *Women of Stature*, when engaging in *Relational Dating or Mating*, here is a list of what we need to know, or better yet, what we cannot ignore, but not limited to such:

- ☐ We must know which God they serve.
- ☐ We must know their core values and beliefs.
- ☐ We must know their family background.
- ☐ We must know what influences their perspectives.
- ☐ We must know their life goals, aspirations, and dreams.
- ☐ We must know what encourages them.
- ☐ We must know their communication style.
- ☐ We must know about their conflict resolution skills.
- ☐ We must know how they handle disagreements.
- ☐ We must know how they handle challenging situations.
- ☐ We must know how they handle rejection.

Fear or Freedom

- ☐ We must know their Spiritual Practices, Beliefs, and Faith.
- ☐ We must know their hobbies and interests.
- ☐ We must know what turns them on or off.
- ☐ We must know how they like sharing.
- ☐ We must know about their experiences, thoughts, desires, and memories.
- ☐ We must know their love languages.
- ☐ We must know their financial propensities and habits.
- ☐ We must know their health and wellness status.
- ☐ We must know about their friendships or social circles.
- ☐ We must know about their social influences.
- ☐ We must know about their past relationships.
- ☐ We must know about their relational behaviors.
- ☐ We must know their current perspectives.
- ☐ We must know about their challenges or struggles.
- ☐ We must know and understand their vulnerabilities.
- ☐ We must know their proactiveness or laziness.
- ☐ We must know their views on parenting.
- ☐ We must know their level of intimacy.
- ☐ We must know their cultural background and traditions.
- ☐ We must know their passions, desires, and hopes.
- ☐ We must know their bucket list of travel adventures.
- ☐ We must know what makes them happy or sad.
- ☐ We must know their areas of trauma.
- ☐ We must know their triggers.
- ☐ We must know their Mental, Physical, Emotional, and Spiritual status.
- ☐ We must know their concerns and fears.

What if they choose not to answer these questions or share information with us? Unfortunately, it may be a reason to pivot, especially if they are not exhibiting basic people skills. Of course, some may not feel comfortable sharing all of this information with just anyone. Still, if one is in a committed relationship or friendship, hiding information about themselves, then something is wrong.

Fear or Freedom

In *The Lady's Code*, when dealing with those in our circle, we cannot settle for surface-level conversations, leaving important matters unaddressed or whitewashed. In the Eye of God, with self-reflection and growth, we need active participation with a zone of safety, allowing a safe place to express our thoughts, feelings, and desires. If our zone of safety becomes a zone of interrogation to use against people, deception will become an apparent spearhead, causing them to shut down on us.

In certain cultures, like mine, we were brought up with a guiding principle ingrained in our upbringing to mind our own business. Growing up in a country setting, I was taught to respect the boundaries of others and to focus on my own life and responsibilities. In contrast, this countrified principle serves me well in various aspects of my life, especially when it has nothing to do with me personally. However, minding my own business in a committed relationship got me into a serious pickle. My adherence to this principle led me down a path of confusion, misunderstanding, carelessness, trauma, and heartache, exposing the limitations of such an approach in a committed relationship to my seeming detriment.

The bottom line is that I was never taught to ask questions as I was growing up, nor was I taught about positive and negative character traits or fruits. As a result, I was operating in a relational deficit, unsure of how to engage in meaningful dialogue. Without a formal awareness of these attributes, I inadvertently overlooked obvious red flags. Unfortunately, my naivety due to my upbringing caused me to accept what was presented to me without questioning, inquiring further, seeking clarity, aligning with the Word of God, or adding Him into the equation. At the time, I did not even know that James 1:5 said this: "*If any of you lacks wisdom, let him ask of God, who gives to all liberally and without reproach, and it will be given to him.*"

Nevertheless, the pickle of my relational deficit was actually a part of my Predestined Blueprint, learning how to strike a balance between respecting boundaries and actively participating in a relationship of TOGETHERNESS, *As It Pleases God*. For this reason, as a part of my personal growth, when something has to do with

Fear or Freedom

me and mine, I ask a lot of fact-finding and probing questions, both of myself and others, while also including God Almighty in the equation.

Whether our deficits pertain to *Relational Dating or Mating*, career choices, or Spiritual Matters, the clarity we seek can often be found through the art of asking the right fact-finding questions and aligning with the Word of God. Moreover, regardless of where we are in life, asking questions of ourselves first is a fundamental step in self-discovery, *As It Pleases God*. Self-querying allows us to dig deeper into our motives, heart postures, fears, mindset, traumas, habits, desires, beliefs, and aspirations, becoming more self-aware, authentic, and merciful to make better decisions. In addition, it also helps us to recognize patterns in our thoughts, words, and behaviors that may be unpleasing in the Eye of God. When operating in such a manner, it has the potential to enhance our relationship with others.

On the other hand, if we find ourselves questioning others more than we question ourselves, we will find ourselves judging more than we understand, tainting our Spiritual Fruits. When we shift our focus outwardly, scrutinizing the actions, thoughts, beliefs, desires, and choices of those around us to make ourselves feel better, we run the risk of clouding our clarity, understanding, and relational skills. Unbeknown to most, judgment often stems from a place of fear or insecurity, causing a lot of defensiveness, lies, manipulation, and projection with a constant cycle of negativity and building unnecessary walls.

Negative fixations of self-doubt, regret, and dissatisfaction from seeming inadequacies or unsuccessfulness will divert our energy from pursuing self-awareness, self-reflection, and self-development, *As It Pleases God*. For this reason, we must keep all things on the positive side of the spectrum, creating a win-win out of a seemingly lose-lose.

According to the Heavenly of Heavens, when engaging in *Relational Dating or Mating*, there should always be a three-way question-and-answer session going on.

☐ We need a self-querying session.

Fear or Freedom

- ☐ We need a relational querying session with others.
- ☐ We need a *Spirit to Spirit* querying session with God.

As life would have it, due to these sessions, *As It Pleased God*, I am now known as The WHY Doctor, unveiling the veiled for a time such as this. Querying sessions of positivity and reversing our negative thoughts, desires, beliefs, words, and behaviors while using the Fruits of the Spirit open our hearts and minds to new possibilities. By building on our strengths and nurturing our abilities, *As It Pleases Him* grants us insights from the Heavenly of Heavens with a Spiritual Awareness surpassing human reasoning.

Before moving on, these sessions are extremely important because fear is the primary culprit of unequally yoked, premature, shotgun, and undeveloped relationships. The fear of not finding Mr. or Mrs. Right causes the best of us to jump the gun on relationships that set us back, Mentally, Emotionally, Physically, or Spiritually.

In the Eye of God, the fear associated with *Relational Dating or Mating* has become an epidemic. In *The Lady's Code*, it is so amazing how fear will cause us to settle for inequality to fill the void of loneliness, insecurity, or depression, overriding our instincts, red flags, or common sense.

As *Women of Stature*, here is Pam's Writing on the Wall dealing with misinformation, conditioning, and judgment. I believe you will find it dynamically compelling as it explores how women with the best intentions often get ensnared in complex situations by not asking the right questions beforehand.

Story of Fears – Pam's Writing on the Wall

Pam was preoccupied with the idea of meeting a man at church, driven by her deep commitment to serving the Lord. Afraid of being alone, she began to picture the kind of partner who would be equally devoted and compatible. In her enthusiasm to find this

Fear or Freedom

person within the church community, she often overlooked the true meaning of being equally yoked.

Her definition of being equally yoked meant having faith in God and consistently attending church. Culturally, this is what she was taught, and she believed it beyond a shadow of a doubt. Her mind was made up with this man-made misconception, forming the very foundation of her identity and influencing her decisions, relationships, and paths. Pam was resolute in her decision to steer clear of any association with an unbeliever, no matter the circumstances. Yet, she was painstakingly unfamiliar with the Fruits of the Spirit, lacked essential people skills, struggled to exhibit Christlike behavior, and had no clarity about her true purpose in life.

More importantly, this woman's unwavering stance on hooking up with a church-goer sheds light on an often-overlooked aspect of relationships. The alignment of presumable and misunderstood core beliefs will sometimes get us into a pickle, putting a sour taste in our mouths with what we now call: CHURCH HURT.

Spiritually Speaking, by Pam choosing not to engage with someone who does not share her faith meant she prioritized her Spiritual Integrity and personal happiness over misinformation or half-truths. Clearly, we all have free will to believe what we like, but we must understand there is a difference between using our faith to please ourselves and outright PLEASING God.

Before we get into the nitty-gritty of Pam's story, please allow me to say this: Just because someone is not attending church does not mean we cannot communicate or fellowship with them using our basic people skills of common courtesy, kindness, and respect while setting Spiritual Boundaries, *As It Pleases God.*

In a world often preoccupied with superficial connections, Pam stood out as a woman on fire for God. Her heart was deeply committed to serving the Lord, and this unwavering faith gave her a watered-down version of purpose and strength. Each Sunday, as she sat in the pews of her church, the vibrant glow of her Spirit resonated with the teachings she held dear. Yet, beneath this passionate devotion lay a significant longing for a relational commitment.

Fear or Freedom

Pam yearned for a partner who shared her commitment to faith as she made her desires clear. Not only did she make them known to God, but also to any man who might cross her path, shunning those who were not actively in church. She approached her faith with enthusiasm and confidence, actively expressing her hopes through her prayers, actions, and conversations.

As the fear of not having a God-fearing man consumed her, she became a little desperate, overlooking the deeper aspects of compatibility. She was not a promiscuous woman or a flirt, yet as the pressure of being single mounted, she began to let her guard down secretly. She stated that as long as the man was in the church, she would work everything else out.

In her eagerness, she had moments of romanticism, imagining a partner who ticked all the boxes without truly discerning whether they were genuinely committed to living a faith-filled life, *As It Pleased God*, or exhibited the Fruits of the Spirit. As Believers, many argue that love can overcome differences, but if God is not in it, *As It Pleases Him*, the healthiest and wisest choice is to remain true to oneself and single.

It was a Sunday morning like any other; Pam had just finished church service, and her heart was full of hope, freedom, and serenity with a church high. As she walked to her car, a church-going man came running after her to meet her, introducing himself as Gary. He was definitely her speck, dressed in a sleek suit, slightly out of breath but with an excited sparkle in his eyes that melted her heart instantly. This woman was so flattered, she could not hide her blushing from smooth-talking, gregarious Gary.

In my opinion, Gary saw Pam coming from a mile away because he approached her with such flattery, making himself extremely hard to resist, as if he had done his homework on her. He came with too many things she liked without having to ask her one question upon meeting her.

Pam had always been a bit skeptical about meeting someone running after her in such a manner. After all, due to lowering her guard because it was the church parking lot, she did not perceive it as being harmful, choosing to ignore the usual caution that guided her decisions and red flags. In addition, she was so flattered

Fear or Freedom

that he selected her from all the other women that she momentarily lost her sense of good judgment.

In spite of everything, life was about taking risks, and this chance meeting felt like a breath of fresh air. As they exchanged numbers and promised to meet later in the week, Pam could not help but wonder if she was stepping into something real or fake. As she drove away from the church parking lot, her heart raced with nervous excitement, feeling as if God had finally answered her heartfelt prayers.

Pam was in Heaven, feeling like Gary was worth the wait without really knowing him. As they chatted more and more, Pam found herself becoming more flattered by the minute. Whether her head would catch up to her heart in time remained to be seen due to the way she behaved. But one thing was clear: Pam was ready for a new adventure, no matter where the journey would lead her.

Gary was a man of wooing words, and he had her nose so wide open that you could run a truck in it! His attentiveness and genuine interest in what she had to say made her feel special, as though she were the only woman in the world.

He promised her marriage, took her to look at wedding rings, brought flowers for her every day, took her fishing, went to the gym with her, etc. He was making serious plans for Pam. She stated that everything was going really fast, but she was happy with him and was willing to make the sacrifice and marry him.

After several months of the relationship, her holy roller church-going man convinced her to have sex with him, and then weeks later, she moved in to save money for their wedding. Everything started to go downhill from there. Her perfect relationship began to turn sour when she realized that all of the money that he was spending on her was money for his mortgage. He had not paid the mortgage in six months; therefore, she had to help him catch up on the payments for the house. Once this was taken care of, he quit his job because he was tired of working. Who does that? An able-bodied man quits his job...come on!

In the realm of relationships, Pam found herself in a challenging situation as she supported her partner's aspirations in the music industry, all while managing the weight of their financial responsibilities. His dream of becoming a successful singer had ignited a passion in him, and Pam, with her unwavering faith and hope, stood by his side even as she was left paying all the bills.

He painted a vivid picture of a future filled with success, happiness, and wealth, where they would live in a luxurious home free from financial worry. He even convinced her that his music career would flourish, and he would soon pay her back for the increasing expenses she had taken on. His ambition felt infectious, and Pam, always the optimist, allowed herself to dream alongside him.

As time passed, reality began to set in. Pam found herself shoulder-deep in bills, managing the household expenses while a full-grown man was in the house. Though she believed in his potential, doubts crept into her mind about him. Pam could not ignore the mounting pressure of supporting both of their dreams. Nor could she shake the feeling of something not being right about this whole ordeal.

This man was in the church every time they opened the door; he was in the mass choir, a deacon in the church, and an avid prayer warrior. He appeared to be a man after God's own heart in public, but behind closed doors, he was a force to be reckoned with. After Pam had dated him for several months, she noticed that something was deeply wrong. She could not place her finger on the problem, but something was not right; therefore, she made him go back to work.

Despite her skepticism, Pam remained supportive, hoping her belief in him would encourage him to work even harder. As the days turned into months, she began to look closer at his actions; she found out he would miss work quite often, his mood swings were out of control, and he appeared distant at times. Although he would get paid, her heart ached whenever she had to dip into her savings or take on extra work to keep their home afloat.

Through open conversations, Pam began to express her feelings. She shared her concerns about their finances, emphasizing the importance of working together toward a common goal and a sustainable future. The dialogue was not easy, but it was

Fear or Freedom

extremely necessary because he always had an excuse about his money.

Pam was a little naive because she was obsessed with getting married to a man in the church, so she overlooked a lot of things. It was not that Pam could not see the *Writing on the Wall*; it was that she did not want to see it!

As a matter of fact, she saw the *Writing on the Wall* the first day she met him, but she ignored it. She realized that just as he pursued her outside of the church, he would likely do the same with other women. With all that aside, she wanted her moment, she wanted to feel special, and she wanted a man. In light of this experience, the mix of excitement and insecurity consumed her because she was not able to distinguish between a genuine connection and one built on momentary infatuation. So, she made a conscious decision to block it out, hoping he would not chase other women and be faithful to her.

One day, she was confronted with the painful awakening of the truth about this man as she got off work early, and to her amazement, she caught him using drugs. He had drug paraphernalia all over the counter. In the quest for fulfillment to have a man of God, she never saw this coming.

When she discovered that her partner was an active drug addict, the experience left her feeling both shocked and scared. Pam had never encountered anyone using drugs before, so it completely threw her off balance. For this reason, she decided to move out of the house immediately.

Pam's unexpected encounter with substance abuse rocked her world. She said that it was like a whirlwind sweeping through her life, uprooting her sense of safety and trust. Nevertheless, at that moment, she realized she had to prioritize her own well-being, cut her losses, and get as far away from this man as possible.

Growing up in a nurturing environment emphasizing the importance of healthy choices and moral integrity, she never anticipated she would find herself facing a reality that shook her to her core. The aftermath of her decision was difficult, filled with uncertainties and a slew of negative emotions to navigate. Amid all this, Pam found solace in her faith with the support of her church.

Fear or Freedom

To complicate things further, this irresponsible man had the audacity to continue to pursue Pam. He scoured every possible place, searching high and low for her, only to find her exactly where she often was—at the church, lost in fervent prayer.

Pam felt utterly heartbroken because she overlooked the clear warnings around her. She struggled to find her way back to God's embrace, feeling lost for not heeding the *Writing on the Wall*. Despite the signs He sent her, indicating that he was not the right one, she mistook those messages for mere selfishness. Nevertheless, in the middle of her prayer, guess who interrupts her...that little holy-roller knucklehead comes into the church, interrupts her conversation with God, sweet-talks her, and begs her back.

Gary opened up to her about the stress he was under and admitted that it was his first time experimenting with drugs. He promised her that he would not do it again. At that moment, they laid their sins on the altar; they both prayed together and pleaded with God for forgiveness. Pam felt as if she begged God to forgive her; therefore, she felt as if she needed to forgive him. From my perspective, she was absolutely correct about forgiving him. Yet, she made one big mistake: She moved back into the house with him, shacking up again, out of the fear of losing him to another woman, the fear of being lonely, and the fear of going back into the dating scene.

All of her fears were overwhelming her...she feared going back, she feared going forward, she feared the embarrassment, and she feared the unknown. At that point, she feared that she had lost her faith in God, as her self-esteem dropped to an all-time low. She was trapped in the fears of her own making, and she could not tell anyone about what she was dealing with. She had to keep the hidden secret that her superficially equally yoked man was not equally yoked with her at all.

He was choking the life out of her with his wayward behaviors as he continued to sing in the choir like a saint. He prayed for people with the laying on of hands as if he were Holy Ghost-Filled and Fire-Baptized from the Heavens Above. And he still kept his position as a deacon in the church. This church was not an

Fear or Freedom

ordinary church—this was a well-known Mega-Church, yet behind his saintly exterior, a darker truth loomed.

Gary was exposing her to a life she thought God shielded her from; yet, she was in it, and she was truly lost and could not tell a soul. At that moment, she finally realized not everyone who walks through the church doors is as they seem. Pam found herself ensnared in reality, contradicting everything she had been taught to uphold. The love she once had for him was fading fast because she knew of his agonizing struggle, threatening to strip her of her very essence, while he continued to play church and play with God as if He could not see the hypocrisy.

Then, a month later, he was back doing drugs again, but this time, Pam knew the signs to look for. She could not believe how he worshiped God like a champ and did drugs like a pauper. She tried to get him into treatment, but he would not go because he had choir practice. She could not understand why choir practice was so important when he really needed help with his drug addiction. The answer came a week later when 2 of the choir members began to fight over him in church.

Pam could not believe he was cheating on her, using drugs, and playing with God. By this time, she knew she had to leave...but her fear had a grip on her that would not let her go. She knew better than to live her life in this manner. Despite what she thought, felt, and experienced, her struggles with loving him were real.

The *Writing on the Wall* was there; she knew what it was saying; still, she continued to ignore what it was telling her because she was secretly hoping he would somehow change. As I questioned her superficial reasons for staying, she finally stated she did not want to start over.

Pam's curiosity was piqued by the inner struggles he faced; it baffled her why God had not healed his pain. With a heart full of compassion, she pleaded with him to open up about his troubles, determined to truly help him. As he started to peel away his emotional layers, he revealed that his addiction to drugs stemmed from unresolved traumas and skeletons haunting him. To her shock and heartbreak, he confessed to a crime he had been acquitted of due to insufficient evidence. Unfortunately, this unveiling left her frazzled, betrayed, scared, and overwhelmed.

As the veil ripped from the top to the bottom, he revealed to Pam that he had taken the life of an innocent man who resisted him during a robbery. In addition, this man was justifying his actions by claiming it was the only way for him to start anew. To her dire chagrin, this was how he bought the house he was staying in. He stated the man's spirit came to haunt him every day, and this is why he cannot keep any money. He also stated he did not have any peace, and he was living with the blood of an innocent man on his hands.

Pam instantly got up and began to pack her bags. Why leave now? She decided to leave because she distinctly remembers being pushed from the top of the staircase a few months back. Although she did not get hurt, the fall had always puzzled her. Beyond a shadow of a doubt, she felt the thrust of the push and knew she was the only person upstairs. Yet, when he picked her up from the bottom of the stairs, she explained what happened; he never said anything to her about his little demons.

After he unveiled the truth about his character, she felt ultimately betrayed, used, and abused. This monster took her kindness as a weakness to appease his selfish behavior. More importantly, she was now able to put the pieces of the puzzle together.

All of his fun-loving threats of loving her so much he would snatch her up were real threats. All of his lackadaisical jokes about causing harm to the mother of his child were indeed real threats. All of the threats he made when he was angry were real threats. By the grace of God, this unveiling was a real eye-opener for Pam; there was no question about whether he would take her life at the drop of a dime. With his troubling history, she refused to let herself become another tragic statistic or victim.

Pam has made the difficult decision to close this chapter of her life. She informs him that she is leaving and urges him not to search for her ever again. As a woman of faith, she shares that she cannot continue to bear the weight of his past, present, or future struggles. He told her that if she left, she could never come back. Pam turned

Fear or Freedom

around, looking him straight in the eyes, and said that she could not live with a person who had no conscience or value for human life.

In addition, she stated that whatever she had to go through to overcome her fears of being alone, she would do it! She refuses to live in a hell-on-earth situation with someone who has ripped her heart out of her chest and stepped on it without giving it a second thought. Then, this holy-rolling jerk had the audacity to tell her that she would be replaced by the next day. Pam then puts her head down, saying a silent prayer—then picks up her keys, bags, and purse, leaving everything else behind. She never came back; she changed her number, address, church, etc., therefore cutting off all contact with him.

Pam's so-called equally yoked relationship went from bad to worse, and she was nothing like him. They were like night and day; she was so angry at herself because God gave her exactly what she asked for. What she feared the most had come upon her—that relationship turned out to be by far the worst relationship she had ever encountered. The whole ordeal dumbfounded her because she would not listen.

It was amazing that she feared committing to someone who was not in the church and still hooked up with a liar, cheater, drug addict, murderer, and thief who is haunted by his demons. This woman was absolutely devastated, as an unequally yoked relationship shattered her hopes. It was not because she did not know it was coming; it was due to the fact that she ignored the *Writing on the Wall*. Plus, when she had the opportunity to walk away, she did, but her fears brought her back to suffer a little more.

After owning her role in the relationship, she realized that she had broken her vow to God of celibacy with a man who crushed her heart to pieces after shacking up with him. Once she owned her first mistake, she was finally able to read the *Writing on the Wall*, understand it, learn from it, and then apply it. It was only then that she was able to walk away to seek real help and healing.

She recounts praying for a man in the church, but now she prays for a man who has the church in him and who exhibits Christlike Character. For this reason, she has become very specific about her wants, needs, and desires, and she is adamant about reading the *Writing on the Wall* with everyone. She believes in exhibiting love, joy, peace, patience, kindness, goodness, faithfulness, gentleness, and self-control. And, if one is not exhibiting those characteristics, she gracefully moves on.

Pam could not understand what would draw her to a man like this. She sought God about this ordeal—she knew if that man saw her weaknesses, then it was her reasonable service to do something about it. As God dealt with her, she realized she was crucifying people who were not going to church without getting to know the contents of their hearts. She was so focused on the outer image of a church-goer and not the character of a Child of God.

After many years of counseling, Pam is now happily married to the real man of her dreams. She had to learn about being equally yoked the hard way, but she is now on the right track, adhering to *The Lady's Code: As It Pleases God*. More importantly, her husband believes, in Ephesians 5:25 with all his heart, "*Husbands are commanded to love their wives as Christ loves the church.*"

She told me that they were an interdependent team, where one was weak, the other was strong, and vice versa, to create wholeness as it relates to their union. I was able to see the true TESTAMENT of their love without them having to say one word. Here are the subtle but effective signs of love I look for in an equally yoked relationship:

- ☐ Submissiveness.
- ☐ Attentiveness.
- ☐ Respectfulness.
- ☐ Gentleness.
- ☐ Helpfulness.
- ☐ Affection.
- ☐ Thoughtfulness.
- ☐ Protectiveness.
- ☐ Understanding.
- ☐ Forgiveness.
- ☐ Oneness.
- ☐ Communication.

Fear or Freedom

Now, the holy roller, he is still going from relationship to relationship and job to job, robbing Peter to pay Paul. His demons still haunt him, as he continues to be a modern-day gigolo who goes to church to pick up women to support his habits. He is one of the smoothest, sweet-talkers ever, priding himself on conning those who are weak enough to believe his lies while secretly following Pam's life via social media.

When we refuse to deal with or acknowledge our fears and insecurities, it creates an emotional block of anger, strife, and unforgiveness, causing chaos and confusion within our very own souls. When we switch out on ourselves, it opens a string of deficiencies that become pretty evident in our actions, thoughts, beliefs, words, reactions, attitudes, and how we live our lives.

Furthermore, it is not necessary to sell ourselves short when all we have to do is become rich in Spirit and in Truth, *As It Pleases God*. John 4:24 gives us the God Code: *"God is Spirit, and those who worship Him must worship in spirit and truth."* In so many words, when we become honest with ourselves about what we do, say, or think, we open the door to learning more about what we do not know without having to pretend as if we know everything. Once we become open to learning in spite of our insecurities, what we know will come across as wisdom through our humbleness and not our overbearingness or wretchedness.

Ultimately, we should never allow our church biases or conditioning to override the Fruits of the Spirit or prevent us from behaving Christlike, period. To avoid getting caught in a situation similar to Pam's, let us deal with our *Crushing Fears* to ensure we get a proper understanding, *As It Pleases God*.

Crushing Fear

In the Eye of God, we have the option to allow our fears to work for us or against us. For the sake of *The Lady's Code: As It Pleases God*, it behooves us to get an understanding of how to cause fear to

Fear or Freedom

become our Divine Power. Fear is an emotion that can often feel overwhelming, making us anxious, nervous, paralyzed mentally or emotionally, paranoid, insecure, and worrisome, amplifying our insecurities. Fear weighs heavily on our hearts and minds during moments of uncertainty, influencing our decisions and relationships, positively or negatively. All this is due to work pressures, family issues, relationship concerns, financial stress, health anxieties, and so on.

However, fear is also a survival or protective instinct as well, helping us avoid dangerous situations, circumstances, and events. For this reason, as *Women of Stature*, we must familiarize ourselves with a few of them, such as, but not limited to:

- ☐ Fear of Failure (Atychiphobia).
- ☐ Fear of Success (Success Anxiety).
- ☐ Fear of Rejection (Anthophobia).
- ☐ Fear of the Unknown (Xenophobia).
- ☐ Fear of Uncertainty (Uncertainty Avoidance).
- ☐ Fear of Abandonment (Fear of Being Alone).
- ☐ Fear of Change (Metathesiophobia).
- ☐ Fear of Losing Control (Atychiphobia).
- ☐ Fear of Public Speaking (Glossophobia).
- ☐ Fear of Social Situations (Social Anxiety Disorder).
- ☐ Fear of Commitment (Commitment Phobia).
- ☐ Fear of Intimacy (Intimacy Anxieties).

Why must we deal with our fears? According to our Divine Design, our bodies respond to fear by releasing hormones like adrenaline and cortisol, which can lead to feelings of anxiety, tension, and panic. Picturesquely, adrenaline floods our system, increasing our heart rate and blood pressure, while cortisol helps to maintain our energy levels in the short term. Too much of this can make us sick Mentally, Physically, and Emotionally, with issues such as anxiety disorders, chronic depression, mood swings, and anger issues.

In our moments of fear, turning to faith, *As It Pleases God*, and using the Fruits of the Spirit is a viable way to combat the harmful

Fear or Freedom

hormones released into our systems, gaining our strength and authority back. With this powerful, bold, and confident approach, we give our bodies time to redirect our hormonal conjectures to release good hormones instead, such as Serotonin, Dopamine, Endorphins, and Oxytocin.

Unbeknown to most, with the use of the Fruits of the Spirit, behaving Christlike, and remaining calm while adding in prayer and meditation, our bodies will naturally release a balance of our happy hormones, feel-good hormones, helper's high hormones, or love hormones.

Are these real hormones? Absolutely! When we embody the Fruits of the Spirit, confronting obstacles with a proactive mindset, *As It Pleases God*, we will begin to reflect a Christlike demeanor. This Divine Stance not only impacts our internal state, but it also influences our Spiritual State, affecting those around us with our mere presence.

When *Crushing Fear*, we must choose freedom over fear. Here is why: Some say fear is 'False Evidence Appearing Real,' which is true, but we must know what is real and what is not, right? Unfortunately, this is indeed where we usually fall short in the Eye of God. How so? We must know what we are working with, good, bad, or indifferent.

In *The Lady's Code*, we define fear as 'Fruits Eaten At Random.' What does this mean? We are somehow consuming our own fruits, and fear is our internal alarm connected to our conscience, letting us know to check our Spiritual Fruits (our actions, reactions, thoughts, beliefs, desires, words, or biases). Blasphemy, right? Wrong. 1 John 4:18 specifically tells us: *"There is no fear in love, but perfect love casts out fear, because fear involves torment. But he who fears has not been made perfect in love."* According to the Word of God, the first Fruit of the Spirit is LOVE, and it is NUMBER ONE for a reason.

Is 'Fruits Eaten At Random' a play on words? Absolutely not! As I stated earlier, there is no law against the Fruits of the Spirit or their usage. Whereas not using them or keeping them to ourselves disrupts the human psyche with divisiveness. Is this Biblical? Like

Fear or Freedom

clockwork, I would have it no other way. In 2 Timothy 1:7, here is what Apostle Paul shares with Timothy about the reason and rhyme of our internal calamities: *"For God has not given us a spirit of fear, but of power and of love and of a sound mind."*

In all simplicity, if we do not have power, if we do not have love, if we are not operating with a sound mind, if we are operating selfishly with zero regards for another, if we are making rash decisions with zero facts or information, and if we are behaving recklessly, the Spirit of Fear has some sort of shackle on us, even if we are in denial.

Conversely, a selfless, sound mind of clarity, wisdom, and self-control, *As It Pleases God*, helps us stay in control, think on or our feet, and make informed decisions to create a win-win out of a seemingly lose-lose, embracing the fullness of life. The bottom line is that God has already equipped us with the internal and external tools to keep us balanced, Mentally, Physically, Emotionally, and Spiritually. All we need to do is use them, *As It Pleases Him*.

Above all, the key is to remain calm, kind, forgiving, merciful, helpful, and loving. John 15:5 wants us to know: *"I am the vine, you are the branches. He who abides in Me, and I in him, bears much fruit; for without Me you can do nothing."* The moment we step out of bounds on the negative side, the release of cortisol can literally put us on the *Wall of Pretense*, faking the funk. Let us talk about pretending in the next chapter.

CHAPTER 8
WALL OF PRETENSE

Perfection, perfection, perfection, we cannot get away from longing for the American Dream of being a perfect person or having the perfect mate, family, job, or business! For this reason, it is common practice to PRETEND. Yes, PRETEND. We fake it until we make it when we are indeed dying inside with total disgust, creating a *Wall of Pretense*. Beneath the surface of our smiles and projected self-assuredness, many are grappling with profound discomfort, struggles, insecurities, traumas, and emotional turmoil, as detected by those mastering the Fruits of the Spirit, *As It Pleases God*.

In all reality, we live in a society that often equates success with confidence, money, power, and followers. However, in the Kingdom of God, it is equated with obedience, humility, forgiveness, using the Fruits of the Spirit, and the ability to master Spiritual Dualism. Above all that we are led to believe, according to the Heavenly of Heavens, our true strength lies in our ability to embrace who we are, with our flaws and all, knowing God did not make a mistake when He created us.

In speaking of Spiritual Dualism, the *Wall of Pretense* can serve as a shield to cope, and it can also become a prison of self-hindrance. For instance, the *Wall of Pretense* can protect us from judgment and

Wall of Pretense

vulnerabilities from the vultures or the wolves in sheep's clothing, allowing us to function day-to-day. At the same time, the *Wall of Pretense* can isolate us, placing us in a box, feeling anxious, overwhelmed, or depressed, as we suppress our authentic emotions and experiences by pretending or being fake.

From the Ancient of Days, since the dawn of human consciousness, and hidden under layers of something else, we often stumble upon darker corners of our psyche without realizing it until we turn on ourselves. Unfortunately, this hidden turning point leads us to confront an uncomfortable truth about ourselves.

What uncomfortable truth must we confront as Believers? The secret disgust we harbor for ourselves that we keep nicely and quietly tucked away. Know this: The interplay of self-criticism and self-loathing will rat us out, even if the *Wall of Pretense* is at its best positionable posture.

Regardless of what wall is erected and for whatever reason, I want to know what is going on between your two ears and what is coming out of your mouth. In mastering Spiritual Dualism, *As It Pleases God*, I want to know if it is positive or negative, good or bad, right or wrong, just or unjust, and so on.

In living our best lives, our internal dialogue determines our actions, reactions, thoughts, feelings, beliefs, and words. The truth of the matter is that most of us do not pay attention to any of this, nor do we care as long as we are getting what we want. Well, our time is up; it is time to get with the Divine Program of becoming accountable and aware of both sides of the coin, Mentally, Physically, Emotionally, and Spiritually.

According to *The Lady's Code: As It Pleases God*, when it comes down to stepping into the ring of life, we have two types of people:

1. Those who believe in themselves.
2. Those who DO NOT believe in themselves.

Unfortunately, when it comes to this factor, we either believe or disbelieve—there is no in-between on this one. The *Women of*

Wall of Pretense

Stature who believe in themselves can indeed circle hoops around those who do not. How so? As long as they are not pompous and remain humble while exhibiting integrity, developing their people skills, and exhibiting the Fruits of the Spirit, they can operate in or out of the Kingdom better than those who are arrogant, rude, disobedient, destructive, and lack integrity.

Is this not a little biased, especially when a *Woman of Stature* has it going on, needing nothing from anyone? The moment we step in or outside of the ring with a super-inflated ego, breaking *The Lady's Code* with selfishness, waywardness, or pride to pounce on the faint or doubtful at heart, it changes the rules of the game, whether we believe in ourselves or not. In the Eye of God, this is where we make costly Spiritual Mistakes, causing us to curse our own hands or curse our Bloodlines unawaringly.

We cannot afford to play clean-up when it comes down to our Bloodlines; therefore, we must take heed to what we are doing, as well as its repercussions, before the deed is done. Why must we take account of what we are doing before the deed is done? We do not want our children of tomorrow to pay for our irresponsible folly of today.

Before I go any further, let me say this: Adhering to *The Lady's Code: As It Pleases God* will do two things:

1. It will make us bitter.
2. It will make us better.

The *Wall of Pretense* says that it is the hidden desires from within to be seen as PERFECT by others that cause the most significant disappointments, disgusts, or blows to our egos when we truly know that we are not perfect. We are able to fool others, but we are not able to fool ourselves, nor can we fool God Almighty.

Why can we not fool ourselves, especially when we are taught to fake it before we make it? The psyche knows and keeps a record of everything, including our thoughts, desires, secrets, weaknesses,

Wall of Pretense

lusts, habits, and all of the sneaky stuff! Therefore, we cannot TRICK the inner man.

Woman of Deceit

In a culture, prizing perfection over uprightness has caused so much confusion among women that I sometimes hang my head down in shame, asking myself, 'How did we get here?' The surface appearances and the curation of identities to become more than we are to feed our egos, instead of doing so to remain humble, require self-examination from a Spiritual Perspective.

Unbeknown to most, the lies we tell ourselves will cause warring of the psyche, instigating an inner conflict of jealousy, envy, coveting, pride, and competitiveness among other women. In *The Lady's Code*, we are required to become transparent with ourselves to circumvent these negative attributes from consuming us, thwarting our people skills, and mangling our fruits.

What is the purpose of transparency with ourselves as Believers, especially when our people skills are top-notch and our fruits are thriving in multiplication form? In the Eye of God, transparency with ourselves is multifaceted, serving not only as Spiritual Growth to understand our true selves and to take accountability, *As It Pleases Him*. Authentic transparency also serves as a Spiritual Gauge of our level of openness and honesty with God, our Heavenly Father, and others to bring forth our Predestined Blueprint. Moreover, it is a game-changer for all, regardless of whether we are a *Woman of Stature* or a woman of deceit.

What is a woman of deceit? Or better yet, how do we determine a woman of such caliber? Without being biased or breaking *The Lady's Code*, I must interject scripture to avoid showing any partiality. "*In the twilight, in the evening, In the black and dark night. And there a woman met him, With the attire of a harlot, and a crafty heart. She was loud and rebellious, Her feet would not stay at home. At times she was outside, at times in the open square, Lurking at every corner. So she caught him and kissed him; With an impudent face she said to him: 'I have peace offerings with*

Wall of Pretense

me; Today I have paid my vows. So I came out to meet you, Diligently to seek your face, And I have found you. I have spread my bed with tapestry, Colored coverings of Egyptian linen. I have perfumed my bed With myrrh, aloes, and cinnamon. Come, let us take our fill of love until morning; Let us delight ourselves with love. For my husband is not at home; He has gone on a long journey; He has taken a bag of money with him, And will come home on the appointed day.' With her enticing speech she caused him to yield, With her flattering lips she seduced him. Immediately he went after her, as an ox goes to the slaughter, Or as a fool to the correction of the stocks, Till an arrow struck his liver. As a bird hastens to the snare, He did not know it would cost his life. Now therefore, listen to me, my children; Pay attention to the words of my mouth: Do not let your heart turn aside to her ways, Do not stray into her paths; For she has cast down many wounded, And all who were slain by her were strong men. Her house is the way to hell, Descending to the chambers of death." Proverbs 7:9-27.

In all simplicity, if we lie to ourselves, it is apparent that we lie to others to get what we want. Plus, we will also lie to God about our heart's posture or intentions to manipulate Him. Here again, in *The Lady's Code*, Proverbs 6:16-19 says that the Lord hates these things:

- ☐ Arrogance.
- ☐ Lying tongue.
- ☐ Hands that shed innocent blood.
- ☐ A heart that devises wicked schemes.
- ☐ Feet that are swift to do evil.
- ☐ Bearing false witness.
- ☐ A person who stirs up strife among brethren.

Just because we are *Women of Stature*, we do not get a free pass on this behavior in the Eye of God. As a matter of fact, we are held to a higher accountability than someone who has never had any home training or Spiritual Training. Why are we not equated the same? Because we know better and choose not to do better, our Spiritual Correction may be a little more rigid.

Wall of Pretense

Of course, it will never seem simple when you are going through it; however, the goal of *The Lady's Code* is to help you become PROACTIVE in the dating or mating phase to eliminate potential headaches or hiccups in the future.

There is no magic formula to finding the right person or ideal situation; however, there are specific messages that are *Written on the Wall*, letting you know the particular types of people who are not for you, as well as the types of people who are.

The *Writing on the Wall* is considered to be God's way of letting us know of things to come after the date is over, or once you are in a committed relationship with a specific type of person. Is this considered judging others? Maybe or maybe not, but I will tell you this: If you settle for the wrong individual, it may cost you more heartache than you may be able to handle. Therefore, it is not good to be unequally yoked. Until you understand this fact, you may go through relationship after relationship looking for something in someone, primarily when you cannot really pinpoint what you are looking for in the first place.

In the quest for meaningful or sustainable relationships, many of us repeatedly enter relationships that ultimately fall short of our hearts' desire due to unrealistic or unfounded expectations from the lies we feed ourselves. Here is a list of deceptively unrealistic examples, but not limited to such:

- ☐ You desire a kind person, but you are unkind.
- ☐ You desire a loving person, but you are unloving.
- ☐ You desire a grateful person, but you are ungrateful.
- ☐ You desire a sweet person, but you are bitter.
- ☐ You desire a respectful person, but you are disrespectful.
- ☐ You desire a peaceful person, but you are chaotic.
- ☐ You desire a positive person, but you are negative.

I can go on for days with this list, so please allow me to Spiritually Align, *As It Pleases God*: *"Therefore, whatever you want men to do to you, do also to them, for this is the Law and the Prophets."* Matthew 7:12.

Wall of Pretense

When we engage in relationships without understanding what is required of us, the Law of Reciprocity can indeed backfire, creating misalignments or hellish encounters of another kind.

Clueless Dating

Navigating the murky waters of relationships can be challenging at times, especially when we exclude God. Meaningful connections are built on compatibility, understanding, and mutual respect, *As It Pleases Him*. Ideally, good, sound relationships are not built on blindness, deafness, or muteness, although we can get lucky at times. But I personally would not depend on luck when it takes the same amount of energy to add God into the equational efforts. Amos 3:3 clearly asks us the question: *"Can two walk together, unless they are agreed?"*

Clueless dating or mating must stop! In my opinion, clueless dating is simply UNWISE. *"He who walks with wise men will be wise, but the companion of fools will be destroyed."* Proverbs 13:20. Frankly, it is totally unwise to think this scripture does not apply to us. From a human perspective, we think the destruction takes place externally, but unfortunately, it is more like internal destruction hidden from the naked eye, spreading outwardly. Simply put, before any external manifestations occur, the internal brewing has already happened, positively or negatively.

You are precious in the Eye of God, and you cannot open yourself up to any and everything. How can the difference be determined according to Kingdom Standards, *As It Pleases God*? It is determined by whether or not you are becoming selflessly sharper with Kingdom Interests or selfishly duller with worldly interests. For sharpness, Proverbs 27:17 says, *"As iron sharpens iron, so a man sharpens the countenance of his friend."* For dullness, Proverbs 1:32 says, *"For the turning away of the simple will slay them, and the complacency of fools will destroy them."*

Moreover, Matthew 13:15 explains the reason for dullness and what to do about it, *As It Pleases God*: *"For the hearts of this people have grown dull. Their ears are hard of hearing, and their eyes they have closed, lest* they should see with their eyes and hear with their ears, lest they should understand with their hearts and turn, so that I should heal them."

In addition, Matthew 18:20 also says, *"For where two or three are gathered together in My name, I am there in the midst of them."* As I come into agreement with you, *Spirit to Spirit* and *As It Pleases God*, I am going to share with you ways on how to read the *Writing on the Wall* to ensure you are not wasting your time or blocking the right person from availing themselves to you.

Now, if you are looking for Mr. or Ms. Perfect, I am sorry to burst your bubble. There is no such thing...no one is perfect! However, there is a Mr. or Ms. Perfect for you with the Spirit of Togetherness and Selflessness, making your baby leap from within. As a Word to the Wise, if your baby runs and hides around a person, BEWARE! Simply put, if your conscience warns you, take heed without justifying your feelings. Once you understand that everyone is a WORK-IN-PROGRESS, you are better able to understand what you are looking for or what you are not looking for in a relationship, be it personal, professional, or Spiritual.

In the Eye of God, I may not have all the answers to every relational question due to our differences. Still, I do have enough information in *The Lady's Code* that will revamp how you think about dating, mating, or relating, how you perceive yourself, how you attract relationships, the ways to develop your people skills, and how to find an exit, *As It Pleases God*.

When dealing with *Clueless Dating* or breaking *The Lady's Code*, we very well may spend years unlearning, relearning, or getting over some things. In the Eye of God, we must truly understand the point of origin if we want to really appreciate who and why we are as a person to become like-minded with those we are in relations with.

What is the purpose of being like-minded as Believers? According to the Heavenly of Heavens, it brings about JOY to our Heavenly Father and the human psyche, helping us to UNITE in outright humility. The Spiritual Alignment of like-mindedness is located in Philippians 2:2-4, saying: *"Fulfill my joy by being like-minded, having the same love, being of one accord, of one mind. Let nothing be done*

Wall of Pretense

through selfish ambition or conceit, but in lowliness of mind let each esteem others better than himself. Let each of you look out not only for his own interests, but also for the interests of others."

As a *Woman of Stature*, I have found that negative experiences and hurt produce baggage, and with every piece of baggage, the unresolved issues get stronger and more frequent, similar to giving birth. For this reason, we must find a way to refuse the baggage we do not want to keep. The best way that I have found is through prayer, Pre-Yoking, and avoiding certain types of people.

On this note, for all the *Women of Stature*, allow me to introduce Alice's *Writing on the Wall*. Her story changed my life forever, causing me to wake up to reality and become extremely mindful of my choices, including *Clueless Dating*, while taking nothing for granted. Although her story may be a little triggering, the Divine Wisdom encapsulated in her Testimony is needed for a time such as this, to maintain our Divine Stature in the Eye of God.

The Eye-Opener - Alice's Writing on the Wall

When I spoke with Alice about her *Writing on the Wall*, I could not believe how she developed a deaf ear to what she needed to avoid. My heart cried out to God when she revealed this story to me. Although this story may be triggering for some, *The Lady's Code* must go forth, *As It Pleases God* to bring healing and open eyes to those with eyesores, muteness, oozing hearts, stiff necks, and unjustifiable deaf ears, zapping the *Woman of Stature* status.

Alice was not accustomed to standing up for herself or for what was right. Yet, she was indeed a very nurturing and caring person who would give you the shirt off her back. Miss Goodie Two-shoes, as a child, made a promise to herself: she would never intentionally hurt anyone or make them feel bad. Over time, this commitment morphed into an unspoken rule that dictated her every interaction, which inadvertently made her weak and vulnerable.

Alice had always been the kind of person who put others first with a natural, deeply ingrained desire to care for others. With a

Wall of Pretense

nurturing Spirit and a heart of gold, she was often the one everyone would turn to for advice, comfort, and support.

Due to her lack of emotional toughness, she broke like glass as she overshadowed her own needs, leading her to remain silent in situations where she should have spoken up. Basically, Alice had a weak backbone that created a sense of desperation for her. She was desperate for love, desperate for a friend, desperate to be seen, desperate to be in control, desperate for attention, desperate to be at the top, desperate, desperate, desperate, and the list goes on.

From a young age, Alice internalized the notion that love equated to physical intimacy. In a world where romance is often sensationalized through movies and social media, she grew up believing that sex was a vital component of meaningful relationships. Unfortunately, this ideology was reinforced by the dynamics she observed in her own life, where love always seemed to come with strings attached, which often involved sexual expectations.

In my opinion, from analyzing her *Writing on the Wall*, she was never educated about the true nature of sex or the potential consequences of premarital relationships, leaving her in the dark about what it really meant, so she was unaware of the Spiritual Implications. In many cultures, discussions about sex and relationships are often shrouded in silence, leaving young individuals like Alice unprepared, unaware, and vulnerable to the complexities and responsibilities that come with them.

With her boyfriend, Oscar, Alice felt an overwhelming pressure to prove her love through her physical presence. Each encounter was tinged with a sense of obligation rather than a genuine connection. To Alice, the act of pleasing Oscar was her only means of demonstrating affection and commitment. This unyielding commitment to physical intimacy as a measurement of love created a toxic foundation for their relationship. While she sought validation through his approval, she unwittingly set herself up for emotional distress.

As Alice confused sex with love more and more, the stronghold became tighter and tighter as she began to love Oscar more than

Wall of Pretense

God himself. Even though she denied this outwardly, she inwardly knew she put God on the back burner for selfish reasons.

After being in a relationship with this man for years, Alice denied the fact that cheating had become his middle name. He would lie to her, and she would believe it. She even believed the lies he told her about getting another woman pregnant until this woman showed up at his place eight months pregnant.

Lo and behold, the pregnant woman knocks on the door; he would not answer it, nor would he allow Alice to answer the door. Every time she knocked, the knock became a little harder, and then it went away. A few minutes later, they heard breaking glass. The pregnant woman had thrown a brick through the window to get his attention. Oscar ran outside and tackled this woman like she was a man.

Alice frantically watched him beat up this pregnant woman, tussling and dragging her in the dirt. She stood there and watched, doing NOTHING. Can you imagine another woman standing by, saying or doing nothing while her boyfriend beat up a pregnant woman with his probable unborn child? Personally, I was dumbfounded, but she stated that she was scared. Then the lightbulb went off in my head...if she was scared, there was a reason for her fear. I did not press the issue, but I had an inclination that he was abusing her.

Let us continue with this *Writing on the Wall*. The neighbors called the cops to report the incident. Right before the police arrived, he came back into the house and made Alice leave, being that she was the only witness to this entire incident and knew all the details. In my opinion, this should have been the *Writing on the Wall* for Alice, but she was too naive to see this man for who he really was.

As a result of the incident, the pregnant woman who was carrying his baby was hospitalized that night. Sadly, her baby began to die inside of her. Alice had to carry a secret of the real reason why her baby, I mean, their baby died. As a matter of fact, she was afraid to say anything because she did not want to lose Oscar.

A few months later, Oscar found another place and moved Alice in with him. They enjoyed spending time with each other; it was

Wall of Pretense

the ultimate relationship Alice always wanted, until he began to push her around. She began to notice that when he became angry, he would become a little violent. It started with a push; she ignored it. Then came the slap; she ignored it. Then came the bloody nose; he apologized for it. Oscar should have become a used car salesman because he sweet-talked his way out of giving her a black eye and a big bloody lip while convincing her it was all her fault.

Alice felt as if this was her punishment for not saying anything about his beating up his pregnant ex-girlfriend. At this point, she had had enough; she packed her things and went to a battered women's shelter. Alice refused to talk to the counselors about her situation. Not only that, ungrateful Alice did not like the living arrangements anyway, so she went back home, hoping things would change, subjecting herself to a hostile environment.

Alice went back to a life of abuse for her version of comfort, attention, and love through her eyes. Unfortunately, this woman was blinded to her reality because she did not have a rule or playbook, nor did she have *The Lady's Code* to guide her. While it is easy for many of us to criticize her for this reckless and unwise behavior, I have to acknowledge that she winged it the best way she knew how.

Alice's journey began in a world where love was not synonymous with safety. She was raised in an atmosphere where emotional comfort was negatively misaligned with instability and turmoil, causing her perception of affection to take on a twisted form. To her, relief was laced with chaos, and attention often came at the cost of her well-being. Through her eyes, love was a double-edged sword, mirroring the toxicity of her past. From Alice's perspective, she wrestled with her definition of real love while struggling to reconcile its true meaning with the bruises scarring her mind, body, and soul.

From the outside looking in, we can pass judgment, but this woman was oblivious to dealing with a manipulative man like Oscar. Plus, her mother encouraged her to stay with him to keep the benefits from him flowing to her. What type of mother would subject her daughter to such an environment for money? Her

Wall of Pretense

mother did not see a problem with him knocking her upside the head to keep her obedient.

Frankly, at this moment, I realized Alice's phenomenon was rooted in a deep-seated belief that love is meant to be earned through suffering, a lesson learned in childhood that is often hard to unlearn without God Almighty. I dropped my pen with a few teardrops, bleeding ink across my tablet. Although it was not stated, if a mother is okay with a man beating up her child, it means that she is abusive as well. I did not press Alice for more information or the details about her mother because she wanted to protect her. However, I did see a pattern for her naivety and cluelessness. So, instead of giving her a side-eye, I became more compassionate and gained a better understanding of her *Writing on the Wall*, as we go deep into the patterned trenches of Alice's story.

Oscar assured Alice that he would change and pursue counseling. For a period, he made significant progress, but once he began to feel comfortable with himself, his anger flared up over minor issues. By this time, the love she had once had for him had begun to fade. In the depths of a turbulent relationship, Alice found herself wrestling with unbearable emotions of hate as she had lost all of her trust in him and his proclaimed betterment.

As Alice grappled with her reality, a profound fear gripped her—not only was she afraid for her physical safety, but the thought of leaving him paralyzed her. As a result, she began to pray a lot, read the Bible for comfort, and ask God to help her with her cluelessness and frailty. In her reality, each prayer was a real lifeline, a way to navigate the overwhelming fear, hate, anger, and uncertainty clouding her sense of good judgment. In addition, praying brought her a sense of peace, albeit temporary, offering her asylum from her chaotic life.

One Saturday morning, in a moment of peaceful desperation, Oscar began to argue and push Alice around because he noticed she was emotionally checking out. He was not accustomed to her not being all into him, showering him with love and adoration. Amid his temper tantrum, while refusing to respond to his negative antics, she decided just to walk away from him to prevent any type of unwanted abuse or confrontation. As soon as Alice

Wall of Pretense

began to walk out the door, he grabbed her, pulling her down to the floor and causing her to fall back on her ankle.

As she lay on the floor, grappling with her disbelief and hurt, she could not help but feel a deep sense of disdain. How could someone who claimed to care for her act in such a violent and harmful manner? Her heart, already heavy with the betrayal, added another layer of anguish as she attempted to rise.

She struggled to get up, her mind racing with confusion and disbelief. Each attempt to push herself off the ground was met with an unsettling realization: she could not put weight on her right leg. Every time she tried to put her weight on her leg, it felt gritty and unstable. As she fought against the pain radiating from her leg, she could not ignore the emotional repercussions of her circumstances. The manipulative betrayal cut deep, leaving scars that may take far longer to heal than her physical injuries.

As Oscar rushed Alice to the hospital, he briefed her on what to say and what not to say. In the aftermath of the traumatizing attack, the hospital refused to treat her because it appeared to be a sprained ankle. After all, she was walking, so they sent her to her primary care physician. Each time she tried to stand, she felt the weight of her reality bearing down on her, intensifying her sense of isolation, rejection, and despair. She told them her ankle was broken, but they did not believe her. But the lie she was forced to tell about falling, they believed.

Once Alice got to her PCP, she was in so much pain, but they still took their precious time to examine her because she did not appear to be in serious condition. Once they realized she had been limping around on a broken leg for almost 6 hours, they immediately took control of the situation, rushing her back to the hospital in an ambulance for emergency surgery.

Oscar had broken her leg in 2 places, and Alice still lied for him, telling the Doctors that she slipped and fell. Nonetheless, they repaired the damage by putting a plate and screws in her fibula and tibia and then placing a cast on her leg. Her doctor said that she would walk with a limp for the rest of her life, but Alice was not claiming that.

Wall of Pretense

After sitting around the house in physical and emotional pain all day long, she became more determined than ever to get out of her cast and out of his house. She had plenty of time on her hands, so she started to plan her escape from him. She put furniture on layaway and silently started looking for a place to live.

One day, Oscar came home from work early, catching her making arrangements to leave him. He started yelling at her, and she politely got up and got her purse while limping out to her car. With a cast on her leg, this joker ran behind her and dragged her back into the house like a rag doll. Alice's conscience was eating at her. All she could think about was when he dragged his pregnant ex through the dirt and how she kept her mouth shut. She began to cry to God like a little baby because she felt as if she was to blame for him killing his unborn child, and now she had to pay the price for her silence.

As her leg began to heal, so did her heart and mind. With grit and determination, she began to push through the layers of pain as God began to strengthen her to walk away from this man and never to return. In the wee hours of the morning, Alice was awakened out of a deep sleep, and a voice said to her, 'GO NOW.' She felt puzzled and a little delusional. The voice spoke again, saying, 'GO NOW.' She then recognized that it was the Voice of God, giving her the signal to run for her life.

Ultimately, this woman ran like there was no tomorrow! She got an apartment soon thereafter. Alice actually said this was the first time she ever felt safe. As she leaned into her faith for support, she enjoyed living on her own without having Oscar breathing down her neck, controlling, abusing, and taking his issues out on her.

A few months later, Oscar found her. He knocked on the door, and her biggest mistake was letting him in. This petty man falsely accused her of taking his movies. Alice, with her newfound independence, got so upset that she yelled at him for the first time in her life.

Unfortunately, this display of assertiveness took a shocking turn. Oscar, unprepared for the confrontation and threatened by the change in their relationship, reacted with aggression. In a

Wall of Pretense

moment of rage and perhaps a desperate bid to reassert his control, he struck Alice. The impact was more than physical; it shattered the fabric of their relationship. Alice literally saw stars, her world spinning not just from the blow, but from the realization that the person she thought she knew came back to violate her even further.

Can you believe that Oscar hits her over movies? Who does that? When she said this to me, I wondered if it was really about the movies. Was it that she got one up on him by leaving? Then again, was it because she gained the courage to stand up to him? Who knows, besides Oscar himself, right?

Nevertheless, when she regained consciousness, her face felt a little deformed. So she went to look in the mirror, and her face was twisted. This good-for-nothing man broke her jaw, knocking it out of the socket. Oscar knew he would be arrested and his career would go down the drain; therefore, he made a powerful threat to kill her if she told anyone.

Alice knew Oscar meant it and would make good on his threats because she saw how he arrested innocent people, she saw how he trumped up charges on drug dealers, how he used his badge to manipulate people, she knew his dirty, hidden secrets, and she held the key to his demise. Knowing all of this, Alice said that she loved her life a little more. So here again, she covered for him. She lied to the doctors, her parents, other people, and most of all, she lied to herself.

To Alice's great disappointment, her face required extensive reconstructive surgery. After they finished putting all kinds of screws and plates in her face, they wired her mouth shut, which gave her the perfect alibi to plead the 5th. The incident served as a harsh reminder of the complexities of relationships, particularly when one person begins to change and reclaim their voice.

As Alice navigated through this turbulent period, she learned a crucial lesson: Independence is not just about having the freedom to do and speak whatever, whenever, however, wherever, and whyever. It is also about recognizing one's value and the need to proactively SET BOUNDARIES regardless of who they are, their job title, or what they bring to the table.

Wall of Pretense

Alice's story is not unique; women have been dealing with control and abuse issues for centuries without gaining the courage to tell the truth. But it resonates with many who find themselves at a crossroads in their relationships, taking two steps forward and three steps back. Her experience underscores the importance of communication and the necessity of mutual respect from all parties involved.

Candidly speaking, independence can be liberating, but it also reveals truths that may be difficult to face. Here is what I mean: Despite whether Alice said anything or not to ruin Oscar's life, she had an underlying issue. Her anger was boiling over, and she had to find a way to get back at him. In emotional turmoil, Alice said her revenge was consuming her every thought, and she was dead set on making her mark without saying one word.

After many months of thinking and pondering, she had the perfect plan. She knew Oscar hated drug dealers, and she knew which one of the drug dealers he hated the most. As a result, she began to date Pablo, one of the biggest drug dealers in town.

Alice could not have had a better plan because this was indeed a low blow to Oscar's ego as he became the laughingstock of the force. Alice used this relationship as a way of getting revenge. Still, after her newness had worn out, Pablo began to use, abuse, mistreat, and cheat on her continuously, causing her plan to backfire.

In my opinion, this woman was on a real cycle of déjà vu. Sadly, Alice dealt with it because she did not want to start over with another failed relationship. Alice knew what he was doing to her was wrong, but she accepted it because she felt as if she was bought, stamped, and paid for! Once again, her mother supported and encouraged Pablo to correct her by any means necessary as long as he padded her pockets. As a result, Alice felt as if she had no one to turn to.

As time went on, Pablo openly engaged in multiple relationships and rejected Alice because he knew she was not going anywhere, because she loved her lifestyle. Unfortunately, this was a tough time for her mentally, physically, and emotionally because all she

Wall of Pretense

wanted was to be loved by someone, or just anyone. Alice felt as if she stepped out of the pot and into the frying pan.

After many physical attacks from this man, she was paralyzed with fear of hitting him back. He got so carried away with abusing Alice that one night, he slapped her out of her chair onto the floor and started kicking her like a dog. There, she lay on the kitchen floor in the fetal position, shocked, crying, and in pain.

Once again, she hears a voice speaking to her. The audible Voice of God said, 'Get up; if you do not stand up for yourself, people will kick you around for the rest of your life.'

Alice immediately stood up, girded up her loins like a roaring lion, wiped her tears away, and said to Pablo, 'Don't you ever put your hands on me ever again; if you do, one of us is going to jail, and one of us is going to hell.' Alice spoke those words with courage and authority, as if it was coming from God himself. It frightened Pablo so badly that he refused ever to put his hands on Alice again.

From that day forward, Alice put her trust in God and Him alone. Regardless of what her mother said or felt, Alice was deadset on breaking the manipulation once and for all. Nevertheless, by the Hand of God, she did move on from Pablo, granting her the ability to put abusive relationships behind her to ensure she was able to deal with the real issues of her past, *As It Pleased Him*.

Alice found out the hard way that unrestrained emotions and feelings can spark a desire to do something very unwise. Nor does she seek revenge on anyone; instead, she gives it to God and leaves it alone without breaking *The Lady's Code*, emphasizing dignity, grace, and the importance of maintaining one's integrity in the face of adversity to embrace Divine Healing, Guidance, and Reflection.

Moreover, Alice decided it was time to leave *Clueless Dating* behind her. Through her experiences, Alice learned that dating without clarity can lead to emotional turmoil and regret, not just for herself but for others involved as well. By stepping back from the dating scene, she took the time to understand her feelings, thoughts, desires, and what she truly wanted in a partner, rather than getting swept away by attraction, revenge, infatuation, fear of loss, or misconceptions of love.

Wall of Pretense

In life, some moments force us to confront the overwhelming slew of our emotions. For Alice, this reality came crashing down one fateful day when she discovered that unrestrained feelings could lead her down a path of recklessness. The experience was a harsh lesson, causing her to reevaluate how she handled her emotions, beliefs, desires, longings, and relationships.

For Alice, before she enters into any relationship, she always asks herself, What is it going to cost? If the cost is too high or the relationship is unequally yoked, she moves on with pride.

Alice's experience highlights the painful reality that love can sometimes become synonymous with performance rather than connection. Because she had never had the opportunity to experience unfiltered love, one that was not contingent upon physical intimacy, she found herself trapped in a vicious cycle of abuse.

More importantly, Alice's story serves as an urgent reminder of the importance of dismantling false beliefs to gain a true sense of self-worth, *As It Pleases God*. In addition, she is living proof that kindness and strength can coexist, making it possible to be nurturing while also advocating for oneself and others.

As God would have it, through her experiences, Alice transformed her vulnerability into EMPOWERMENT, advocating for her needs while still caring for those around her. In doing so, she not only found her voice but also paved the way for others to do likewise. Today, Alice stands tall, embodying a splendid blend of compassion and courage, inspiring those around her to explore the balance between kindness and self-advocacy.

Before ending this chapter on the *Wall of Pretense*, prior to embarking on a personal or professional journey, or even a Spiritual Journey with anyone, you must make sure you are ready. The last thing you need is someone taking advantage of your frailty, naivety, or lack of understanding.

The essential message is clear: If you are not fully prepared to date, connect, or build relationships, *As It Pleases God*, it is crucial to take the time to enhance your people skills or apply the 80/20 Rules you will learn in the next chapter before stepping into the

Wall of Pretense

unknown. This Spiritual Groundwork will safeguard you against deception and its potential pitfalls.

Lastly, in *The Lady's Code*, here is what you must know: "*A prudent man sees evil and hides himself, the naive proceed and pay the penalty.*" Proverbs 27:12. In the realm of personal relationships, awareness of potential pitfalls is vital when using our Spiritual Discernment faculties, *As It Pleases God*.

As *Women of Stature*, we must understand the importance of recognizing red flags in our interactions with others to prevent naivety, emotional distress, financial loss, or damaged relationships. For this reason, let us take a deep dive into the Relationship 80/20 Rule to ensure a path leading to safety, grace, wisdom, resilience, and success.

CHAPTER 9

RELATIONSHIP 80/20 RULE

When it comes to the real matters of the heart, unchecked or ungoverned emotions can cloud our sense of good judgment, especially if they are negative, unfruitful, or debasing. Whereas, in the Eye of God, every relationship has the potential to shape us positively or negatively; however, as *Women of Stature*, we must know the difference between our emotional woes hindering our progress and our emotional toes, taking us to our next. In this chapter, we are going to take a deep dive into the Relationship 80/20 Rule to ensure we understand why we do what we do, and why we are not doing what we should, *As It Pleases God*.

In our relationships, good, bad, or indifferent, we will find ourselves in situations where, despite our best intentions, we cannot help the ones we love. In the midst of loving on any level or with any devil, we can control who we AVOID!

In dealing with different types of relationships, there are a lot of people who will make it to the avoid list we had high hopes for. But, as we all know, when dealing with our Predestined Blueprinted Purpose, *As It Pleases God*, we cannot take everyone with us. For the record, our personal avoid list is not designed to devalue anyone—it is a means of choosing to protect ourselves

Relationship 80/20 Rule

from influences that do not align with our Spiritual Values or developmental well-being. Still, it is our responsibility to do our part in kindly weeding out the wolves in sheep's clothing without them knowing they have made it to the chopping block or cutting their ears off, like Peter in Matthew 26:51-54, with acts of violence.

Why should we not let people have it, especially if it is well deserved? First, if we are not exhibiting the Fruits of the Spirit, *As It Pleases God*, we are just as guilty as they are for behaving like them. Secondly, suppose we do not exhibit self-control, giving the matter to God. In this case, we must ask ourselves, 'What do we deserve?'

Here is what 1 Timothy 6:5 shares with us about letting people have it: *"Useless wranglings of men of corrupt minds and destitute of the truth, who suppose that godliness is a means of gain. From such withdraw yourself."* Thirdly, if we have not done our part to avoid them, then they are not fully at fault. Nonetheless, without offending anyone, please allow me to align this with scripture: *"Now I urge you, brethren, note those who cause divisions and offenses, contrary to the doctrine which you learned, and avoid them."* Romans 16:17.

In *The Lady's Code: As It Pleases God*, there are indeed those we need to keep at arm's length, but we can approach all things using the Fruits of the Spirit and behaving Christlike. Clearly, this is not a reflection of our love for them to woo them but rather a strategy for self-protection, emotional clarity, common sense wisdom, and healing to bring about peace, unity, and fulfillment, *As It Pleases God*. On the other hand, there are certain people we cannot just get rid of, such as family members, co-workers, ride-or-die individuals, etc., so we must learn how to deal with difficult people.

How do we deal with those we love and cannot avoid? We can choose to limit the time we spend with them or steer conversations away from sensitive, negative, or triggering topics. All in all, we must develop our communication skills to reverse engineer conversations from negative to positive at the drop of a dime without offending, complaining, nagging, or rehashing faults. How is this humanly possible? If we focus on creating a win-win

Relationship 80/20 Rule

in our interactions using the Fruits of the Spirit, the lose-lose of the interaction will begin to lose its power, naturally.

In any relationship, be it romantic, family, work-related, or totally platonic, effective communication is the foundational bedrock upon which understanding, agreement, teamwork, and connection are built. Although no one is perfect, and we all stand to be corrected ourselves, we must operate on *The Lady's Code* Relationship 80/20 Rule. As *Women of Stature*, a person must exhibit 80% or more of the positive characteristics and 20% or less of the negative characteristics that we can live with, in order to remain in our inner circle. All others must remain in the outer circle.

If we do not know what the acceptable positives and negatives are, it is time to get to know them. If necessary, make a checklist for both. What if we do not have time to do a checklist? Do you mean to tell me you do not have time to understand what you deem as positive or negative? Could this really be the problem why our divorce rate is at an 80% failure rate? Wait, wait, wait, I have another question: 'Do you really know the difference between positive and negative character traits?'

As my ear has been to the ground, what I have found is that most of us pretend to know positive and negative character traits in wordable format, but do not really know them in actionable form. In *The Lady's Code*, we make sure we know how the charactorial wordable format plays out in the actionable form, but putting them into actionable word pictures. This method gives the mind an example to use when the character trait presents itself in reality.

How do we make this actionable stuff make sense? For example, achieving a degree in a certain area is an important milestone, but action is required. It is imperative to recognize that while advanced degrees symbolize dedication, knowledge, and hard work, they can sometimes become just pieces of paper without practical experience to accompany them. In all simplicity, in the real world, we need actionable experience to become effectively and confidently usable in our field of expertise.

As *Women of Stature*, it is only wise to make a checklist to become familiar with positive character traits across the board that are essential for building strong character and healthy relationships,

Relationship 80/20 Rule

As It Pleases God. While simultaneously knowing the negative character traits designed to form cracks in our relational foundation from pleasing ourselves. As Proverbs 10:9 says, *"He who walks with integrity walks securely, but he who perverts his ways will become known."* For this reason, we must know what integrity is or is not, period! Now, if one cannot live with a character trait that falls into that 20% negative category, that is a zero-tolerance item; leave them alone.

In *The Lady's Code*, there may be a few unacceptable characteristics or zero-tolerance items, but we must know what they are. The zero-tolerance category will not be the same for everyone; once again, we must know what they are. One must decide what characteristics fall into this category because everyone is unique, with different backgrounds and traumas. Do not compromise if something is a sore spot, trigger, or vice, but under no circumstances does one need to mistreat anyone regarding a negative characteristic. Politely move on with grace, kindness, and integrity. *"Having your conduct honorable among the Gentiles, that when they speak against you as evildoers, they may, by your good works which they observe, glorify God in the day of visitation."* 1 Peter 2:12.

In our fast-paced world, if one desires a relationship based on 70/30, 60/40, 50/50, 40/60, and so on, rest assured, there will be a decline in the quality of this relationship, and it may not be a pretty picture. The lower we decline on the positive characteristics, the more we are settling or compromising, and the more issues we will have to wrestle with, especially when it comes to relatable communication. In all simplicity, if we cannot see eye to eye, we are destined to go toe to toe in due time.

When we find ourselves holding on to the memories and pleasures of past relationships, we will tend to have more problems that contribute to our dissatisfaction. It is hard to have a relationship with someone we cannot communicate with or who is constantly comparing us with others. Sooner or later, someone will start complaining.

Most of the time, complainers do whatever it takes to flatter others to get favors in return, with fewer boundaries, only to find

Relationship 80/20 Rule

out the complainer is never satisfied anyway. I have found that when there is a complaint, there is already a conceived thought of something better, positively or negatively! If there were no thoughts of something better, there would not be a complaint.

Complaints often arise from a sense of dissatisfaction or discontentment with something, someone, or our current situation, with a preconceived aspiration of something better than what we have, be it true, false, or indifferent. Realistically, complaints can be viewed as a form of feedback, a request for change, a reason for concern, or a call for attention to issues that matter to us. For this reason, positivity and clarity are important to ensure our complaints of for the betterment and not for the downfall while using our words carefully.

If we use our complaining as a grumbling or nagging session, rest assured, it will bring forth challenges, frustration, contention, and confusion among those involved. It is only wise to keep all of our negative bickering to ourselves or find positive words to express ourselves.

What if we do not have positive or good words to express the way we are feeling? With all due respect, it is time to expand our vocabulary. Plus, with the power of Google, I do not accept excuses on this matter. Actually, Proverbs 10:19 shares with us: *"In the multitude of words sin is not lacking, but he who restrains his lips is wise."*

Here is the deal before you let it all hang out: As a *Woman of Stature*, find yourself a quiet place alone, and then ask Google how to say what you want to say positively. Then, you can save it to your phone to keep a list of the conversion process. Doing so will help you to reverse engineer your negative complaints into positive statements. As Titus 3:2 tells us: *"To speak evil of no one, to be peaceable, gentle, showing all humility to all men."*

A woman who chooses her words carefully and strategically not only enhances her credibility and relatability but also embodies a sense of sophistication, poshness, and poise highly esteemed by the human psyche. How do I know? Proverbs 16:24 says, *"Pleasant words are like a honeycomb, sweet to the soul and health to the bones."* Regardless of our repertoire, positive words offer emotional

Relationship 80/20 Rule

sustenance to ourselves and others. When we speak kindly, we create an environment where individuals feel valued and appreciated, even if correction must occur. Believe it or not, effective communication to uplift and inspire ranks among the most critical skills for professional success in or out of the Kingdom of God.

In contrast, harsh, demeaning, or negative words cause harm, initiate trauma, and create unnecessary rifts within the human psyche, breaking connections, trust, and safety in our relations while increasing stress and anxiety. For this reason, Colossians 3:8 tells us: *"But now you yourselves are to put off all these: anger, wrath, malice, blasphemy, filthy language out of your mouth."*

When we allow ourselves to become too mentally entangled in someone or something without God, only to please ourselves with zero self-control, ignoring the *Relationship 80/20 Rule*, rest assured, emotional bondage will soon follow like a thief in the night. Most often, it will take more than we are willing to give, but know this: *"For 'He who would love life and see good days, let him refrain his tongue from evil, and his lips from speaking deceit.' For the day of the Lord will come as a thief in the night."* 1 Peter 3:10.

In *The Lady's Code*, our willingness to put away dead, evil, and deceitful things provides us with the power to cope and eliminate our sensitivities of being misunderstood. As long as we are willing to understand ourselves, *As It Pleases God*, every day provides us with an opportunity to live better than we did the day before.

As *Women of Stature*, if we allow ourselves to live in victory by being properly connected, *As It Pleases God*, while owning our truth, the *Relationship 80/20 Rule* will work for us and not against us. Moreover, it gives us the ability to properly manage our inner and outer circles and deal with our past appropriately, *As It Pleases Him*, opening the door to succeed at dating, mating, or relating on any level.

In addition, in *The Lady's Code*, once we are able to put our past into its appropriate perspective, it then gives us a better understanding of a few items, but not limited to such:

Relationship 80/20 Rule

- ☐ WHY should we date, mate, or relate.
- ☐ With WHOM we should or should not date, mate, or relate with.
- ☐ HOW we should date, mate, or relate.
- ☐ WHERE we should date, mate, or relate.
- ☐ WHEN should we date, mate, or relate.
- ☐ WHAT type of individual can we relate to, date, or mate in the friendship, relationship, partnership, or foe process!

By striving to live honorably, *As It Pleases God*, we will enable *Divine Wisdom* to be at our beck and call as we use our work-in-progress status to grow GREAT for the Kingdom of Heaven in the Spirit of Excellence.

Divine Wisdom

In the intricate tapestry of relationships, according to the Cycle of Life, we often encounter challenges and obstacles testing our bonds because 80% of our results come from 20% of our efforts. According to the Ancient of Days, the other 80% of our efforts are encapsulated in time and chance, according to our Predestined Blueprint, which has everything to do with Divine Alignment. Ecclesiastes 3:1 even tells us: *"To everything there is a season, a time for every purpose under heaven."* The bottom line is that if it is not our season, we must prepare for it…our time and chance will come; now the question is, 'Will we be ready?' According to *Divine Wisdom*, Proverbs 21:5 says, *"The plans of the diligent lead surely to plenty, but those of everyone who is hasty, surely to poverty."*

For me, I focus more on a person's plan rather than what they are doing. You see, most of us just do things without a plan, but *Divine Wisdom* teaches us to plan through documentation and pursue it with justifiable actions. When you prepare for your own season of growth and change, you will become more stable, Mentally, Physically, Emotionally, and Spiritually.

Relationship 80/20 Rule

Above all, if Jesus had to prepare for you, what makes you any different? Here is what I mean: *"In My Father's house are many mansions; if it were not so, I would have told you. I go to prepare a place for you. And if I go and prepare a place for you, I will come again and receive you to Myself; that where I am, there you may be also."* John 14:2-3.

What about using prayer instead of having a plan? You can pray until you are blue in the face, but with *Divine Wisdom*, if you do not plan, prepare, or document as instructed when seeking and knocking on Heaven's Door, you will become limited with your Kingdom Usability. Here is the Spiritual Seal according to Revelation 3:20: *"Behold, I stand at the door and knock. If anyone hears My voice and opens the door, I will come in to him and dine with him, and he with Me."*

Why the limitations, especially as Believers? Okay, this will be a lengthy answer, but stay with me here—I am about to shake up some things for your Heaven on Earth Experience. First, when it comes to Spiritual Matters of the Kingdom of God, your memory is not that good without documentation, regardless of whether you consider yourself a genius or not. As a matter of fact, in putting all abiding preconceived notions and sidebar jokes aside, real geniuses are known by what they DOCUMENT and NOT by what they remember. In addition, the person getting the LAST LAUGH is the one who documented their instructions, testimony, testament, plans, Q & A's, or blueprint, giving them the right to proclaim Psalm 126:2. *"Then our mouth was filled with laughter, and our tongue with singing. Then they said among the nations, 'The Lord has done great things for them.'"*

In squashing this memory matter once and for all in accordance with *Divine Wisdom*, if you do not remember the Heavenly Agreement for your reason for being here on earth in the first place, why would you chance remembering Divine Instructions? Wait, wait, wait, do not answer this yet; let us take it to scripture. Habakkuk 2:2-3 gives you a point of reference on what to do: *"Then the Lord answered me and said: 'Write the vision and make it plain on tablets, that he may run who reads it. For the vision is yet for an appointed time; but at the end it will speak, and it will not lie. Though it tarries, wait for it; because it*

Relationship 80/20 Rule

will surely come, it will not tarry.' " All in all, as one *Woman of Stature* to another, please write your plans, instructions, thoughts, or whatever down; you will thank me later!

Secondly, limitations determine if you can document and follow instructions while coming into AGREEMENT, having a single mind, focus, respect, and commitment to God, *As It Pleases Him*. Basically, it determines our level of agreement to selflessness over selfishness, love over hate, workability over corruptibility, positive over negative, righteousness over unrighteousness, self-control over the lack thereof, and so on. Moreover, in mastering Spiritual Dualism as such, Amos 3:3 has a question for you: *"Can two walk together, unless they are agreed?"*

Lastly, limitations determine whether you are divided or stable. James 1:8 admits, *"A double-minded man is unstable in all his ways."* Limitations in the Eye of God determine character...do you abide by the rules, or are you deadset on breaking them? There is no better way to find out what you are working with than by erecting a limit. For example, if you are seeking *Divine Wisdom* for your potential soul mate, the limitation is to keep your legs closed and your britches up. Can you withstand this limit? If you can, *Divine Wisdom* will work on your behalf. If you cannot, then you get what you get, nor should you open your mouth to complain!

The Power of Agreement is what *Divine Wisdom* looks for in those becoming POWERHOUSES in the Kingdom in the Spirit of Oneness. Matthew 18:19-20 reiterates: *"Again I say to you that if two of you agree on earth concerning anything that they ask, it will be done for them by My Father in heaven. For where two or three are gathered together in My name, I am there in the midst of them."* Truly, in the Eye of God, this is how Divine Power Teams are selected, built, nurtured, and sustained. Now, being that we are not perfect and we are all a work-in-progress, the *Relationship 80/20 Rule* is designed to help us on this Spiritual Journey toward GREATNESS.

In the *Relationship 80/20 Rule*, there is always a hidden positive message or nugget of wisdom in everything we go through. Still, it is our responsibility to find it by asking fact-finding questions to reverse the negatives. Here is the deal: If we focus on 20% of our

Relationship 80/20 Rule

negative experiences, conflicts, misunderstandings, or frustrations, they have enough power or 'get up and go' to overshadow 80% of our positive moments, achievements, successes, wins, or whatever. So, we should never give negativity the fuel to cloud our lives without a positive counteraction, *As It Pleases God*.

What are the fact-finding questions to ask? They are the *What, When, Where, How, Why,* and with *Whom* questions that are answered in the Spirit of Truth. By asking fact-finding questions, we engage in a deeper exploration of what is going on between our two ears and develop like-mindedness. Philippians 2:2 specifically says, "Fulfill my joy by being like-minded, having the same love, being of one accord, of one mind." Whether it is becoming like-minded with ourselves, others, or our Heavenly Father, queries are a necessity for *Divine Wisdom* to rest in our bosoms, *As It Pleases God*. Here are a few questions to begin with, but not limited to such:

- ☐ What is the problem or issue?
- ☐ How did it become a problem or issue?
- ☐ Who is involved?
- ☐ Why are they involved?
- ☐ When did this occur?
- ☐ Where did this occur?
- ☐ Why did this happen?
- ☐ What does the Word of God say about this?
- ☐ What can I learn from this situation?
- ☐ How can this challenge or strengthen our bonds?
- ☐ What are the underlying needs?
- ☐ What emotions are driving this conflict?
- ☐ How can I contribute positively to the resolution?
- ☐ What is the win-win?

As a rule of thumb, it is best to write our questions and answers down until we become an expert in our self Q & A in our *Spirit to Spirit* Relational Sessions.

Relationship 80/20 Rule

When we can ask God, ourselves, and others the right questions, we can extract the answers from within with confidence, without having to put ourselves or God in a box of limitations. By far, our Spiritual Queries give us the ability to diagnose our own lives, issues, and challenges from a Biblical Perspective. Meanwhile, building our Spiritual Credibility and overcoming barriers with our relations and people skills, *As It Pleases Him*.

For me, problems or issues are like treasure chests of *Divine Wisdom* in need of being positively extracted and converted. As a *Woman of Stature*, in my *Spirit to Spirit* Relational Sessions, I expect the wisdom to come forth *As It Pleases God*. As a result, I get *Divine Wisdom* instead of standard or average wisdom, which is what I am sharing now in this book, *The Lady's Code*.

Why do I get *Divine Wisdom* as such? Because I BELIEVE and AGREE, allowing my tongue to become the pen of a ready writer! What is more, I open my Spiritual Eyes to SEE and my Spiritual Ears to HEAR, thus saith the Lord, while opening my heart to share freely as I am doing right now in the Spirit of Love and Unity. Here is the scripture I stand on, "*My God shall supply all my needs according to His riches in glory by Christ Jesus.*" Philippians 4:19.

Does this really work for anyone? Absolutely. First, all we have to do is create a mind map and document while asking the right fact-finding questions to extract the positive information and nuggets of wisdom. Secondly, operate with the Fruits of the Spirit with a work-in-progress mentality. Thirdly, pray, repent, forgive, and fast on occasion. Fourthly, add the Holy Trinity into the equation with outright humility. Lastly, cover all of it with the Blood of Jesus while placing a Spiritual Demand for *Divine Wisdom* to come forth, while aligning whatever it is with the Word of God.

What makes *Wisdom Divine*? When WISDOM comes from the Heavenly of Heavens to the earthly realm that cannot be purchased, it is Divine. If it comes from a man with the accumulation of knowledge, understanding, and experience that can be purchased, it is not Divine. In all simplicity, whatever comes from the Heavens Above as a GIFT is Divine.

Relationship 80/20 Rule

Spiritually Speaking, when dealing with anything Divine...there is a price, and if one is not ready to account for the cost, stick with regular wisdom instead. Luke 14:28 says, *"For which of you, intending to build a tower, does not sit down first and count the cost, whether he has enough to finish it?"*

When dealing with God for real, for real, He does not play around with lukewarmness, pompousness, and disobedience. Here is what Revelation 3:15-16 wants us to know about becoming stagnant, complacent, self-satisfied, straddling the fence, and Spiritually Indifferent: *"I know your works, that you are neither cold nor hot. I could wish you were cold or hot. So then, because you are lukewarm, and neither cold nor hot, I will vomit you out of My mouth."*

According to *Divine Wisdom*, in manifesting God's Holy Presence, we are not Spiritually Fine if our fruits are rotten and mangled while pretending they are not or while justifying and rationalizing their condition. As *Women of Stature*, there is a call to action to work on using the Fruits of the Spirit without making excuses, pretending, or lying about our condition.

By golly, if we do not know what the Fruits of the Spirit are as described in Galatians 5:22-23, then we have work to do in evaluating our lives honestly and *As It Pleases God*. Now, the question is, "If you are not reflecting His Divine Presence, then what are you reflecting?" Divine Minds wants to know...or better yet, do you know?

The point of the matter is that if God cannot get the Fruits of the Spirit to willfully flow out of us where there is no law, He will not trust us with *Divine Wisdom* with many Spiritual Laws protecting and governing it. According to the Ancient of Days, *Divine Wisdom* is Spiritually Guarded by the Heavenly of Heavens with all types of Spiritual Laws, smiting us down at the drop of a dime for illegal access. For this reason, Jesus serves as Spiritual Atonement for us, but it does not grant us Keys to the Kingdom without being Spiritually Trained, Tested, Vetted, Nested, and Commissioned.

On the other hand, if we go to the dark side to gain illegal access, there is a price and a sacrifice that must be made, and the Blood of

Relationship 80/20 Rule

Jesus will NOT cover this matter. Though we may not suffer a physical death, the psyche will take a plummeting blow for illegal entry or taking Spiritual Shortcuts into the Realm of the Spirit.

What is the big deal about Divine Access, primarily when we have free will? We have free will indeed. In the same way, we have boundaries, the Realm of the Spirit exercises those same rights but on a DIVINE LEVEL. For example, if you owned a Fortune 500 Company, you would not allow a kindergartener to run it, would you? Absolutely not. Although this is a no-brainer for most, for some odd reason, we expect our Creator to give us Divine Access while we cannot manage our Spiritual Fruits, *As It Pleases Him.*

In all simplicity, if we have a problem handling our humanness, we cannot handle the Realm of the Spirit with folly flowing through our veins; it will yoke us to the core, having us for lunch. So, do not play around with the dark side, period! Besides, I do not need to tell you what is dark; you already know!

Still, let us put scripture on the matter of Spiritual Abuse or Misuse: "*Now God worked unusual miracles by the hands of Paul, so that even handkerchiefs or aprons were brought from his body to the sick, and the diseases left them and the evil spirits went out of them. Then some of the itinerant Jewish exorcists took it upon themselves to call the name of the Lord Jesus over those who had evil spirits, saying, 'We exorcise you by the Jesus whom Paul preaches.' Also there were seven sons of Sceva, a Jewish chief priest, who did so. And the evil spirit answered and said, 'Jesus I know, and Paul I know; but who are you?' Then the man in whom the evil spirit was leaped on them, overcame them, and prevailed against them, so that they fled out of that house naked and wounded.*" Acts 19:11-16.

Clearly, God does not expect us to be perfect, but our heart and mind postures must be on point and cued up, *As It Pleases Him*, especially when proclaiming to walk by the Spirit. Or, we must at least make our best attempts to do what is right without abusing or exploiting Him, ourselves, or others. If not, the Cycles and Vicissitudes of life will read us as a canker sore, especially when idolatry is involved.

On behalf of *Divine Wisdom*, here is what we need to know about idolatry, abuse, misuse, and lying on God: "*Your riches are corrupted,*

Relationship 80/20 Rule

and your garments are moth-eaten. Your gold and silver are corroded, and their corrosion will be a witness against you and will eat your flesh like fire. You have heaped up treasure in the last days. Indeed, the wages of the laborers who mowed your fields, which you kept back by fraud, cry out; and the cries of the reapers have reached the ears of the Lord of Sabaoth. You have lived on the earth in pleasure and luxury; you have fattened your hearts as in a day of slaughter. You have condemned, you have murdered the just; he does not resist you." James 5:2-6. For the record, I do not wish ill will upon anyone; I am just the Messenger because the time of REPENTANCE is readily upon us! Take heed.

When dealing with the Divine Realm of the Spirit, you cannot swing it high and low, doing whatever with whomever, and not become Spiritually Chastised. There is an extremely high accountability that you do not want to play around with.

Nevertheless, once we are faithful over the small nuggets, God will trust us with the Secrets of the Kingdom and the Bags of Gold if we have the correct heart and mind postures, *As It Pleases Him*. Here is the Spiritual Seal in *The Lady's Code*: *"His lord said to him, 'Well done, good and faithful servant; you were faithful over a few things, I will make you ruler over many things. Enter into the joy of your lord.'"* Matthew 25:21.

Once again, to turn our average things into Divine, *As It Pleases God*, we CANNOT become DISTRACTED from being about our Father's Business.

Distracted

In the realm of personal growth and commitment, the *Relationship 80/20 Rule* contains the Spiritual Aspects of development and evolution with our Heavenly Father, offering profound insight, wisdom, understanding, and knowledge from the natural to the Supernatural. To embody this commitment, we must cut the cord on any leash preventing us from engaging in God's Divine Will or our Spiritual Journey, *As It Pleases Him*. However, for this matter right here, although we have free will, self-will does not count

Relationship 80/20 Rule

when dealing with our Predestined Blueprint due to the Spiritual Timestamp.

What is a Spiritual Timestamp? The Spiritual Timestamp refers to the specific moments or seasons in our lives when we should seize opportunities to fulfill our Divine Purpose according to our Predestined Blueprint. Ecclesiastes 3:1 emphasizes, *"To everything, there is a season, a time for every purpose under heaven."*

In all simplicity, God's Divine Will overrides self-will, even if we make a free will choice to do our own thing or the wrong thing. To be clear, He will not violate our free will because He did not create us as robots. Instead, it places us in a rigorous cycle of repetition in a hell-on-earth experience as opposed to our Heaven on Earth Experience. Unfortunately, this is one of the reasons Believers loving God walk around feeling empty while pretending to be full.

Personally, I am tired of the lies and the whitewashing of what is really happening. As *Women of Stature*, the bottom line is that if you need to sever ties, cutting the cord with certain people, do it. If you need to curtail specific behaviors or habits, do it. If you need to cast down negative thoughts or beliefs, do it. If you need to sever a soul tie, do it. If you need to keep your legs closed, do it. Whatever needs to be cut, cut it, period.

Why is cutting negative cords so important for Believers? Unfortunately, they can choke the life out of your purpose before it becomes Divine, *As It Pleases God*. The goal of the enemy is to prevent you from getting to the Divine Stage of Spirituality, where you are Divinely Covered and Protected by being in Purpose on purpose.

How do we make being in Purpose on purpose make sense? Please allow me to explain the difference: In *The Lady's Code*, we have a self-willed purpose, doing our own thing with no Spiritual Blueprint, only what we create on our own. And then, we have a Divine Purpose (The Will of God) with a Heavenly-Orchestrated Pre-Written Blueprint with instructions engraved on the tablet of our hearts, which is called our Predestined Blueprint. Frankly, this is one of the reasons God is extremely concerned about our heart postures. What does this mean in layman's terms?

Relationship 80/20 Rule

Negativity, rotten fruits, and debauchery can cover our hearts with a cloud, stone, grease, or mud of our own choosing.

We all have a Predestined Blueprint (Reason for Being). Unfortunately, it is just that we do not remember because we are Spiritually Veiled. Until God Almighty removes the Spiritual Veil, *As It Pleases Him*, it must remain until we become Spiritually Aligned, according to Kingdom Standards.

As *Women of Stature*, once we are Spiritually Unveiled, *As It Pleases God*, it is a whole new ball game. Plus, there is no reason to showboat at this point, because when the Lion of Judah comes forth, making our silence our POWER, we become the Spiritual Go-To.

Conversely, if the Spirit of Showboating occurs, it means we are still Spiritually Veiled with a *Distracting Spirit*. If this happens, it is time to step into our Prayer Closet, *Spirit to Spirit*, to purge this negative or distracting energy to maintain our Spiritual Covering or to remain in Purpose on purpose.

Our Predestined Blueprint is Divinely Protected, and if we get to this point, the Heavenly of Heaven steps in to GUARD our reason for being. Whereas, if we are out of purpose, doing our own thing, we will have normal, adequate protection, not Supernatural. Either way, we must still do our part in getting rid of anything negative or debauched.

My goal is to get you to the Supernatural State with Divine Power, putting your enemies to boot. But to truly get to this point, we must serve and honor God, *As It Pleases Him*. In addition, we must also prioritize our *Spirit to Spirit* Relations and Spiritual Growth to develop Spiritual Mastery. Once we become ONE with the Holy Trinity, here are a few things to master to weed out *Distractions* to open the Spiritual Floodgates of Transformative Power, but not limited to such:

- ☐ We must master Prayer, Fasting, and Meditation.
- ☐ We must master Spiritual Dualism.
- ☐ We must master the Fruits of the Spirit.
- ☐ We must master Repentance and Forgiveness.

Relationship 80/20 Rule

- ☐ We must master Behaving Christlike.
- ☐ We must master Overcoming Obstacles.
- ☐ We must master Selflessness and Humility.
- ☐ We must master Extracting Wisdom.
- ☐ We must master the Law of Reciprocity.
- ☐ We must master the Art of Sharing.
- ☐ We must master the Spiritual Tilling Process.
- ☐ We must master Boundaries and Limits.
- ☐ We must master the Power of Unity.
- ☐ We must master the Power of Agreement.
- ☐ We must master converting all things into a Win-Win.

When we become preoccupied with worldliness, we will find ourselves in a state of compromise while appearing right in our own eyes. 1 Corinthians 7:35 tells us why: "*And this I say for your own profit, not that I may put a leash on you, but for what is proper, and that you may serve the Lord without distraction.*"

Serving our Heavenly Father, *Spirit to Spirit*, with an undistracted connection, is the goal. If someone or something is preventing us from doing so, it could be an idolatrous distraction. Whether in singleness, marriage, or anything in between, we have an obligation to spend quality time with God for Spiritual Development, *As It Pleases Him.*

The *Writing on the Wall* says that we need to pay attention to the people around us. We must also determine if they have a *Build Up* or a *Tear Down Mentality* to govern how we should deal with them, how much we need to distance ourselves, or how close we should get to that individual. Remember, everyone has a role to play in our lives, but we never want to play ourselves short or become silenced as if we do not have a voice of reasoning. According to the Heavenly of Heavens, we must always learn, grow, and share regardless of our environments, situations, circumstances, or events while understanding what the *Writing on the Wall* is saying and what type of caution needs to be exhibited.

Relationship 80/20 Rule

What is considered a *Tear Down Mentality*? It is a secretly insecure person who allows their mind to run wild with negativity, lies, and self-created debauched scenarios, similar to a dream killer. Are they not the same? No, a dream killer slays or distorts the vision of an individual due to perceptions, biases, conditioning, traumas, and so on. In contrast, the tear-down mentality is a mindset that underhandedly attacks the mind of another with negativity, brainwashing, manipulation, deflecting, chaos, and spreading rumors.

Here is the deal: A person can possess one of the two (dream killer or tear-down mentality), or they can be consumed by both (dream killer and tear-down mentality), which becomes a Deceptive Spirit (A Lying Spirit) or a Jezebel Spirit (A Controlling Spirit). In the Eye of God, they are all fueled and undergirded by the negative attributes of jealousy, envy, pride, greed, coveting, pompousness, revenge, or competitiveness with a trail of rotten fruits. Most often, we do not realize we are operating in such a manner until we use the Fruits of the Spirit as a measuring gauge or mirror.

For instance, when it comes down to building quality relationships, a secretly insecure person will try to do everything possible to make a secure person appear as if they are weak, as if they are a failure, or as if they are unsuccessful. These are the deflective people who will throw rocks, hide their hands, and distract us while trying to help us find the culprit.

On the opposite side of the coin, according to *The Lady's Code*, a secure person or a *Woman of Stature* would open their hands, doing everything possible to make sure the people around them become better, stronger, and wiser than they were the day before. They will also create a win-win situation out of everything, regardless of the haters, the wolves in sheep's clothing, or their secret competition.

While in the Spirit of Excellence, *As It Pleases God*, we must always pay attention to our actions, thoughts, beliefs, desires, and words because they give us subtle clues about our negative slippages. According to the Heavenly of Heavens, they also provide us with an opportunity to self-correct using the Fruits of

Relationship 80/20 Rule

the Spirit. In my opinion, it is like On-The-Fruit-Training, helping us to avoid secret distractions.

Distractions and stolen thoughts from a hellion are subtle ways that the enemy gets us off track from doing what we need to do. We must understand whether or not our stress is really stress or whether our stress is a distraction from a hellion on wheels. It is for this reason that the *Writing on the Wall* advises us to avoid a Hellion at all costs. Should we not stand our ground? In the Eye of God, we must choose our battles wisely.

Suppose you are in a relationship with someone who looks for trouble or fights all the time. It is best to RUN. "*A violent man entices his neighbor, And leads him in a way that is not good.*" Proverbs 16:29. It is not that you are running out of fear; you are running to protect your sanity. If you do not, you will become like them in due time. According to the Ancient of Days, this is like quicksand; it will suck you under when you least expect it.

In our daily lives, we will encounter a multitude of personalities with varying people skills, each bringing their own set of thoughts, beliefs, desires, behaviors, and attitudes to our interactions. So, it is not uncommon to find ourselves in situations where we witness trifling or wayward behaviors or conversations. Whether in personal relationships, at work, in social settings, or even if you pretend to be down with the okey doke, you know precisely when someone is exhibiting trifling behavior. If it is ignored or unaddressed, you will be drawn in by default under the guilt-by-association clause. "*Do not be deceived: "Evil company corrupts good habits.*" 1 Corinthians 15:33.

What do you do when peace is boring to a hell-raiser and hell-raising is repulsive to a person of peace? The answer is BACK AWAY. Then focus on living by example while setting realistic boundaries based on 1 Corinthians 5:11: "*But now I have written to you not to keep company with anyone named a brother, who is sexually immoral, or covetous, or an idolater, or a reviler, or a drunkard, or an extortioner—not even to eat with such a person.*"

Why should we not eat with them, especially if they are good people? We have free will to choose the company we keep. Just

Relationship 80/20 Rule

keep in mind that we cannot change what people are accustomed to, nor do we want to compromise our integrity or allow false expectations to be levied against us. In short, they do not give something for nothing. Proverbs 23:6-8 advises, "*Do not eat the bread of a miser, Nor desire his delicacies; For as he thinks in his heart, so is he. 'Eat and drink!' he says to you, But his heart is not with you. The morsel you have eaten, you will vomit up, And waste your pleasant words.*"

Nevertheless, in *The Lady's Code*, we are known by our FRUITS. As *Women of Stature*, we want our good fruits to remain, *As It Pleases God*, without being *Distracted* by ill-gotten gain, bogus innuendos, or false expectations. "*Better is the poor who walks in his integrity Than one perverse in his ways, though he be rich.*" Proverbs 28:6.

If one is willing to sell their souls at the drop of a dime, then *The Lady's Code* is not for them. Why are they excluded, especially when they have free will and are Believers? I exclude no one; everyone has equal rights to glean from this book. Still, I am required to speak the truth in love.

No matter how much we try to conceal our true nature by putting on a mask or assuming a title, it carries no weight in front of God Almighty. Our actions, words, thoughts, beliefs, desires, and intentions are what truly matter in the Eye of God. Therefore, it is crucial always to be true to our values and beliefs and not just pretend to be someone else for the sake of gaining approval or recognition.

Ultimately, it is our authenticity that defines us and sets us apart from the rest. A real *Woman of Stature* is grafted into Christlike Character traits, *As It Pleases God* and not the highest bidder. Please allow me to Spiritually Align: "*No servant can serve two masters; for either he will hate the one and love the other, or else he will be loyal to the one and despise the other. You cannot serve God and mammon.*" Luke 16:13.

If you are serious about building quality relationships, *As It Pleases God*, take a moment to evaluate what you are going to allow in your circle or who needs to leave. Doing so will enable you to make the right moves at the right time to protect yourself, your job, family, friends, and most of all, your sanity. In *The Lady's Code*, by

Relationship 80/20 Rule

maintaining a positive mental attitude, you open yourself up to discovering incredible opportunities that can greatly enhance your life. Additionally, a positive outlook can help you overcome hidden insecurities lurking in precarious places within your relationships.

In our increasingly fast-paced, microwave, and interconnected world, distractions lurk at every corner, making no one exempt from them, even if we pretend we are. Furthermore, the key lies in discerning which influences are beneficial and which are detrimental. As a fundamental part of the human experience of Spiritual Dualism, you must know what to do when they arise, why you are doing so, and learn from everything and everyone. Among these experiences, you cannot lose hope; so, before moving on, here are a few things to do when *Distracted*, but not limited to such:

- ☐ Identify the challenge.
- ☐ Invite the Holy Spirit into the matter.
- ☐ Cover the matter with the Blood of Jesus.
- ☐ Determine if it is positive or negative.
- ☐ Weigh your options.
- ☐ Find the applicable scriptures associated.
- ☐ Apply the applicable Fruits of the Spirit.
- ☐ Address the situation if necessary.
- ☐ Use the resources at your disposal.
- ☐ Determine the action plan and the end goal.
- ☐ Document the lesson, wisdom, or growth spurt.
- ☐ Document strategies (what worked or did not work).
- ☐ Keep it moving in the Spirit of Excellence.

Is it really this easy? Sometimes yes, and more often no, but positive CONSISTENCY is what makes us GREAT in the Eye of God. Remember, regardless of the *Distraction*, every experience is a stepping stone, leading you to your Divine Cornerstone.

In painting a picturesque view of a familial *Distraction*, with Daisy's *Writing on the Wall*, I could not hold back the tears. Once again, this story may be triggering, but for *The Lady's Code: As It*

Relationship 80/20 Rule

Pleases God, it must be shared on the Wall for the sake of many in transition for a time such as this.

The Real Daisyrella - Daisy's Writing on the Wall

In the heart of rural America, the image of a 'good ole country girl' often raises visions of wide-open fields, animal farms, warm familial bonds, aromatic, greasy meals, and simple joys of freedom. However, the story of Daisy challenges this tranquil perception to the hilt, bringing her life from the background to the forefront in *The Lady's Code*. Although she never knew her story would make it to the printed pages, God had a different plan.

In sharing her journey with me, she said the scars of our experiences may shape us temporarily, but they do not have to define us if we choose to rise above, transform, and share the testimony to enhance the lives of others for the Greater Good. Now, here we are, getting ready to dig into *Daisy's Writing on the Wall*, removing the Spiritual Veil, *As It Pleases God*.

Daisy was brought up in a household conditioned to embrace acceptance over inquiry, whether good, bad, or indifferent. From a young age, she learned life was meant to be endured rather than questioned, while being told to suck it up. Her parents, perhaps unknowingly, cultivated an environment where her curiosity was stifled, and distractions were to be ignored. As a result, this mindset left Daisy navigating her childhood without the necessary communicative tools and people skills to understand her surroundings.

Unbeknownst to her, Daisy's upbringing took place in a profoundly negative and hostile environment, filled with individuals whose behaviors ranged from selfishness to outright aggression, control, and rudeness. In examining Daisy's narrative, this is my personal analysis from a psychological perspective. However, we must explore the transformative power of her story and how we can extract and convert its essence into actionable insights for our own healing, *As It Pleases God*.

Relationship 80/20 Rule

As a child, Daisy grew up in an extremely toxic environment with hateful people, and did not know it. She grew up in a hostile environment and did not know it. She grew up in a selfish environment and did not know it. She grew up with bullies and did not know it. She grew up in an abusive environment, which she knew. Sadly, with this knowledge, Daisy bears the scars, both visible and invisible, serving as reminders of her troubled childhood experiences.

Growing up, Daisy never once heard her mother or father say, 'I love you' to her. Can you imagine never being hugged by your parents? Can you imagine never being kissed by your parents? Can you imagine never receiving affection from your parents? These are some of the things Daisy could only dream of having. Daisy was tortured by the longing for affection from her parents as she watched her other siblings receive what she could only long for.

One day, Daisy reached her breaking point; she had had enough. She was hanging on by a thread and knew it. As Daisy confided in me a little more with tears in her eyes, she whispered to me, saying she was beyond tired of being told she would never amount to anything. I am asking myself, 'How can a child get to this point at such a young age?' 'Should kids not be out playing and having fun?' 'What the heck is going on here?'

This child was tired of her two-faced kinfolk; she was tired of the backbiting, and most of all, she was tired of being beaten for things she did not do. As misunderstandings and false accusations became her reality, she admitted she was not the most perfect child, but she was definitely not as bad as her ruthless siblings. Actually, she was the best child of them all, having to take care of them, cooking, cleaning, doing laundry, and everything as if she were an adult maid. In my mind, I am thinking, 'Is Daisy a real Cinderella Story?' Or, better yet, 'Does she deserve her own Daisyrella Story?'

The injustice in Daisy's life stifled her Spirit, making her feel trapped in a life determined to crush her dreams, especially after being put out of the house and having to sit outside in the cold with nowhere to go. It seemed as if she were the only child being put out of the house constantly for ridiculous reasons.

Relationship 80/20 Rule

I asked her, 'Did you do something to warrant being put out of the house?' She said if burning a pot of rice warranted being put out of the house, then she was guilty. If refusing to wear old-fashioned clothes to school warranted being put out of the house, then she was guilty. If defending herself from being beaten up by her siblings warranted being put out of the house, then she was guilty. If telling the truth when asked and refusing to lie for her mother warranted being put out of the house, then she was guilty.

Sadly, this young girl slipped into a state of depression as she was beaten to a pulp after refusing to intermingle with her hateful siblings. She felt as if she had nothing else to live for and was tired of being distracted by hatefulness, so she decided to end her life. Daisy gave up on herself! She took a whole bottle of her mother's pain medication to make her pain go away.

God's hand was indeed on this child. He did not allow her to take her own life, but He made her so sick she would think twice about doing this again. Daisy vomited to the point where she felt as if she was going to vomit her guts out. As a child, she did not know how to pray, but at that point, she found the words to ask God to take the pain of vomiting away while vowing never to attempt suicide ever again.

The sad thing about this situation is that nobody knew she took the pills. They did not know because they did not care. How can a child take a whole bottle of prescription pain pills, and nobody knows anything about it? How did she get her hands on them? Did her mother not realize the pills were missing? Whatever information Daisy was hiding from me or whomever she was protecting, somebody knew something! This child is riddled with pain, vomiting, and suffering, and no one does anything or takes her to the doctor. I was appalled; in my opinion, this is child neglect!

Okay, let me finish the story: When Daisy makes a promise, she is adamant about keeping it. After she vowed to God, she took beatings like a champ; her parents thought something was wrong with her. Daisy learned how to find peace within her very own soul.

Relationship 80/20 Rule

The most amazing thing about Daisy, she learned how to create the life she wanted MENTALLY. While her body was in a negative situation, she focused on mastering the power of her mind as a child. Not an adult, a child! She also learned how to take herself out of a situation mentally and emotionally while around hateful people to protect herself physically. With her dedication to herself, she refused to allow anyone to break her willpower to succeed at living her life or allow anyone to get into her head with negativity.

Above all, Daisy stands out as a powerful testament to the strength of the human Spirit. With a heart full of compassion and a mindset on healing, she absolutely refused to allow her mother's unresolved traumas and recklessness to become her burden. In doing so, she exemplifies the importance of personal boundaries and the desire to create a healthier future by choice.

As a young child, amazingly, Daisy learned how to change the channel of negativity to focus strategically on the positive. She also knew that when she became an adult, she could choose her attitude, values, beliefs, actions, and reactions regardless of her genetic makeup or upbringing. The way she was made to feel as a child, she does not wish on her worst enemy; therefore, she proactively safeguards herself from the atrocities of hateful people. The choice to break away from the negative cycle of trauma is not an easy one. Still, it is an act of self-love leading to generational change and breaking hidden or unspoken generational curses.

Ultimately, Daisy's journey is a powerful declaration that healing is a personal choice and that we all have the power to define our paths, free from the burdens of the past. In my opinion, if a child can successfully do this, in *The Lady's Code*, there is no excuse for a full-grown adult not to do likewise.

As Daisy's confidence grew, she faced the world with a renewed sense of purpose. She transformed her pain into a driving force, channeling her experiences into advocacy for others who felt voiceless and powerless. As an adult, Daisy has kept her promise to God and herself, refusing to become distracted by the naysayers.

No one believes this really happened to her because she does not look like what she has been through. She is a very beautiful, nice,

Relationship 80/20 Rule

loving, peaceful, and pleasant person who prides herself on integrity and kindness, even among not-so-nice people. Daisy takes nothing for granted, priding herself on growth and transformation. She said that if God, her Heavenly Father, can deliver her from that situation, she must serve and live for Him without bowing down to anything lesser.

As life has it, the fruit will never fall far from the tree; therefore, it is going to take discipline and perseverance to overcome or alter a negative DNA structure or mindset to a positive one. One thing you must remember is that an undisciplined lifestyle will hinder you from achieving your goals.

In contrast, as *Women of Stature*, a disciplined lifestyle will free you to achieve anything your mind can conceive. For this reason, you must become very cautious about what you watch, listen to, read, and think about, as well as the people with whom you associate in your inner or outer circle.

If Daisy can overcome without having *The Lady's Code* at her fingertips and become a *Woman of Stature*, so can you with *The Lady's Code* in hand! Her last words to me were, 'No one can stop GREATNESS from within you, but you!'

Oh, by the way, did I mention, as God would have it, to the chagrin of her entire family, and defying the black sheep odds, Daisy now stands out as a remarkable, humble, and prominent figure. She has emerged as an unexpected beacon of light for her family, who, unbeknownst to her, are transforming their lives with her mere presence.

Daisy's personal revelations and choices create an atmosphere of encouragement, hope, and introspection among her relatives. This shift is fascinating: they seek her advice on everyday dilemmas, fixing the fractures and cracks in their own lives.

Although Daisy pretends to be seemingly unaware of her family's secret admiration, still, from my perspective and according to the *Writing on the Wall*, she knows. They absorb her insights, gradually self-correcting negative behaviors that once permeated family gatherings, prompting them to seek self-improvement and growth. Each subtle adjustment in their actions allows them to evolve, fostering a sense of unity that once felt elusive.

Relationship 80/20 Rule

This phenomenon highlights the power of living by example, illustrating how true change often comes from within. In the family's eyes, Daisy is a role model who has unintentionally become the catalyst for change for millions of families. She said casually, 'While her life was difficult and challenging, somebody has to get this healing party started, so it may as well be her.' As I concurred with her, her last statement was so profound, 'No one should ever mistreat a child because we do not know who that child may become. Nor do we know what God is using to train them to become who they already are.' In a moment of awe, I dropped my pen to allow her statement to resonate within the depths of my soul.

Here is what I heard from Daisy's statement: Parents are really assigned to train their children to become what they already are. This principle is rarely spoken about in or out of the Kingdom of God, which leads me to believe it is time to do something about it. Ultimately, we are responsible for properly training our NEXT, the Kingdom's NEXT, or the NEXT Generation. What NEXT means to you is between you and God Almighty.

When we believe in our potential, we can redefine our stories, prove naysayers wrong, and ultimately transform our lives for the better, especially when knowing what to do, *As It Pleases God*. For this reason, let us read *Malcolm's Writing on the Wall* to ensure we find the strength to rise above adversity and forge our own paths like my precious Daisyrella.

Love on Layaway - Malcolm's Writing on the Wall

The central theme in *The Lady's Code* is the evolution of one's self-awareness and growth that emerges through the challenges of relationships. When faced with setbacks, such as a broken heart or a relationship that did not go as planned, individuals often engage in profound self-reflection, positively or negatively. In *Malcolm's Writing on the Wall*, we are going to touch on both.

Whether single, married, or anything in between, dating, mating, and relating involve a learning process for everyone. Even

Relationship 80/20 Rule

if you are currently dating the person you are married to, you will likely need to add some excitement to keep things interesting and actionable. This may involve planning date nights, communicating openly, doing chores together, vacationing, supporting them during tough times, and so on, to nurture your connection, *As It Pleases God*.

To be clear, dating, mating, or relating is not about singleness; it is really about ONENESS with the person you love and care about to bridge the gap, fostering love, respect, and understanding. When I talk about a gap, I am referring to the differences, misunderstandings, and challenges arising in any relationship.

In reality, each person brings their unique experiences, backgrounds, and emotional baggage, resulting in a wide array of gaps in need of addressing. The length and depth of these gaps depend largely on how you handle your interactions and the value placed on your relationship. Therefore, I am going to empower you with some information that will prevent you from burning bridges you may need to cross periodically.

The *Writing on the Wall* says that the way in which you think today determines what tomorrow holds for you, as well as what type of package it comes in. Of course, you cannot control everything that happens, but you can control how you deal with it and your perception.

According to the Heavenly of Heavens, renewing your mind on a daily basis with the Word of God, prayer, repentance, forgiveness, and meditation play a vital role in how you deal with God, yourself, and others. As we begin to read *Malcolm's Writing on the Wall*, do not forget that when laying the groundwork in a relationship, you should never limit your ability to think outside, inside, around, and through the box, nor should you crush another human being just because you can.

Dee hired a private detective to find out if her fiancé was cheating on her. The detective then asked, 'Why are you getting married, knowing that it is a possibility that he is cheating on you?' She said, 'Because I have money, and He does not, and I am the shot-caller in this relationship!' The detective scratched his head

Relationship 80/20 Rule

in amazement. Even though the detective took the case, he was appalled at her attitude.

This smug chick did a thorough background and credit check on her fiancé, Malcolm, to see if he was worthy of her time and effort. The detective did not catch him cheating; he had no criminal background; however, he did have a few mishaps on his credit, which Dee gave him the 3rd degree about. As a matter of fact, Dee postponed their wedding, started to date other men, and refused to marry Malcolm until he was able to get his credit straight.

Malcolm was devastated; he could not believe she could throw away true love for a credit score. He was so in love with Dee that he would worship the ground she walked on. However, Dee kept him around as the maintenance man to fix whatever was broken. As a matter of fact, he even went a step further to keep her car clean and properly maintained. Malcolm gladly did so because his love was not easily turned off.

Even though he was a mechanic, he did not allow his occupation to prevent him from treating Dee like a QUEEN. When she got around her friends, she began to treat Malcolm like a servant; she even allowed her friends to talk about him and treat him like a junkyard dog. To add insult to injury, she always appeared cold and uncaring, as if he were a nobody, but when she needed something, she would always apologize and kiss up to him. However, after she got what she wanted, she was back to her old selfish ways again.

Although Dee spoke down about Malcolm being a mechanic, he allowed her criticism to inspire him to open up his own mechanic shop. After a couple of years in business, Malcolm no longer had to come home with dirt, grease, and oil under his fingernails. And, now that everything is going well for Malcolm, Dee wants to get married.

On their wedding day, Malcolm finds out that Dee invited all of her ex-boyfriends to the wedding. So, instead of Dee being with her husband at their wedding, she hung out with all of her exes, totally ignoring her husband. Dee acted as if Malcolm did not exist; this was supposed to be the happiest day of Malcolm's life, and it

Relationship 80/20 Rule

turned out to be his worst nightmare. Malcolm's mother sobbed because she knew that her son was in love with someone who was not in love with him. Unfortunately, she only married him for the money.

Malcolm grew tired and weary, loving someone who did not love him. He thought he could buy her love, but it did not work—he only bought himself more agony. He thought he could change her, but it made Dee worse, becoming more ruthless by the day.

In my opinion, Malcolm seemed to be a man after God's own heart, trying everything to please his wife. While Dee, on the other hand, did everything to make him leave her. While simultaneously making it clear that she did not love him and she couldn't care less about the relationship. In reality, this fragile man knew he could not live like this for the rest of his life, but he refused to allow her to make him feel as if he were worthless.

Malcolm's life had once been filled with hopes and dreams, but after her recent statement, it had been overshadowed by intense pain and heartbreak, vacillating between anger and despair. His world felt as though it was unraveling, and the love he once cherished now seemed like a distant memory. His wife's open infidelity left him emotionally battered, navigating a turbulent sea of unwavering betrayal while desperately trying to hold onto the fraying threads of their relationship.

After years of being mistreated, abused, and misused, Malcolm decides to hire an investigator, and he unknowingly hires the same investigator his wife had hired several years earlier. Amazingly, the investigator remembered this case because of Dee's arrogant attitude. As the investigator grew to know Malcolm personally, he finally told him about the statement Dee had made several years ago about her having the money and being the shot-caller in the relationship. Malcolm could not believe she would say something of such. However, he played it cool while the investigator did his job.

One week later, the investigator catches Dee on tape with four different males; they all appear to have money, they all wined and dined her, and they all had feely, touchy relationships in public. Malcolm remembered seeing those same four guys at the wedding.

Relationship 80/20 Rule

He was outraged; he wanted to hurt Dee, but he could not allow Dee to turn him into someone or something that He was not raised to be. Although Malcolm wanted to cheat, and he was tempted to do so to get even out of revenge. Nevertheless, he chose to play it smart.

In moments of silence, Malcolm found comfort through self-examination. He also reached out to friends and family for support, and through his conversations, he realized the importance of self-worth. In addition, he also understood that he deserved love based not on the fragile hopes of reconciliation but on mutual respect, togetherness, and honor. This unfortunate experience shaped him, transforming the agony of betrayal into lessons of resilience, self-discovery, and the profound importance of honoring one's own heart. Ultimately, this is what Malcolm's *Writing on the Wall* wants us to know:

- ☐ He became 100% sure that he was done with the relationship with Dee.
- ☐ He gave himself some time to heal.
- ☐ He refused to feel like a victim.
- ☐ He began to set a guard over his heart.
- ☐ He did not engage in another relationship.
- ☐ He kept an open and guarded mind.
- ☐ He started asking questions regarding how she really felt about their relationship.
- ☐ He asked her about her expectations in the relationship. He was offended by her answers, but he kept his cool.
- ☐ He never confronted her about her infidelity. He gave her enough rope to hang herself.
- ☐ He learned how to control his emotions and act normal.
- ☐ He started paying attention to everything.
- ☐ He kept his business to himself.
- ☐ He did not indulge in any form of name-calling.
- ☐ He prepared for separation while she was out cheating and doing her thing.

Relationship 80/20 Rule

- ☐ He opened a separate account and opened credit cards in his name only. (Do not empty out someone's bank account; only take what belongs to you!)
- ☐ He started looking for a place to stay.
- ☐ He made a copy of her address book, online contacts, and important documents.
- ☐ He began to document everything, and he password-protected it as well while taking an extra step to store it in a safe deposit box.
- ☐ He planned for his divorce without abandoning his home.
- ☐ He got an attorney and filed for divorce.

Once the divorce papers were served, Malcolm moved out of the home he once shared with Dee, marking the end of a chapter in both their lives. The decision to separate had been a long time coming for him, but the reality of the situation hit hard. As he packed his belongings, memories of happier times flooded back, reminding him of what once was.

Dee had been fine with the divorce. After all, she was the one who had strayed, finding comfort in the arms of other men while being for the streets. As the initial shock of the divorce subsided, she began to confront the implications of her actions, masking the pain of their failed marriage and the insecurity of not being wife material from the start.

The men she had turned to during her marriage scattered, leaving her to deal with her cheating ways on her own. Plus, they were not looking for a commitment; they were only looking for one thing and having a good time. The men she had turned to were not interested in picking up the pieces of her heart, nor were they paying any bills.

The truth of the matter is that Dee felt as if Malcolm would never leave because he loved her more than he loved himself. As life would have it, once Malcolm started to love himself and the ground He walked on, Dee lost her power to control, use, and abuse the only true love of her life.

Relationship 80/20 Rule

In a heartwarming turn of events, experiencing the ups and downs of life, Malcolm is now remarried, and he has four beautiful children. In addition to his flourishing family life, Malcolm proudly owns a well-known full-service tire franchise, where he has established a reputation for top-notch quality customer service.

His business has become a cornerstone of the community, not just for the services it offers but also for the trust and relationships he has built with his customers. His story is indeed one of resilience, hope, and the power of second chances while living by example and exuding good people skills.

Dee, on the other hand, is struggling with the consequences of her decisions. In a cruel twist of fate, Dee lost her job and, subsequently, her social network. With mounting credit card debt, she found herself working menial labor—cleaning hotel rooms for just above minimum wage.

This new chapter in her life was not just a demotion in work status; it represented a humbling fall from grace. The vibrant lifestyle Dee once led became a distant memory as she struggled to make ends meet in an environment filled with financial strain and emotional turmoil.

Dee would not tell anyone that while she was busy judging Malcolm's flawed credit and financial insecurity, she was living on credit. She is now traumatized that she has a hard time paying for a lifestyle she no longer has any recollection of, as she lives in abject poverty. At the same time, Malcolm has become a millionaire, refusing to bail her out of debt.

Dee had the same opportunity to treat Malcolm right but chose not to do so, causing her to get a side-eye from God. *"For the love of money is a root of all kinds of evil, for which some have strayed from the faith in their greediness, and pierced themselves through with many sorrows."* 1 Timothy 6:10. As *Women of Stature*, and according to *The Lady's Code*, never allow money, fame, power, or status to cause you to mistreat anyone. Because *"A man with an evil eye hastens after riches, And does not consider that poverty will come upon him."* Proverbs 28:22.

Can Dee overcome her atrocities? Absolutely! She is no different from anyone else because we have all fallen short. The

Relationship 80/20 Rule

final point is that Dee treated Malcolm the same way her mother treated her father. She was conditioned to behave as such, as it became her normal, which blinded her to her wrongdoings, breaking *The Lady's Code*. Nonetheless, it was her responsibility to change the trajectory of these negative behaviors.

Malcolm's *Writing on the Wall* serves as a poignant lesson on empathy, humility, and the unpredictable nature of life. It challenges the social tendency to judge others based on their financial choices while overlooking one's own vulnerabilities. Dee's experience illustrates the danger of judging others too harshly, especially when one's own circumstances can change at any moment. On this note, let us move on to the *Wall of Overcoming* to ensure we are properly equipped when life gets to lifing.

Wall of Overcoming

The *Writing on the Wall* says that owning our mistakes or faults in life is a great way to safeguard our integrity while keeping our natural instincts intact. Negative Environmental conditioning does not have to plague us if we do not accept it! All that is required is that we place our mindset on a different currency to redirect, recycle, or reform a negative into a positive.

In *The Lady's Code*, our philosophy is to keep it simple and stop allowing people to chat in our ears before we have a talk with God about whatever we want to overcome. If we find ourselves hurt about something or someone, when speaking with God, we must evaluate the three sides of the story:

- ☐ Our side.
- ☐ Their side.
- ☐ The truth.

Doing so allows us to understand our role in the situation, circumstance, or event. Plus, it allows us to repent, forgive, give thanks, understand the situation, add God into the equation, take

Relationship 80/20 Rule

our power back, document the lesson, and move on as if we have never been hurt before.

Do we have the power to reverse negative conditioning into positive? Absolutely! We have more POWER than we give ourselves credit for. In *The Lady's Code: As It Pleases God*, we must change our MINDSETS to overcome anything that is not conducive to our Predestined Blueprint. The Bible tells us: *"And do not be conformed to this world, but be transformed by the renewing of your mind, that you may prove what is that good and acceptable and perfect will of God."* Romans 12:2.

The key is to use the *Wall of Overcoming* to unveil the reason for our being. If we use it for selfishness or selfish gain, it will backfire. Why would it backfire, especially if we are trying to overcome negative conditioning? According to *The Lady's Code*, we must overcome with selfless humility and not pompousness.

If the psyche is running the show, it indicates that our Spirit is not ONE with the Holy Spirit, which causes conflict from within us. Simply put, we may overcome one negative thing to replace it with another negative. In this case, in the Kingdom, we consider this a double-negative, when it should be negative to positive or a lose-lose to a win-win.

How do we make the *Wall of Overcoming* make sense as *Women of Stature*? We are in charge of the energy we harness or release from within...meaning, we have choices! According to the Heavenly of Heavens, when choosing to overcome and understand, *As It Pleases God*, here are a few things to know, but not limited to such:

- ☐ Know who you are dealing with (Know your audience).
- ☐ Know what you are dealing with (Know the issue).
- ☐ Use relatable analogies or examples.
- ☐ Paint a relevant, picturesque view for understanding.
- ☐ Ask and encourage questions, creating dialogue.
- ☐ Listen more than you speak.
- ☐ Clarify what you heard.
- ☐ Exhibit gratefulness for the experience.
- ☐ Come into agreement or non-agreement.

Relationship 80/20 Rule

Overcoming a setback has to become a mindset of clarity and unwavering faith. If we do not develop clarity of mind with understanding and faithfulness, we will continue to live with the setbacks over and over again without doing anything about them. In *The Lady's Code*, setbacks are hidden lessons to bring us into the Spiritual Classroom.

Suppose we do not understand what God is trying to say to us, what He is trying to teach us, what direction He is trying to lead us in, what corrections we need to make in our lives, or what has become an idol in our lives over Him. In this case, the lesson will continue to repeat itself until we get it. Therefore, there is no reason to blame anyone for our setbacks or the cycle of déjà vu.

Why can we not pass the blame, especially if it is justified? In the Eye of God, the lesson is never about them; it is always about us. Our learning curves are about us, and our Spiritual Fruits are about others. On the *Wall of Overcoming*, the analogy of an ice cream parlor is a fitting illustration of what is for us and what is for them.

For instance, we, as entrepreneurs, own an ice cream parlor for our livelihood to sustain ourselves with a form of income (the business is about us). So, we must make ice cream as a product to serve to others (the product is for our customers). If the owner were to consume all the ice cream themselves, the business would quickly falter, resulting in the loss not only of an income source, soon going out of business, but also losing community connections and loyal customers. The analogy also applies to consuming our own fruits without learning and growing, *As It Pleases God*.

In the Kingdom of God, in the same way a business is built on a product or service, so are we. Here is what Galatians 5:13 instructs us to do: *"For you, brethren, have been called to liberty; only do not use liberty as an opportunity for the flesh, but through love serve one another."*

What are we serving up? I do not have a clue...only the server, servee, and God can answer this question. However, when overcoming adversity, it is wise to begin serving up the Fruits of the Spirit and behaving Christlike.

Why is it so wise to serve up the Fruits of the Spirit? In a world often marked by chaos, division, envy, jealousy, coveting, competitiveness, pride, and strife, we need a counterbalancing

Relationship 80/20 Rule

system as a form of guide, mirror, or measurement to better understand what we are serving to ourselves and others. Gratefully, in curbing our negative behavioral tendencies, the Fruits of the Spirit provide the apparatus to interject positive interactions. Once again, they are foolproof, and against such, there is no law according to Galatians 5:22-23. Anything else we serve up has one.

In light of overcoming, we are invited to consider how we can actively serve up the Fruits of the Spirit in our daily lives. Whether through small acts of kindness, loving gestures, exhibiting patience, an authentic smile, or an expression of thankfulness, we have countless opportunities to uplift ourselves and those around us.

For our redemption and inheritance, *As It Pleases God*, He wants us to use the Fruits of the Spirit to increase, grow, and multiply with wisdom, strength, and stature. The fruit of our actions and wisdom, paired with Spiritual Understanding, equip us to navigate life's challenges and to make serviceable choices aligning with the Greater Good. Is this Biblical? Absolutely. I would have it no other way.

Colossians 1:9-14 concurs, *"For this reason we also, since the day we heard it, do not cease to pray for you, and to ask that you may be filled with the knowledge of His will in all wisdom and spiritual understanding; that you may walk worthy of the Lord, fully pleasing Him, being fruitful in every good work and increasing in the knowledge of God; strengthened with all might, according to His glorious power, for all patience and longsuffering with joy; giving thanks to the Father who has qualified us to be partakers of the inheritance of the saints in the light. He has delivered us from the power of darkness and conveyed us into the kingdom of the Son of His love, in whom we have redemption through His blood, the forgiveness of sins."*

But more importantly, if Jesus served us with His life, why can we not serve Him in goodness, righteousness, and truth? Wait, wait, wait, before answering this question, please allow Mark 10:45 to tell us what He did for us: *"For even the Son of Man did not come to be served, but to serve, and to give His life a ransom for many."*

Relationship 80/20 Rule

We have to look from within to find the lesson, and once we find the lesson, it is wrapped in Divine Wisdom. From my perspective, a setback for me is wisdom being handed to me on a silver platter. I eat it up, and I share it to activate the Law of Reciprocity.

I was once told that I needed to break what I am saying down so that a little child could understand complex ideologies. So, let me explain, activating the Power of Clear Communication regarding matters dealing with setbacks. When I am served a setback, obstacle, or difficult situation, I become a STUDENT, learning the lesson and getting an understanding, *As It Pleases God*. Then, I turn around to become the TEACHER who empowers others to open The Floodgates of Wisdom, making what I learned become Divine Wisdom instead of normal wisdom. How so? I have the Holy Spirit backing me and the Blood of Jesus covering me as I use the Fruits of the Spirit to prepare the TABLE for the next person. Doing so with *The Lady's Code: As It Pleases God* at the forefront, I place a Spiritual Seal on my OVERCOMING. How do we make this make sense? Here is the Spiritual Seal: "*And they overcame him by the blood of the Lamb and by the word of their testimony, and they did not love their lives to the death.*" Revelation 12:11.

Seedtime and harvest apply to our setbacks as well, and they cannot hold us back if we simply set them up to become a BLESSING for ourselves and others. Suppose we can find a way to learn from our setbacks and create a win-win situation by looking for the positive without focusing on the negative. In this case, Divine Wisdom will be waiting to provide us with the substance or provisions needed to overcome the situation, circumstance, or event.

As *Women of Stature*, a setback is a distraction designed to keep us blind, confused, and frustrated with ourselves. Nevertheless, when we exercise wisdom, compassion, and due diligence when dealing with a setback, we are better able to maneuver around obstacles to achieve our desired goals.

Here is a prime example: If we crush an ant mound, we will never see them weeping or settling for defeat. They will rebuild that mound by any means necessary, regardless of whether we

Relationship 80/20 Rule

want them there or not! It is sad to say, but it is only death that will stop an ant from rebuilding its empire.

Hunger Pains' Writing on the Wall

If something or someone rains on our parade, simply dry off, regroup, get a strategy, and go for it again! This *Writing on the Wall* brings me to this one story: I ran into this woman some time ago, and her child was having a hard time financially because she was in recovery from a major illness. She saw that her child was losing a lot of weight, and the woman blew it off as if her child was on some sort of diet.

Then, one day, her child could not take the hunger pains anymore; therefore, she swallowed her pride, asking her mom for something to eat. Her mom gave her a piece of meat and a soda to drink. Some people would take this as an insult, but this child was so hungry that she was grateful for whatever was given to her.

A week later, upon her routine visit to her mom's house, she noticed her mom was trying to get rid of her quickly. Then, she started asking questions about why she was trying to get rid of her. The mom then said she was taking someone out to dinner. This child felt so hurt because she had nothing to eat all day.

The mother she loves so much is feeding someone else's child without even extending any sort of invitation to feed her own. Although very hurt, this child did not form any resentment; she still loved and helped her mom with no strings attached. Nevertheless, she stopped asking for food and placed her needs in the hands of God, reciting this scripture: *"And my God shall supply all your need according to His riches in glory by Christ Jesus."* Philippians 4:19.

The following week after the incident, this child was helping her mom without having one morsel of food in her belly. She did not say a word to anyone about it; she just continued to do a good deed for her mother. Then, a stranger walks up and offers to help her, but she realizes the stranger is not really a stranger. She had met him before.

Relationship 80/20 Rule

Out of the blue, this person then offered to buy her lunch; she said that she would accept on one condition—he had to buy lunch for her mom as well. He gladly accepted, and the mother felt so embarrassed about the incident that she hung her head down in shame. From a guilty conscience, the mom does offer to feed her child later on that day, without her daughter having to ask for food.

Is it an atrocity not to provide for your own? Maybe or maybe not...this woman's child placed her faith in God, and He not only provided a meal for this child at that moment, but He also gave her a husband as well.

God used this situation for this woman's child to find the man of her dreams...he was that child's BOAZ. This child never had to go hungry another day in her life. She could not ask for a better man; he loves her in a way no man has ever loved her.

It was not about the hunger or the meal; it was about this child's faith meeting up with her famine. The only way this child could get to her blessing was through her mom's atrocious behavior. As life would have it, the love this child displayed despite disappointments was her BLESSING in disguise, even when people looking from the outside thought otherwise.

A true winner will not stop because of a setback, sickness, or lack. They simply find another way. In *The Lady's Code*, we leave no stone unturned, regardless of how it may appear. Your best bet is to refrain from settling for mental defeat, do what you have to do to overcome your setbacks emotionally, and keep yourself moving physically to ensure you do not have any regrets about giving up on yourself.

Oh, by the way, on the *Wall of Overcoming*, if you add a little repenting, forgiving, prayer, and the Fruits of the Spirit to it, you will indeed enhance your Spiritual Powerhouse, causing the Spirit of Defeat to flee.

According to *The Lady's Code: As It Pleases God*, this is like the icing on the cake that bridges the triumphant gap, commencing all things to work together for your good. *"But those who wait on the Lord shall renew their strength; They shall mount up with wings like eagles, They shall run and not be weary, They shall walk and not faint."* Isaiah 40:31.

CHAPTER 10

WHERE IS THE LOVE

In recognizing our worth or when we are in pursuit of genuine connection, there are times when we feel true love has eluded us. In reality, the truth is, 'True love resides from within.' In a relationship, as we all know, like attracts like. If we do not truly love ourselves unselfishly, we will find that we unknowingly drive away the people who are attempting to extend their love toward us. While at the same time, attracting those who contribute to the hurt, trauma, or disgust. Consequently, it is not that love does not exist; it is a matter of two things:

- ☐ It is a matter of whether or not we REJECT the love coming our way by self-doubt, self-sabotage, or false expectations.

- ☐ It is a matter of whether or not we EMBRACE love through self-confidence, self-manifestation, agreement, or realistic expectations.

If we are not sure how to love, then we need to learn. It is perfectly okay to pick up a book or take a class on love. If we have never experienced love, then we need to find it within ourselves first.

Where Is The Love

How do we go about the process of loving ourselves, *As It Pleases God*? First, we must ACKNOWLEDGE that love is a deliberate choice. Secondly, we must AGREE with ourselves that love requires trust, action, and respect. Thirdly, we must AVOID lying or deceiving ourselves, others, and most of all, God.

On the journey toward self-love, *As It Pleases God*, the best way to begin is by making a list of the good and bad truths about ourselves. Once completed, we can move on to making another list of the positive and negative attributes we possess. Then, move on to the following list of the right and wrong habits we have. Once completed, for each attribute listed on the negative, bad, or wrong habits list, we must find the FEAR associated with it, which prevents us from loving ourselves and others as we should.

Why do we need to make a list? We do not have to do anything. We all have free will to do whatever we like; it is only a mere suggestion. Making lists helps us keep track of what is going on from within the psyche, or it helps us own our truth a little better, allowing God to guide us, *As It Pleases Him.* Here is the scripture to write on top of your list: *"Trust in the Lord with all your heart, and lean not on your own understanding; In all your ways acknowledge Him, and He shall direct your paths."* Proverbs 3:5-6.

According to *The Lady's Code*, if we want true love or become effective at sharing love, we must become WILLING to give it with no strings attached. Now, here is the catch: To give love, we must possess it. We cannot drink from a well that is all dried up or full of fear, hatefulness, bad habits, and negativity. Blasphemy, right? Wrong. *"A righteous man who falters before the wicked is like a murky spring and a polluted well."* Proverbs 25:26.

Most often, real or true love is not discovered when you are desperately pursuing it. When you recognize what you want and do not want in a relationship, it is easier to attract what you desire. If you do not know or if you are oblivious to what you want, you will begin to attract anything and everything through a trial-and-error process. Sometimes, you may get lucky, but the chances are you will go through multiple relationships.

Where Is The Love

Rest assured, with multiple relationships come multiple hurts, multiple heartbreaks, multiple traumatizations, and multiple everything. By the time you get to the perfect person for you, you are all wounded, battered, used up, and exhausted from your previous relationships; therefore, the additional baggage weighs down the current connection.

Having a successful relationship depends on a lot of factors; so, in *The Lady's Code: As It Pleases God*, I will give you the answers to some of your WHYS in life. It will better prepare you to deal with dating, mating, and relating on a more sophisticated or intellectual level to keep dead-end relationships at bay. Now, before I move on, forget about the idea of a flawless relationship!

Why should we not expect a flawless relationship? No one is perfect, and every relationship requires commitment and work! Unfortunately, false expectations have the greatest potential to ruin awesome connections with assumptions and a lack of acceptance.

You must give your mind a clean slate when it comes down to love. *The Lady's Code* wants to evolve your way of thinking, dating, mating, relating, and looking at love. If you have not noticed by now, love spelled backward is EVOL...think about it! The *Writing on the Wall* is designed to help you evolve into greatness in every aspect of your life, personally, professionally, and Spiritually.

When I talk about the perfect partner or mate, I am referring to the perfect one for you. The ideal person for your wants, needs, desires, and Divine Blueprint. Of course, once again, no one is absolutely 100% perfect in all things, but I will say this: 'There's somebody for everybody.'

Now, let me ask you, 'Do you question if every person you meet is the one?' If you do...STOP! Here are the questions that you need to answer:

- ☐ Are you looking for a soul mate?
- ☐ Are you looking for a life partner?
- ☐ Are you looking for a business partner?
- ☐ Are you looking for your BLUEPRINTED partner?
- ☐ Are you looking for a placeholder?

Where Is The Love

- ☐ Are you looking for a buddy?
- ☐ Are you looking for a friend?
- ☐ Are you looking for a roommate partner?
- ☐ Are you looking for someone for sexual pleasure?
- ☐ Are you looking for a bed warmer?
- ☐ Are you looking for someone for material gain?
- ☐ Are you looking for someone to have a great time with when you are not working?

Once you answer these questions, it is your responsibility to trust God to bring what you are looking for. If you keep questioning if they are the one...you are not really trusting God! When the person who is right for you enters your life, there will be no question about it! The *Writing on the Wall* will reveal whatever you need to know; all you need to do is PAY ATTENTION while loving the skin you are in.

The Forbidden Fruit - Carrie's Writing on the Wall

Have you ever had an overwhelming desire for something that was strictly forbidden? Did the desire consume your every thought? Did it drive you insane not to have it? Did you sacrifice your soul to have it? Did you secretly do something you cannot tell anyone about just to have a piece of what was forbidden?

When we talk about the forbidden fruit, Adam and Eve often come to mind. Since the fall, we have had to battle against the sweet temptation of having what is not good for us. Of course, we often like to blame Adam and Eve for our shortcomings. However, they cannot assume responsibility for what we willfully choose.

As you very well know, promiscuity is everywhere—in our churches, in our schools, on the job, and in our very own homes. A lot can be determined by a person's character, values, and standards, including their mental, emotional, physical, financial, and sexual wants and desires. If we do not want to get caught up, we must become totally aware of the types of people we need to avoid.

Where Is The Love

According to *The Lady's Code*, we must become ever so cautious about torturing ourselves to become something or someone we are not designed to be. Nor should we engage in fighting for a lost cause when God is drawing us out of something. For this reason, there is no better time than now to introduce *Carrie's Writing on the Wall*.

Carrie's story resonates deeply with many who have faced the painful realities of conditional love. For years, she loved a man named Ricky, pouring her heart and soul into her Forbidden Fruit. However, her devotion was met with a harsh reality: Ricky's love was contingent on her appearance, a fact that would haunt Carrie long after he walked out of her life.

Ricky viewed Carrie as a trophy, someone to show off rather than a partner to cherish. His obsession with her weight transformed their love into a suffocating cage as he tortured her mentally. He did not care whether this woman starved herself or not; all he wanted was for his trophy to be a size six or below.

When Carrie's weight fluctuated to a size ten, Ricky would act as if she were a fat slob, and he would tell her that she needed to stop eating. In addition, her Forbidden Fruit, Ricky, would make her watch him eat as punishment, as if her worth was tied to the number on a scale. This cruel game of control left her feeling perturbed, but she was thankful to at least have a man.

As the days turned into months and months into years, Carrie found herself navigating through bouts of self-doubt and anxiety while dealing with the fact that Ricky was only in love with her body. She tried desperately to comply with Ricky's demands, engaging in extreme diets, skipping meals, and obsessively counting calories, but her genetic makeup was not having it. She also went to the extreme of secretly having liposuction.

Carrie went over the hill with this diet thing just to prevent Ricky from cheating on her. When she visited her parents' house, she could not stop eating. She ate up everything; her parents knew something was wrong, but she would never admit she had a problem.

One night, Ricky got into bed with a T-shirt on, which made Carrie suspicious. She then asked, 'Why are you sleeping with a shirt on; you never did that before?' He reluctantly responded, 'It is cold in here.' So, Carrie blew it off and did not push the issue.

The following day, she went into the bathroom; she glanced toward Ricky, just stepping out of the shower; her heart sank. He had deep scratches all over his back. At that moment, the room seemed to close in on her. In a state of shock, Carrie just broke down and started crying like a two-year-old, with every teardrop carrying the weight of betrayal.

Unfortunately, this was Carrie's moment of truth: Ricky had been with another woman. He offered no apology or explanation; he just stepped over her while she was sitting on the floor, sobbing. Carrie knew she should have walked away at that point, but she could not bear the fact of losing her man to another woman because she could not stay off her eating binges and on a diet.

This cheating episode pushed Carrie over the deep end. She would not eat for days; this woman had anorexia and was in denial. Ultimately, this deeply wounded and traumatized victim of emotional and mental abuse secretly battled anorexia and bulimia on her own. She did not want help because she would have to explain why she was torturing herself over a man. Until one day, she was forced to do so when she suffered a heart attack. All of the diet pills, binging, purging, and not eating had caught up with her. She almost died with her little secret.

The most amazing thing about this little ordeal, Ricky never came to see her. Although he called, he never came to the hospital to check on her; he just made up some lame excuse to take advantage of the time she was out of the house. While in the hospital, she did not appear to be anorexic, so the doctors overlooked this fact, nor did she volunteer any information. However, they did ask her about taking any form of diet pills. Of course, she denied it, which caused her heart attack at such a young age to become a mystery to the doctors. Nevertheless, Carrie knew the truth.

After Carrie had gotten out of the hospital, she made a promise to herself that she was not going to take any more diet pills and starve herself. And, by making this commitment to herself, she gained weight.

Where Is The Love

Ultimately, Ricky became uncomfortable with her weight gain because her brickhouse body was not bricking anymore, and he did not want to be seen with her. Even though Carrie felt bad about the way he was treating her, she knew she had to start loving herself, even if it meant gaining weight and losing her man.

After the wake-up call, Carrie believed that as long as she loved herself, she had to let the chips fall where they may. After all of the torture and pain Carrie endured, she still lost Ricky to another woman anyway. After many years of pain, she finally accepted it was indeed a part of God's plan for her life.

Carrie is still a very pretty young lady; however, she is still trying to overcome the mental and emotional torture she endured. Even though she did not tell me everything, what she did say was enough to form this *Writing on the Wall* on her behalf.

She is now eating healthy and working out while treating herself really good. Slowly, she began to embrace her body, celebrating not only her well-being but also her strength and character. Though she is no longer a size ten, she has learned to love the skin that she is in as she inspires other women to do likewise. She learned her worth was not defined by her dress size but by her kindness, intelligence, and resilience.

Now, for the Forbidden Fruit: Ricky has his size two trophy wife, who is running around town dropping it like it's hot because he can no longer scratch her back or blow her back out. Being that Ricky has established the foundation of this relationship on LUST and not LOVE, he has to deal with his wife traumatizing and criticizing him over his manhood. While at the same time flaunting her male friends with benefits all over social media. Unfortunately, this once confident man's wife is causing him to second-guess his self-worth and role in the relationship as she runs the show, neglecting him, telling his business, and treating him like a pauper.

Here is the plot twist: This joker has the nerve to beg Carrie to come back to him for a do-over; go figure! Laughter consumed me when Carrie shared that her Forbidden Fruit wants a do-over. I responded, 'He wants to do what when his pecker cannot peck anymore?' As the tables have turned and thickness is really

Where Is The Love

trending, He now realizes his once trophy was always the REAL TROPHY, regardless of her size.

Her last statement to me was, 'I have completely blotted him out of my life, and there is no going back. I have set the bar really high, and He can never have a taste of the GOOD FRUITS of my TREE ever again. He broke the foundation of love for lust, so lust must serve its just reward, and I want no part of that.' My response to Carrie was, 'You go, girl!'

In a world often obsessed with perfection, women like Carrie are often accustomed to valuing themselves through the lens of another to define their beauty. Not realizing that when God created us, He did not make a mistake. We are not a one-size-fits-all. Each individual is inherently unique, designed with purpose, and infused with amazing qualities, making them who they are.

God has created each of us with a natural setpoint, fluctuating between 5-10 pounds depending on various factors like genetics, food selections, activity levels, stress levels, and lifestyle choices. The goal is to find this point, eat healthily, find your purpose, and stay active...if someone does not like you, it is not your problem; it is theirs.

Above all, if you decide to lose weight or even get a boob job, butt implants, liposuction, facelift, botox, or whatever...do it for yourself, period! You should never do these things to your body for someone else, to capture someone's attention, to be accepted, to compete with another person, or to look like them. Once again, please do it for yourself!

Carrie's experiences underscore the importance of loving ourselves unconditionally. If someone does not like who you are or your size, keep it moving in the Spirit of Excellence because one man's trash is another man's goldmine. Above all, love should liberate, not imprison.

In the liberation of love, *As It Pleases God*, make sure you do a few things to build a solid foundation, ensuring your good fruits do not become *The Forbidden Fruit*, but not limited to such:

- ☐ Place God first.
- ☐ Pray, repent, forgive, and meditate.

Where Is The Love

- ☐ Usher in the Holy Spirit.
- ☐ Cover all things with the Blood of Jesus.
- ☐ Apply the Word of God.
- ☐ Worship together.
- ☐ Communicate Effectively.
- ☐ Seek help when needed.
- ☐ Practice active listening.
- ☐ Stand in agreement with ONENESS.
- ☐ Practice delayed gratification.
- ☐ Speak positively.
- ☐ Look for the good or win-win in all things.
- ☐ Establish boundaries.
- ☐ Build trust.
- ☐ Seek understanding.
- ☐ Exhibit humility and respect.
- ☐ Use the Fruits of the Spirit.
- ☐ Behave Christlike.

In *The Lady's Code: As It Pleases God*, we must talk about the sensitive subjects most Believers do not want to speak about. Yet, it is gripping the *Women of Stature* like there is no tomorrow. So, we have to lay it on the table...we need to unveil these issues. We are going to discuss:

- ☐ The Wall of Friends
- ☐ Friends with Benefits Theory
- ☐ Friends without Benefits

If these topics do not apply to you, then you can skip these sections because I am going to drive home *The Lady's Code* in this area. Some of the terminology may get respectfully R-rated. So, buckle up...this STRONGHOLD must be broken.

Where Is The Love

Wall of Friends – Pat and Frank's Writing on the Wall

We often keep the act of cheating to a minimum by creating friendships with those other than whom we are dating, mating, or relating. However, the *Writing on the Wall* says that having friends with benefits allows us to have several friends at the same time without someone feeling the sting of being cheated on or rejected.

Yet, if you are having sex with your friends, then are they really friends? Friends usually appreciate each other socially and emotionally with no strings attached. Now, when we start adding the benefits into the equation, the appreciation becomes physical, emotional, and sometimes social. Having a friend with benefits is nothing more than having an open relationship or a 'Booty Call' for the lustful, lonely, and desperate.

Of course, having an open relationship or answering a 'Booty Call' is commonly frowned upon, but it is quite common nowadays. Furthermore, this is a great way to try it before you buy it. If they do not satisfy you, then there is no need to waste your time, right? Well, in the Eye of God, it comes with soul ties and yokes.

Some people think that if you do not know what you want, then you should have an open relationship. Still, we have free will to choose our relationships, and we also choose our hard as well. Then again, if you have what you want, having a friend with benefits is a great way to cheat on your mate legally.

Sadly, this is why we are becoming so caught up in multiple relationships, providing little or no substance besides sex or a superficial prostitution ring for those who choose to sell themselves short. Is this not a little insensitive? Absolutely not! What is insensitive is when we let it all hang out, pretending to be goody two-shoes as if God is blind or we can get one over on Him.

In the real landscape of modern associations of today, those who proclaim to be okay with open relationships or arrangements are lying to themselves. How do I know? The emotional attachments coming with doing the do without a covenant weigh

Where Is The Love

on the human psyche, causing silent division from within and making us long for more of whatever. Here is what Hebrews 13:4 says about this matter: *"Marriage is honorable among all, and the bed undefiled; but fornicators and adulterers God will judge."* For this reason, 1 Corinthians 7:2 tells us what to do: *"Nevertheless, because of sexual immorality, let each man have his own wife, and let each woman have her own husband."*

Do we not have grace in the matter of doing the do? Of course, we have grace, but it does not exempt us from Spiritual Transfers. For the record, grace is for Spiritual Refinement; it is not designed for us to ENGAGE in sexual gratification of our lusts continually. It is designed for us to TURN AWAY from sexual immorality. Please allow me to Spiritually Align this according to 1 Corinthians 6:18. *"Flee sexual immorality. Every sin that a man does is outside the body, but he who commits sexual immorality sins against his own body."*

How do we prevent Spiritual Transfers when doing the do? *As It Pleases God*, we must abstain until there is a marital covenant. Here is what 1 Thessalonians 4:3-5 says, *"For this is the will of God, your sanctification: that you should abstain from sexual immorality; that each of you should know how to possess his own vessel in sanctification and honor, not in passion of lust, like the Gentiles who do not know God."*

On this note, let us read *Pat and Frank's Writing on the Wall* to unveil what it is saying to us, painting a picturesque view on our *Wall of Friends*.

On one lovely afternoon, in the local library, a remarkable story began to unfold. It was Pat's birthday, and she had decided to treat herself to a quiet day filled with books and a hint of self-reflection. Little did she know that fate had a delightful surprise in store for her—a little surprise named Frank.

While browsing her favorite aisle, her eyes not only caught a glimpse of her favorite books but also a charming guy who seemed equally immersed in reading the same genre. As their eyes met, Pat felt an instant connection, and they struck up a conversation. As life would have it, there was an effortless conversational flow, as if they had known each other for years.

Where Is The Love

In the newness of their blossoming relationship, Pat soon realized just how easy it was to fall under Frank's enticing innuendos. He knew exactly how to rope her in, filling her days with joy and laughter. They spent hours discussing their favorite books, sharing dreams, and fashioning a vision for their future. He cooked, cleaned, pampered, and catered to her. Pat had finally found a man she could really relate to. Frank seemed to resonate with her on every level, and she felt seen and understood in ways she had not been understood before.

As days turned into weeks, one morning Pat had to make a quick trip to the other side of town, so she called Frank from her cell phone, and somehow the lines crossed. She was able to hear Frank candidly talking to another woman as if he were dating her as well. Pat could not believe how candidly she heard his whole conversation.

A few minutes later, Pat called Frank again, and he answered. She explained how she had heard his conversation with another woman, and, of course, this prime-time gigolo did not believe her. She then asked if she could stop by; he claimed he did not have time to entertain her company, not realizing she had just heard him invite someone else over. Therefore, she knew he was up to no good.

After several months of keeping Frank at arm's length, in her moment of weakness, she allowed him to stop by to bring her dinner. Afterward, he walked outside to make a phone call, and she could hear him screaming at what appeared to be another woman, but she did not want to jump to any conclusions.

Frank walked back into her house as if nothing ever happened, had sex with her, and then left. Pat felt so dirty; she did not expect him to leave right away; she thought he would at least hold her all night.

To add insult to injury, she did not hear from him for weeks at a time. As a woman of God, Pat was on this emotional roller-coaster with her emotions because Frank was treating her like a prostitute. He would feed her, expect sex from her, and then leave. He did not call her until he wanted another sexual fix, as she compromised her Spiritual Walk with God to satisfy a man

Where Is The Love

who did not want her.

Like clockwork, Frank called a week later, wanting to take Pat out to lunch; she reluctantly declined because she felt as if Frank only wanted one thing. She then asked him about their relationship, and he responded, 'We are just friends, and whatever happens, happens.'

After he made that statement, she knew that he had played her for a fool. She was having sex for love, and he was having sex for fun! So much for a friend with benefits! As a result, his actions taught her how to think and act like a *Woman of Stature* without breaking *The Lady's Code*. Doing so helped her to maintain her glamour and glitz without giving up her goodies while being the 2nd woman prostitute, side chick, or whatever fits his fancy. Pat is now on the 'No Commitment, No Goodies' plan.

In a world where modern relationships often blur the lines of commitment, love, and fulfillment, it is vital to acknowledge that not every person is worth holding onto or entertaining. Pat believes that if women can keep their legs closed long enough, they are better able to tell if a man is interested in them or if they just want sex. She firmly believes there is no need to stay in an unfaithful, unfulfilling, and uncommitted sexual relationship with someone who couldn't care less if she had a pot to piss in while leading her straight into the Pit. Nor does she deal with anyone who displays a blatant disregard for her well-being and happiness.

Pat later finds out Frank firmly believes in the *Friends with Benefits Theory*, and this is why he is still single and ready to mingle with anyone, anything, and for any reason. How could she not know what he was all about? Pat never asked! She assumed...and unfortunately, the soul tie from this particular relationship was not worth sacrificing her relationship with God.

Continuing to engage in a casual relationship containing false expectations, where one partner is unfaithful and uncommitted and the other is faithful and committed, can have serious consequences. As a rule of thumb, in *The Lady's Code*, we should never force or beg someone to accept or love us.

According to the Heavenly of Heavens, authentic love and

Where Is The Love

acceptance must flow to us freely to prevent the build-up of emotional baggage, toxic mess, negativity, and darkness.

What is the purpose of not allowing our emotional baggage, toxic mess, negativity, and darkness to build up in our lives as Believers? Unfortunately, according to the *Wall of Friends*, negative pileups lead to issues with trust, self-esteem, clarity, and even a decline in our overall well-being. All of this leaves us feeling depleted, worn out, unworthy, lost, or even fearful, overshadowing our sense of authentic self-worth, self-awareness, selflessness, and purpose.

Over time, the weight of unmet needs, unresolved trauma, and the pain of betrayal can create a barrier between the individual and their potential to obtain real love and happiness, *As It Pleases God*. And then again, a toxic relationship can push people over the edge, causing them to implode, explode, or collapse when they least expect it, especially when dealing with *Friends with Benefits*.

In a world where relationships often define our experiences, breaking free from unhealthy or draining relationships is necessary. Primarily, the ones that no longer serve us give us an opportunity to reclaim our power back and transform ourselves for the Greater Good. In addition, it also paves the way for healthier, more fulfilling connections, *As It Pleases God*. As we journey through this process, we must get an understanding of the *Friends with Benefits Theory* to ensure we do not get caught up, settling where we do not belong.

Friends with Benefits Theory – Spiritual Transfers

In order to make the *Friends with Benefits Theory* work, both parties must be in 100% total agreement with it. If one person wants a relationship and one person wants a friendship with a little nookie on the side, it is not going to work. Someone is going to get their feelings hurt, or someone is going to feel used or manipulated.

In the Eye of God, this is a very promiscuous type of relationship, and extreme caution needs to be exercised when having casual sex with multiple partners. Why must we exercise extreme caution? For each partner, there will be a soul tie or yoke attached. Every time we lie down with someone who is not our husband, a Spiritual Bonding or Deposit occurs, making us weaker vessels in or out of the Kingdom of God.

However, it will work for you if you just want to have sex without the baggage of relationship complications, the responsibility of a commitment, or when you are dealing with a person who does not have it like that. However, the baggage of the soul tie or yoke will still occur. What does this really mean? Whether we like the person or not, the Spiritual Transfer will still happen. So, whatever is going on within them, we make an agreeable bond to it.

The strength or type of bond will vary from person to person. For example, if someone is consumed with the Jezebel Spirit (A Controlling Spirit), this same Spirit will transfer to us the moment intercourse takes place. Now, the level of penetration may vary depending on the condition and self-control of the psyche. Unfortunately, the more we engage, the more it consumes us. Now, if we have another partner consumed with the Spirit of Saul (A Rebellious Spirit), the same penetration will occur. So, not only do we have the Jezebel Spirit to contend with, but we also have the Saul Spirit to deal with. The more partners we have without releasing those Spirits, the weaker and weaker we become. And, next thing we know, we are behaving like we are fully possessed, especially behind closed doors.

What is a Spiritual Transfer? Spiritual Transfers refer to the process of transferring Spiritual Energy or Power from one individual to another, positively or negatively. Transfers can happen through various means, such as prayer, meditation, laying on of hands, words, thoughts, sexual relations, or other Spiritual practices. Nonetheless, we must have the right types of transfers, keeping us in the LIGHT.

Meanwhile, if we go to the dark side without Spiritual Covenants, *As It Pleases God*, this is where we run into problems. Why do we have problems in this area as Believers? Chastity was

Where Is The Love

not used as one of the Fruits of the Spirit to safeguard the Spiritual Transfer.

Just because chastity is not spoken about much, it does not mean it does not exist. Some things are best left for marriages to remain pure in the Eye of God. Why marriage? The bed becomes undefiled because a Spiritual Covenant is involved as they become ONE, allowing them to swing from the chandelier, climb the walls, or drop it like it's hot. Really? Yes, really! Once again, *"Marriage is honorable among all, and the bed undefiled; but fornicators and adulterers God will judge."* Hebrews 13:4.

Being that Spiritual Transfers are a sensitive topic, please allow me to align how this works if we go to the dark side: *"When an unclean spirit goes out of a man, he goes through dry places, seeking rest, and finds none. Then he says, 'I will return to my house from which I came.' And when he comes, he finds it empty, swept, and put in order. Then he goes and takes with him seven other spirits more wicked than himself, and they enter and dwell there; and the last state of that man is worse than the first. So shall it also be with this wicked generation."* Matthew 12:43-45. Most think this is a fabricated story, but it is as real as real could get!

Here is the deal: Spiritual Transfers enter through the gates or openings of the eyes, ears, nose, mouth, and sexual organs. Wherever there is a HOLE, in the Eye of God, it is a portal of entry. Thus, if we DO NOT protect them, *As It Pleases Him*, we can 'get got' through our lack of understanding. Personally, I wish someone had taught me this when I was younger...it would have saved me from a lot of issues, traumas, and setbacks. Therefore, as *Women of Stature* of *The Lady's Code*, we need to know this information to equip ourselves better before knocking the edge off with the wrong person or a straight-up, well-kept demon with a veil of pretense.

Just remember, anyone you have sexual relations with definitely holds the possibility of you developing an emotional bond, especially if the sex is good. For this reason, you must set rules, boundaries, and limitations to ensure that you are both on one accord. Why should we set rules, boundaries, and limitations, especially when having free will? What you do not know can hurt you. *"Run from sexual sin. No other sin affects the body as this one."* 1

Where Is The Love

Corinthians 6:18. Of course, no one wants to hear about this rule. It is indeed the hardest one to abide by, but it is the most crucial one.

In addition, it is the number one reason why we have problems in our love lives...yes, sexual immorality is asking for trouble. We cannot think for a minute that we can indulge in this sinful behavior and live in total peace. It is not going to happen! We will have trials and tribulations in this area; it is to be expected!

Bonding without a Spiritual Covenant in or out of the Kingdom has implications of inner beatdowns, especially when you are Spiritually Weak and do not know you are in this state or are in denial of it.

Make no mistake about it...If we take a moment to look around us, emotional scarring is out of control, sexual diseases are out of control, and promiscuity is out of control. We are hooking up with mere strangers over the internet. Are we not destroying ourselves? Are we not creating our own bed of hurt, betrayal, and confusion? These are some of the questions we must ask ourselves when dealing with our sexuality and love.

Now, if for some reason we fall short, we cannot beat ourselves up over it...no one is above temptation. We simply need to dust ourselves off, repent, forgive, pray, ask for mercy, and keep it moving without allowing the temptation to get into our heads. Always remember what 1 Corinthians 10:12-13 shares with us: *"Therefore let him who thinks he stands take heed lest he fall. No temptation has overtaken you except such as is common to man; but God is faithful, who will not allow you to be tempted beyond what you are able, but with the temptation will also make the way of escape, that you may be able to bear it."* Simply put, look for the way out!

What if there is no way out? God will always provide a way of escape or another way of doing what needs to be done, *As It Pleases Him*. On the other hand, if we are pleasing ourselves, then it may appear as if there is no other way out, based on the lies we tell ourselves.

As a Word to the Wise, if we can pinpoint the lie, the truth will avail itself by default. James 1:13-15 says, *"Let no one say when he is*

Where Is The Love

tempted, 'I am tempted by God'; for God cannot be tempted by evil, nor does He Himself tempt anyone. But each one is tempted when he is drawn away by his own desires and enticed. Then, when desire has conceived, it gives birth to sin; and sin, when it is full-grown, brings forth death."

Although I used Acts 19:11-16 earlier when discussing playing with Spiritual Matters that we do not understand. However, it is also a perfect *Writing on the Wall* of Spiritual Weakness. "*Now God worked unusual miracles by the hands of Paul, so that even handkerchiefs or aprons were brought from his body to the sick, and the diseases left them and the evil spirits went out of them. Then some of the itinerant Jewish exorcists took it upon themselves to call the name of the Lord Jesus over those who had evil spirits, saying, 'We exorcise you by the Jesus whom Paul preaches.' Also, there were seven sons of Sceva, a Jewish chief priest, who did so. And the evil spirit answered and said, "Jesus I know, and Paul I know; but who are you?" Then the man in whom the evil spirit was leaped on them, overpowered them, and prevailed against them, so that they fled out of that house naked and wounded.*"

Why did they leave naked? Unfortunately, this was their portal of weakness. When nakedness is used in the Bible, it usually refers to sexual relations. If we are swinging it high and low with ladi, dadi, and everybody, and think we can contend with the enemy, he will take our weaknesses and use them against us. So *seven sons of Sceva* were stripped, chastised, and brought to shame for casting out evil Spirits without having a personal *Spirit to Spirit* Relationship with God, the Holy Spirit, or covered by the Blood of Jesus. On the other hand, if you go to the dark side for temporary power, you will eventually turn on yourself.

The moment you think this will not happen to you, it means it is happening, especially when you have *Friends With Benefits*. Thus, it would be best if you had Spiritual Protection and Discernment, *As It Pleases God* in this area. Also, get an understanding of this: "*Flee sexual immorality. Every sin that a man does is outside the body, but he who commits sexual immorality sins against his own body. Or do you not know that your body is the temple of the Holy Spirit who is in you, whom you have from God, and you are not your own? For you were bought at a price; therefore*

Where Is The Love

glorify God in your body and in your spirit, which are God's." 1 Corinthians 6:18-20.

According to *The Lady's Code*, I cannot stop anyone from doing what they choose to do—have at it! You are entitled to your free will to lay, play, and slay however and with whomever. Still, I must prepare you with the information and understanding of the implications from a Spiritual Perspective and as a *Woman of Stature*.

If you are on the *Friends With Benefits* program, make sure you are not using the words: honey, baby, sweetheart, dear, sweet thing, boo, my boo, sweetie pie, I love you, etc., to ensure your *Bed-Buddy* does not become your *Bugaboo*. Why should we not use terms of endearment as such? It may cause things to become a little complicated if one person starts to develop more feelings than the other.

As a rule of thumb, be very cautious when introducing your *Friends With Benefits* to your friends and family members; it could really complicate things. Why should we exercise caution with this matter? Remember, there are soul ties and yokes involved with the potential to have emotional or mental hiccups.

The *Writing on the Wall* warns that this should be your secret anyway, because a *Friends With Benefits* is no more than a convenient sexual arrangement in exchange for monetary gain, a date, a meal, a movie, and so on, with the potential to ruin your credibility and trustworthiness. Also, you never want to ruin your reputation around the people you love and respect.

Those who settle for the *Friends With Benefits* blah, blah, blah.... You must guard your heart. When a person does not value your feelings, then more than likely, they will not value your body, meaning your sex is going to play out really quickly. If someone can run in and out of your body with no emotions, just think about what they could do to your heart and mind once the thrill is gone.

The *Writing on the Wall* wants you to know that your body is your TEMPLE; therefore, you need to decide how much value you place on it. As a word of caution, when your *Friend With Benefits* finds that special someone who does not break *The Lady's Code* or refuses to settle for the *Friends With Benefits* arrangement, trust me, you might as well kiss them goodbye.

There are many misconceptions in life, and discipline is not one of them. When we allow ourselves to meander through life doing whatever we want without any accountability, we are setting ourselves up for the ultimate disappointment. A carefree and careless demeanor does not necessarily mean we do not care; it is our actions that tell us how much we genuinely care.

When we find ourselves running from responsibility, rest assured, we will have unresolved issues in that particular area as well. Irresponsibility and recklessness are totally unacceptable in the Eye of God. When we become truly responsible for ourselves, we are better able to take responsibility for our relationships, especially for those whom we proclaim to care about. Of course, with responsibility comes discipline.

Discipline is required to achieve anything worth having, and without it, we will not get much accomplished. When we find ourselves surrounded by incomplete projects, incomplete relationships, or incomplete anything, our guards should automatically go up. Ultimately, this is a sign of having too many distractions, and too many distractions impede our discipline.

Furthermore, the lack of discipline leaves room for bad habits to take over and control our lives, and the one thing we must never do is lose our ability to govern ourselves, *As It Pleases God*. For the most part, this is where our problem lies because, most often, we do not know what is happening to us. So we get into the habit of doing and trying anything in hopes it will work in our favor.

With God's side-eye on this uncanny behavior, it will cause us to overthink, overanalyze, over-spiritualize, under-spiritualize, or overdo as we become traumatized by this *Friends With Benefits* arrangement. In all simplicity, it makes it more difficult for us to commit, even if we think we are worthy of a commitment.

Friends Without Benefits

The Lady's Code: As It Pleases God promotes the *Wall Without Benefits* based on the Spiritual Elements of self-control. As *Women of*

Where Is The Love

Stature, if you are single, this is the way to go if you really want to have a successful friendship or relationship, *As It Pleases God*. Please understand that we do not live in a perfect world, nor are we expected to be 100% perfect as well.

According to the Heavenly of Heavens, a relationship that starts as totally platonic friends will have a better chance of succeeding than any other relationship across the board. Why is the success rate better? There are no Spiritual Soul Ties or Yokes established in the Eye of God. In addition, this type of relationship allows you to get to know a person mentally and emotionally first. Therefore, the relationship is NOT based on LUST.

If a committed relationship cannot survive without any physical contact, foreplay, going out, affection, gifts, and so on, then you may want to question this relationship. In the Eye of God, this is the very reason why *Friends without Benefits* works best for those who really want to attract their soul mate. When someone is your best friend, you are able to communicate with them better than just being lovers.

In addition, without involving sexual relations, we can see people, places, and things for what they are without becoming Spiritually Puzzled or Frazzled. When we become experts in constructing our lives from the inside out, we can maintain a sense of balance when people, places, and things come to rock our boats, disrupting our lives. This sense of knowing keeps us from self-destructing when things do not go our way or when we do not get what we want, need, or hoped for. In the pursuit of excellence, it also helps us to self-correct, preventing us from becoming open bait or falling into the hidden traps of self-defeat.

Friends without Benefits can help us pinpoint those who are Spiritually Puzzled or Frazzled by a few factors:

- ☐ Their lack of self-control.
- ☐ Their loose lips.
- ☐ Their trigger-sensitive anger.
- ☐ Their unwillingness to love and forgive.
- ☐ Their egotistical demeanor.

Where Is The Love

- ☐ Their ability to become very chaotic when they cannot get their way.
- ☐ Their envy, jealousy, and coveting of others.
- ☐ Their competitiveness to outdo others or the way they compare themselves.
- ☐ Their negativity or hatefulness.
- ☐ Their stifled creativity.
- ☐ Their ability to find fault in others without offering a helping hand, mercy, or compassion.
- ☐ Their inability to share or help others when it is in their power to do so.

In the world of instant love and matchmaking, the *Wall Without Benefits* is a necessity. As a rule of thumb, with instant anything, we must exercise extreme caution. Matthew 26:41 says it like this: *"Watch and pray, lest you enter into temptation. The spirit indeed is willing, but the flesh is weak."*

In *The Lady's Code*, we as a whole need to become stimulated Mentally, Physically, Emotionally, and Spiritually in a teamified effort. If not, as *Women of Stature*, we will become a reflection of Samson, looking for love in all the wrong places, getting our strength zapped for laying our heads in the wrong lap.

As a forewarning, never seduce a person physically into committing. Why should we not use our bodies as leverage? It is a recipe for disaster. Seduction gets old when a person does not have the proper Emotional, Mental, or Spiritual support to sustain a seduced commitment.

In the complexity of relationships, the allure of physical attraction works most of the time. Still, it can often blur the lines between a genuine connection and outright manipulation. While seduction might seem like a pathway to achieving certain desires or commitments, using our bodies as leverage is not only morally questionable, but it is a self-created or self-induced trap.

How is enticement a trap? Please allow me to counteract this question with another. When our sex gets old, while our body parts get loose and worn out, our grip is not as tight as it was

Where Is The Love

formerly, or we begin to sag and drop; what do we have to work with? As *Women of Stature*, we need to know the answer to this question; if not, it is time to go back to the drawing board, *As It Pleases God*. While initial attraction may spark interest at first, it rarely sustains a relationship in the long run without the foundational support of freedom, respect, communication, and trust, along with stimulation using the Fruits of the Spirit.

When the initial surface-level thrill wears off, if our character sucks, our sex will fall into the same category in due season with all types of neglect, fostering insecurity, jealousy, resentment, disappointment, and turmoil. And while we think we have it going on in this area, our partner has mentally or emotionally checked out without having the guts to make mention of it. Therefore, if someone becomes hell-bent on getting us into bed without getting to know who we are from the inside out, rest assured, something in the pot is not clean.

According to *The Lady's Code*, true intimacy, *As It Pleases God*, extends far beyond the physical realm. Unbeknown to most, intimacy is more about seeing into someone Emotionally, Mentally, and Spiritually to develop a bonding *Spirit to Spirit* Connection. As *Friends Without Benefits*, they are indeed the vital components of a fulfilling relationship.

On behalf of the Heavenly of Heavens, here is the proper order for Divine Intimacy: We must surrender our will under God, first and foremost. Secondly, stimulate the mind positively. Thirdly, stimulate the emotions. With these three steps: If the person does not make our baby leap or make our inner child feel safe, BACK UP. And, lastly, through our Divine Alignment, *As It Pleases God*, the body will come to us by default without having to beg, fight, manipulate, or trick people into loving us. If *The Lady's Code* is out of this order, we will find ourselves backtracking or playing clean-up, especially when God has given us the option to get it right the first time.

Even if we presently have friends with or without benefits, casual connections, lost friendships, unresolved issues, or if we have fallen by the wayside in some way, we must assume total

Where Is The Love

responsibility for our choices, roles, and actions. In addition, we must communicate with God, ourselves, and others, expressing our needs, wants, and desires when applicable. Then, we need to become like Samson in the grinding mill with a plan, navigating challenges, learning to evolve, and moving with intentionality. As *Women of Stature*, this will give us the ability to gain strength in silence, *Setting Standards* to make a comeback to take our rightful position, *As It Pleases God*.

CHAPTER 11

SETTING STANDARDS

Do you have standards? Are you constantly updating your standards? Do you know why setting standards is essential? Are you aware of the benefits of having standards? In *The Lady's Code: As It Pleases God*, we must *Set Standards* to preserve our integrity.

As *Women of Stature*, our confidence or integrity lies in our ability to understand the true essence of who we are, *Setting Standards*, and sharing the Fruits of the Spirit, *As It Pleases God*. On the other hand, if we erect standards selfishly without Him, we will begin to judge or bully others into circumventing their assurance to make us feel better temporarily. Unbeknownst, the cycle continues as we spoil our own fruits without realizing it while dealing with all types of insecurities.

What I have found on my journey through life is that we put off things until tomorrow, yet our tomorrows become another tomorrow. For example, we are set to start a new project on a particular day, but we find ourselves saying, 'I will start tomorrow.' When the next day appears, we procrastinate. Then we say to ourselves again, 'I will start tomorrow.' The never-ending cycle of tomorrow comes and goes until we change our mindset to incorporate the NOW. If we take a moment to look at

Setting Standards

NOW closely, we will notice it reads WON in reverse! In my opinion, our change lies in the way we see the NOW and the choices we are making to WIN.

Backwardness is symbolically plaguing today's generation without us realizing what is happening until it is too late. Then we find ourselves hiding, running for cover, or trying to backpaddle to fix what we could have gotten right only if we *Set Standards*.

In the Eye of God and *The Lady's Code: As It Pleases Him*, it is okay to play our hands close to our chests. Nonetheless, when doing so, we must know what we are doing and the reasons why, while placing the Holy Trinity at the forefront. Thus, if we do it out of fear, arrogance, greed, or bad intentions, we create a disservice to ourselves and others, as it becomes a blockage instead of a source of protection or a guide.

In all simplicity, *Setting Standards* cannot be all about us, nor can we wallow in the past. We cannot build with old materials; we must remove the old ones and use the new ones. According to scripture, *"Neither do men put new wine into old bottles: else the bottles break, and the wine runneth out, and the bottles perish: but they put new wine into new bottles, and both are preserved."* Matthew 9:17. Most would think this is hard to do, but it is not. It is very simple if we learn Proper Protocol, Spiritual Principles and Laws, and *Set Standards* in alignment with the Kingdom, as well as applicable Scriptures and the Fruits of the Spirit.

Setting Standards that *PLEASE God* can inspire us to strive for a meaningful and fulfilling life. By aligning our actions with God's will, we can become better versions of ourselves and contribute to the Greater Good. When our countenance changes to deface our values, it is our responsibility to shift it back to what is conducive to our Predestined Blueprint or reason for being.

The moment we positively allow our conscience to become our guide, *As It Pleases God*, we can save ourselves from making the wrong decisions, thinking the wrong thoughts, saying the wrong things, or going down the wrong path by *Setting Standards*. In all reality, when we are looking for perfection, we tend to place ourselves in an inner prison that will keep us in bondage,

Setting Standards

continually trying to change, bully, degrade, or control others based on our superficial perceptions or biased expectations.

Standards or not, we must understand that no one is perfect, and we are all a work-in-progress, regardless of how we rationalize or deny it. In my opinion, if or when we choose to work on ourselves, it is always best to pray and ask for the ideal person, situation, circumstance, or event to help us grow. As opposed to forcing someone or something to become what it is NOT, or having to lower our standards to fit in. If we do, we will find the presumably perfect person, situation, circumstance, or event that will break us down to the core or traumatize us.

Why would we become traumatized as Believers? When we take God out of the equation or outright violate the will of another person who is not our child, we tend to deviate from Godly to worldly standards. In short, this means that we are setting false expectations for ourselves and others.

In *The Lady's Code*, we will always have something to work on or work at; therefore, we should not become so hard on ourselves when we fall short. What do we do if we fall short? We need to pick up the pieces, dust ourselves off, look for the good, add God into the equation, focus on the positive, and keep it moving in the Spirit of Excellence. Is it really this simple? Sometimes it is, and there are other times we must put in a little more work. If we need to do more, here is *The Lady's Code* checklist to adjust our mindsets, but not limited to such:

- ☐ Repeat this: "*I lift up my eyes to the hills. From where does my help come? My help comes from the Lord, who made heaven and earth.*" Psalm 121:1-2.
- ☐ Assume responsibility, even if it is not our fault.
- ☐ Opt out of playing the victim role.
- ☐ Unveil or narrow down the issue, problem, situation, or vice.
- ☐ Ask fact-finding questions in the What, When, Where, How, Why, and Whom formation.
- ☐ Understand the lesson, blessing, or testing.

Setting Standards

- ☐ Decide how it can be transformed into a win-win.
- ☐ Repent, forgive, and give thanks.
- ☐ Determine how it can help or benefit someone else.
- ☐ End with: "*I can do all things through Christ who strengthens me.*" Philippians 4:13.

We cannot go wrong opting to have a Spirit-Led life and allowing God to cause everything to work for our good. What does this mean for us? The piece that did not work in one phase of our lives will work in another one once we get into the right groove, *As It Pleases Him*.

According to *The Lady's Code*, I do not buy into the 50/50 relationship. As a *Woman of Stature*, I buy into the concept of the 100/100 relationship. One must be able to give 100% of oneself to make a relationship work. If not, how well does one expect a relationship to work when they are giving half of themselves? Here are a few ideal qualities that we should possess under the 80/20 Rule for ourselves. If one does not possess these qualities, it is not fair to expect them from someone else.

- ☐ Stability.
- ☐ Interdependent.
- ☐ Teachable.
- ☐ Flexible.
- ☐ Respectful.
- ☐ Encouraging.
- ☐ Positive.
- ☐ Loving.
- ☐ Joyful.
- ☐ Peaceful.
- ☐ Kind.
- ☐ Patient.
- ☐ Good.
- ☐ Faithful.
- ☐ Gentle.
- ☐ Control of Self.

Setting Standards

- ☐ Affectionate.
- ☐ Giving.
- ☐ Humorous.
- ☐ Resourceful.
- ☐ Cooperative.
- ☐ Open & Honest.
- ☐ Confident.
- ☐ Wise.
- ☐ Sincere.
- ☐ Supportive.
- ☐ Interesting.
- ☐ Loyal.
- ☐ Resourceful.
- ☐ Unselfish.
- ☐ Not Abusive.
- ☐ Protector.
- ☐ Not Lazy.

Why do we need a list? In *The Lady's Code*, lists are ideal for *Setting Standards*. We all need a little reminder from time to time, especially when life is lifing.

Personally, I need a checkup from the neck up as well...I am not just a writer; what I share with others is what I expect from myself, and I will self-correct immediately. There is no way that I can convey this type of information without going through some things...yes, some real stuff causing permanent battle scars! For this reason, I break things down with checklists and charts for the up-and-coming *Women of Stature*. I have not gone through all of this NOT to leave a BLUEPRINT for *The Lady's Code* behind, getting other women like myself prepared, *As It Pleases God*. Prepared for what? Prepared for anything life or the enemy throws at them.

Setting Standards

Who Is Really Winning

As life would have it, along with having standards, we must have rules. Of course, the rules of dating, mating, and relating are made and broken every day. Actually, they have now become a cat-and-mouse game to find out who is the strongest, slickest, or most intelligent at playing the game of love.

However, some people or circumstances are exceptions to the rule. Still, in the Eye of God, you will need to set some limits and boundaries to protect yourself. Then again, it is also done to prevent you from wasting valuable time with people who are not conducive to you or where you are going in life.

In my opinion, it is always best to forget about the game of deception because you can never win with bad energy, bad blood, or rotten fruit, even if you think you are ahead of the game or have won a few battles.

Why can we not win, especially when we are indeed winning? We will eventually turn on ourselves from the inside out, even if we seem to be presently winning. In the Eye of God, winning is a MINDSET, and the true test is whether or not we are winning behind closed doors or when no one is looking. If we cannot control what is going on between our ears and between our legs, then we must ask, 'Who is really winning?'

Remember, the psyche keeps track of our atrocities and uses them as weapons to control us behind closed doors with the lust of the eyes, the lust of the flesh, and the pride of life. What if it does not? Anything we do outside of the Will of God will fall under one of these categories, with a sidebar of power, money, sex, status, and fame.

The Lady's Code: As It Pleases God warns that if you want to use these Spiritual Rules, Principles, and Protocols to play mind games or to manipulate others, this is not the book for you. Meeting people when dating, mating, or relating is not a laughing matter. If you are not careful or honest with yourself, you can get caught up! Once this happens, it can affect you in ways that could cause you to become labeled as damaged goods.

Setting Standards

It is for this reason that one must date with a mission while making their intentions known without misleading or playing games with anyone. Let me say this before I move on: The Law of Reciprocity is in full effect. The games you play today can affect you or your family tomorrow; therefore, you must become ever so conscious of what you are doing and the reasons why.

Now that I have that out of the way, being true to yourself about how you are feeling about a particular relationship determines the reality of the outcome. Trust that your hormones can become very deceptive when you allow yourself to go with the flow, causing you to leap into a relationship with someone you may find incredibly desirable but who is not really the right one for you.

Dating, mating, or relating out of guilt or coercion is a big no-no! Never allow someone to force you to stay with them or love them; if your heart is not in it, walk away! Please do not wait until you become tied up with houses, cars, finances, and children before you decide it is not going to work. It is your responsibility to determine that before you get intertwined with everything, making it difficult to walk away when the mask comes off. Yes, the mask. If you do not know anything about the mask, then live a little longer.

When in the dating, mating, or relating phase of a relationship, everyone plays their role. As life would have it, they are usually always on their best behavior in order to get what they want; however, it is your responsibility to read the *Writing on the Wall*. If you do not pay attention and you allow the sex to get to your head to blind you to reality, then the joke will be on you. So, take heed in this process.

How do we take heed as Believers? By making a list of your likes and dislikes as you go. Yes, keep track of the relationship; do not wait until things start going wrong for you to start paying attention. If you do while having googly eyes, it may be too late by this time.

Setting Standards

Wall of Masks

Essentially, in the newness of a relationship, it is tough to distinguish the difference between love and lust. Yet, you can feel the attraction; therefore, it is up to you to determine which one it is. The next question is how to do this, right? Okay, let me answer the question. You must know your wants, likes, and dislikes in order to get a full understanding of the individual while staying out of the sack. Having sex changes the rules of the game, preventing you from seeing their fruits clearly.

In *The Lady's Code*, if you want to play by your rules as a *Woman of Stature*, you must keep your legs closed or pants up! You do not want your emotions tied to a person you do not fully know, nor do you want to have a Spiritual Transfer to occur. Why should we not become emotionally tied up? It makes it so much easier to detach when there are NO strings tied together, or when there are zero overwhelming, yokable bonds binding us to emotional or mental anchors.

Having soul ties is downplayed quite often; actually, most people do not give this a second thought, but I am going to say this: 'It is a real occurrence that should NOT be taken lightly.' In the dating process, getting your soul tied up with people you do not fully know or understand breaks all types of rules when it comes down to violating your Spiritual Temple (your body). Besides, bad relationships are a result of bad decisions, and you need to OWN this fact before you can perfect it! Therefore, you must ask yourself fact-finding questions first! Secondly, create healthy distances that allow you to foster personal growth and self-awareness.

In the presence or absence of yokable bonds, people are rehearsed. They will tell you what they think you want to hear, or they will repeat to you what YOU have told them you are looking for in a relationship. Do you actually think for a minute that someone will tell you, 'I am really crazy' or 'I am really F****d up?' The answer is NO. They will not tell you until you are drawn in, and when it is harder to let go. Listen, the first encounter with people will most often be their 'Masked Best!' You must also learn how to read between the lines with the Fruits of the Spirit, with

Setting Standards

your lips closed and your mind open, with a smile on your face, *As It Pleases God.*

Have you ever noticed that new relationships frequently show more emotions than old ones? Why does this happen? Possibly the lack of energy, but most often, it is because the newness has worn off, and the masks cannot remain hidden. More than likely, the attraction to the person under the mask has decreased the level of enthusiasm in a relationship. Sometimes, it is the little things in a relationship that turn a person off, such as snoring, forgetting, untidiness, weight gain, disabilities, financial status, occupation, etc. It causes a person to focus their attention elsewhere, such as working, sleeping, working out, bickering, cyber dating, infidelity, and so on.

Personally, it is for this very reason that I unveil my quirks, weaknesses, and flaws before my qualities. Why would I do that? If a person cannot accept my flaws, they cannot accept me, period! There is NO negotiation in this area—it is all of me or nothing. Why am I serious about this factor? It is because I know the TRUTH. What is the Truth? We all have flaws, and we are all a work-in-progress. For me, a person will not get to the diamond without knowing the impurities, grime, or dirt covering it.

Listen, our imperfections are hidden under layers of superficial facades and lies we have been conditioned to cover up through passing judgment, pointing fingers, or looking down on others. So, *The Lady's Code: As It Pleases God* requires someone to see through me and be as transparent as possible due to my God-Given Mission.

As we move on, when the thrill is gone in a relationship, the energy will soon follow. In my opinion, one will not put much energy into something or someone who has been deceptive. Therefore, it is always best to be open and honest about who you are and why you are.

If you have not noticed, I did not say to tell them what you WANT in a mate. In the initial stage of the relationship, you must keep this to yourself as you allow the Holy Spirit to bring the attraction to you. Why do we need to keep this to ourselves, especially when we are required to communicate effectively? The Holy Spirit has the *Spiritual Code* of what you truly need, want, and

Setting Standards

desire. If they go through Him to get to you, He will give the Spiritual Manifesto to pierce your heart, causing your inner child to respond positively.

This approach helps to alleviate the actors or actresses, wolves in sheep's clothing, and pretenders because you have not revealed to them what mask to wear to capture your heart. Does this principle work? Absolutely! It helps to bring out the natural qualities of the prospect in question. Nevertheless, it is your responsibility to pay attention to see if it aligns with your heart's desire.

When one allows God to bring the desires of one's heart, one does not have to tell a person what they are looking for. If they do not already know or possess the qualities, then it is a possibility that they may not be the ONE. When operating with the Holy Spirit, He does not miss the mark. He knows you better than you know yourself. So, if you are not aware of the desires of your own heart, you may miss the Spiritual Cues or red flags.

Rest assured, it is hard to pretend when the expectations are not set on your behalf or theirs. Simply put, if they do not know what they want, and you do not either...this is a recipe for disaster in due time. Why would there be a clash? You will bump heads because the expectations change based on what you feel, think, or see at the present moment, making you wishy-washy. Frankly, this is why dating, mating, or relating with someone is essential in the filtering process, sifting out the genuine deal from the raw deal, the bad deal, and the fake wannabe.

Once real love comes your way, you will not be able to stop thinking about this person. Trust that when the inner man is leaping from within, there will not be a question about it; however, you must control it to ensure you are able to think and function rationally. Let me say this: Uncontrollable love jones will cause you to do unwise things if left unchecked. Therefore, you must go through the same process of reading the *Writing on the Wall* and its varying FRUITS to ensure you do not get caught up.

Remember, no one is perfect, but you must pay attention to the *Writing on the Wall*; you never want to fall in love with the image of the person and not the real person or their counterfeit. Even if you

Setting Standards

feel that this is the right person for you, you must still guard your heart and follow *The Lady's Code: As It Pleases God.*

As *Women of Stature*, there is no need to rush or lose your marbles; take your time. Why should we take our time, especially when the competition is fierce? There is no competition when we place God first, *As It Pleases Him*. What belongs to you will be, and what does not will leave, period. *"But those who wait on the Lord Shall renew their strength; They shall mount up with wings like eagles, They shall run and not be weary, They shall walk and not faint."* Isaiah 40:31.

When embarking upon our relationship quest, we must commit to persevering through all obstacles, regardless of how we feel. Actually, we must consistently think of greatness by learning how to present ourselves strategically without becoming overbearing, desperate, pompous, or weak. We must also know and understand our purpose for doing what we are doing. It also helps us find out what we like and do not like in a relationship, be it personal, professional, or Spiritual. And then, repeat this scripture as a Spiritual Seal: *"Trust in the Lord with all your heart, And lean not on your own understanding; In all your ways acknowledge Him, And He shall direct your paths."* Proverbs 3:5-6.

Basically, we need to find out who needs what we have to offer. By knowing this, we are then able to create a sense of urgency or hunger for what we are offering. Of course, with experience and perseverance, we are then able to update, enhance, or make our simple plan outstanding by knowing seven things, but not limited to such:

- ☐ Know yourself and your Divine Purpose in life (not the self-made or self-created purpose).
- ☐ Know how you can make a difference.
- ☐ Know what you want and do not want.
- ☐ Know the impact of what you have to offer.
- ☐ Know your competition and WHY.
- ☐ Know how you are going to create the urgency for your qualities.

Setting Standards

☐ Know how you are going to share what you have to generate positive results in your life, *As It Pleases God*.

We must master our qualities by diligently getting to know what is in our hearts while making the adjustments to love, serve, and assist those with whom we have a relationship.

As the competition challenges us, we must know and understand what we have to offer without becoming insecure and weak about it. In *The Lady's Code*, we do not have to buy our mate. If a man can be bought with material gain by a woman, he is not worth it, and if a woman can be bought with material gain by a man, she is not worth it. We should never buy love; we should share our love by doing simple things 'just because' for those we date, mate, or relate to.

We must keep our gifts as inexpensive as possible. What is the purpose of doing so? We can pinpoint if they are grateful or ungrateful. Most of our divorces today are centered around unreconcilable differences relating to power, money, sex, selfishness, and ungratefulness.

As a rule of thumb for the *Women of Stature*, love is not something that can be bought; it is a chosen feeling coming from the heart and cannot be measured by material possessions. The Bible teaches us to love one another unconditionally without expecting anything in return. It is important to value relationships based on mutual respect, trust, gratefulness, and affection instead of material possessions. Clearly, this will prevent us from losing out before we really begin.

Some relationships may work, and some may not, so we must keep our budgets to a minimum. For the record, I am not saying we should not help the person we are in a relationship with, because we should. If they are suffering, and we sit back and let them suffer, something is DEFINITELY WRONG, and one should find an exit with this individual.

What if it is not our responsibility to help them? In the Eye of God, **SHARING** is required of us. *"And do not forget to do good and to share with others, for with such sacrifices God is pleased."* Hebrews 13:16.

Setting Standards

"Whoever oppresses the poor shows contempt for their Maker, but whoever is kind to the needy honors God." Proverbs 14:31. On the other hand, all I am saying is that we should not **BUY** or **PROSTITUTE** them, nor should we allow ourselves to become **USED**. It is time out for the gold-digging mentality or using someone's condition to control them for our benefit, or stroking the ego.

Standing In The Gap

Have you ever had someone stand in the gap for you? Do you stand in the gap for others? Wait, wait, wait, do you even know what *Standing in the Gap* is, according to Kingdom Standards? Well, before we move to the *Wall of Temptation*, it is only fair for me to *Stand in the Gap* for you, providing the Divine Wisdom necessary to withstand the enemy's wiles.

What if we do not need you to *Stand In The Gap*? If you did not, you would not be reading this book. You see, this is not an ordinary book; this is a Spiritual Testament of Divinely Spoken Words from the Heavenly of Heavens; therefore, in order for me to Spiritually Download, *As It Pleases God*, I must *Stand In The Gap* for the Kingdomly NEXT, passing the Divine Mantle. In all simplicity, this is not for me; it is for you! Now, once you get what you need, you must do likewise with another to form a Spiritual Seal (mark of authenticity and commitment), solidifying what you gleaned.

What if we hoard this information? What harm could it do? We have free will to do whatever we like with the information received. Nonetheless, we do limit its potential impact, especially when operating in such a selfish manner.

Here is the deal: The way the Kingdom of God works, we must activate the Law of Reciprocity to *Stand In The Gap* for another. In *Setting Standards*, we are not here to fix anyone; that is God's job. Unfortunately, this common pitfall of fixing others causes us to play demigods in the lives of others or make ourselves out to be idols to them while having the nerve to lie about it. When *Standing In The Gap*, we are here to share and serve others with profound

Setting Standards

knowledge, understanding, wisdom, and Spiritual Insight, *As It Pleases God*, for the uplifting and growth of another.

Conversely, suppose we decide to stunt the growth or create an even wider gap for our benefit. In this case, we will get a Spiritual Side-Eye from our Heavenly Father with an onslaught of all types of temptations galore.

According to the Heavenly of Heavens, the goal is to build a bridge, stairway, or highway of continual flowing, beneficial, and relevant Divine Information, Wisdom, and Insight to feed God's sheep. Why is this not a one-and-done process? Everyone's gap is not created equal, nor are they the same.

When *Standing In The Gap*, we need the Divine Presence of the Holy Spirit with the Covering of the Blood of Jesus to make the proper delivery of timely information. Doing so ensures we are not operating with dated material. Picturesquely, we cannot use a dial-up connection or method of operation when a broadband or fiber-optic connection is required. As *Women of Stature*, we must remain on a Spiritual Learning Curve, becoming better, stronger, and wiser to ensure that when we have to pour into another, it is pure and authentic.

When we pour into another, we do not want what we pour out to be muddy, tainted, or toxic because it stains the human psyche to its detriment with scarring residue. In the Eye of God, it must be pure, clear, and concise...although they may get wet, once they dry off, the penetration becomes wefted into the fibers of their being for the Greater Good without having a negative residual residue. Here is the pattern to follow according to Titus 2:7-8: *"In all things showing yourself to be a pattern of good works; in doctrine showing integrity, reverence, incorruptibility, sound speech that cannot be condemned."*

Whether we are filling in the gap, having our gaps filled, or *Standing In The Gap*, Philippians 4:8 says, *"Finally, brethren, whatever things are true, whatever things are noble, whatever things are just, whatever things are pure, whatever things are lovely, whatever things are of good report, if there is any virtue and if there is anything praiseworthy—meditate on these things."*

CHAPTER 12

WALL OF TEMPTATION

Have you ever noticed that the things that you cannot have tasted better than what you have an abundance of? Like clockwork, it never fails. The *Writing on the Wall* says, 'Temptation is Sweet,' which means that Proverbs 9:17 was not lying when it said, *"Stolen water is sweet, and bread eaten in secret is pleasant."* Therefore, I am going to begin this *Wall* with a statement: 'The best way to catch a Bee is with honey.'

If we do not believe in temptation...we will if we are put in the right situation, with the right person, with our type, at the right time, or when we are about to lose our mate to another person. Only then will we understand the Power of Temptation. Plus, it is easy to say what we will not do until our fleshly desires get a taste of something really sweet that our taste buds like.

In the realm of living real life, if someone says to me that they do not have a type, I know they are lying, and I do not trust them as far as I can see them. Why is trust not extended to them? While it may seem like a harmless statement, I perceive it as a red flag, leading to distrust. We are all both consciously and subconsciously prewired and conditioned with likes and dislikes hidden in the word called PREFERENCES. What we attract is an intricate interplay of our genetic makeup, natural science,

Wall of Temptation

psychology, conditioning, biases, and experiences, which leads to liking certain types of music, art, foods, colors, and so on. Therefore, if someone lies about this, then it is fair to ask, 'What else are they lying about?'

For this reason, in *The Lady's Code: As It Pleases God*, I stay far away from those with an anything-goes mentality or those who do not have any standards whatsoever, particularly concerning their character, behaviors, values, method of operation, and personal standards. And so should you! Proverbs 25:28 warns us: "*Whoever has no rule over his own spirit is like a city broken down, without walls.*"

How do we pinpoint an anything-goes mentality? We must pay attention to their fruits, using basic discernment and integrity. It does not take a rocket scientist to determine right from wrong, good from bad, just from unjust, and so on. However, when choosing your circle, *As It Pleases God*, it is best to choose those who uplift and challenge you to grow for the Greater Good.

The fear of temptation loses its grip when you are 100% committed to the success of your relationship, friendship, or marriage. However, just because you are committed does not mean that temptation does not exist or that your spouse, mate, or date will be 100% committed to the success of the relationship as well. As *Women of Stature*, when you become 100% honest with yourself about what you feel, you are better able to deflect or deflect what is tempting you and causing you to break *The Lady's Code*.

Here is the truth about the *Wall of Temptation*: We all have secrets, we all have desires, we all have fantasies, and we all have temptations we dare not act upon or tell anyone about. How do I know? Because we are human! We are all tempted by something; if we are not, then we have to live a little longer. However, our temptations should never outweigh our victories. By engaging in introspection and psychological exploration, we can gain a more profound understanding of our motivations, desires, behaviors, habits, and the essence of who we are becoming. What does this mean? Self-examination is crucial for authentic growth.

Wall of Temptation

The Psyche's Attempt To Control

When we question our thoughts, desires, words, biases, and behaviors, we start to peel back the layers of our psyche, revealing the underlying emotions, thoughts, insecurities, traumas, and experiences driving us or patterning our lifestyles. Even if we are in denial, the show still must go on with or without our participation. Moreover, if we do not participate in counteracting the negatives to the positives, we will remain stuck on the negatives.

Being that the psyche is very complex and fickle and not easily understood, it often has the 'one up' on us because we do not use the Fruits of the Spirit as we should.

Should it not be Fruit of the Spirit instead of Fruits of the Spirit? From a Kingdomly Perspective, Fruit of the Spirit is ONE, meaning we already possess them all, *As It Pleases God*. Whereas, as we are a work-in-progress, we must divide them into Fruits as a plural because we do not have it all together yet; therefore, when dealing with the psyche, you must use them one by one for the multiplicity of issues, which equates to the Fruits of the Spirit.

Please allow me to paint a picturesque view when pluralizing our Spiritual Fruits: For example, before we go a mile, we are required to take steps; each step leads up to the mile, but until we get there, our steps are counted, one by one. Then again, in a Calendar, we have months and days to make up one year, and there is no way to get to the complete year without days and months, unless we are removed from the elements of time. Nevertheless, here is the Spiritual Covenant from Genesis 8:22: *"While the earth remains, seedtime and harvest, cold and heat, winter and summer, and day and night shall not cease."* This concurs that we are stuck with Cycles and Seasons from the Divine Order set forth in Genesis 1:14: *"Then God said, 'Let there be lights in the firmament of the heavens to divide the day from the night; and let them be for signs and seasons, and for days and years.'"*

What do our Spiritual Fruits have to do with months? In all simplicity, if we are a part of the Divine Tribe and desire Divine Healing from the Heavenly of Heavens, this is how we need to be Spiritually Aligned for the Movement of God. Here is what Revelation 22:2 says, *"In the middle of its street, and on either side of the*

Wall of Temptation

river, was the tree of life, which bore twelve fruits, each tree yielding its fruit every month. The leaves of the tree were for the healing of the nations."

If we approach the psyche as if we have it all together, it will have us for lunch based on what is occurring in our days, nights, cycles, and seasons. Why would this happen? It is warring for control; therefore, it keeps track of our comings and goings, even when we think we are slick or have outsmarted God. James 4:1 says it best: *"Where do wars and fights come from among you? Do they not come from your desires for pleasure that war in your members?"*

Is this not all a play on words using the Fruits of the Spirit? Maybe or maybe not, but if we have NOT tamed our psyche or know nothing about it, then it is only WISE to listen up. The Spiritual Shakedown is upon us, and if we are not using the Fruits of the Spirit, *As It Pleases God,* the impact will have a bullseye on our hearts and minds. Science cannot help us, the government cannot help us, nor can the best psychiatrist help us with the Spiritual Matters readily upon us.

For the sake of the *Wall of Temptation,* here is a viable example from a Divine Perspective on how the psyche turns our Spiritual Fruits against us:

- ☐ We are advised to LOVE God, ourselves, and others, but we selfishly allow hate to rule and reign as we fight over power, money, sex, fame, status, and followers.

- ☐ We are directed to be JOYFUL, but we choose not to take advantage of it because we are too busy fighting over who is right and who is wrong.

- ☐ We are instructed to be PEACEFUL, yet we are deadset on warring with God, ourselves, and others, with jealousy, envy, pride, greed, coveting, and competitiveness driving our actions, thoughts, beliefs, desires, and conversations.

- ☐ We are told to be PATIENT, but anxiety dominates our mind, body, and soul with instantaneous everything without Spiritual Discretion, Discernment, or Alignment.

Wall of Temptation

While simultaneously opting to create our own illusion of blessings with bodacious acts of idolatry or playing demigods.

- ☐ We are urged to be KIND, but unkindness has become our liberating go-to as we run around like hellions on wheels without a conscience, doing whatever, whenever, however, and whyever.

- ☐ We are advised to exhibit GOODNESS, but we always find ourselves doing bad things while justifying our thoughts, actions, desires, and biases.

- ☐ We are taught to be FAITHFUL, but unfaithfulness has become our secret plague as if God is not watching, as if He does not exist, or as if He made a mistake.

- ☐ We are taught to be GENTLE, but abrasiveness permeates our words, thoughts, actions, and reactions, causing us to lose respect for God, ourselves, and others.

- ☐ We are warned to exude SELF-CONTROL, but the lust of the eyes, the lust of the flesh, and the pride of life are driving us out of control.

Exploring our psyche with the Fruits of the Spirit can serve as a stepping stone towards growth and development to become a Divine Cornerstone in the Eye of God. Conversely, without using them, *As It Pleases Him*, life will begin to read us as a plague, mangling our fruits to the core. Is this Biblical? Once again, I would have it no other way. Matthew 21:19 says, "*And seeing a fig tree by the road, He came to it and found nothing on it but leaves, and said to it, 'Let no fruit grow on you ever again.' Immediately the fig tree withered away.*"

Wall of Temptation

Weighing the Risk - Jim and Lucy's Writing on the Wall

According to *Jim and Lucy's Writing on the Wall*, most individuals who indulge in the act of temptation usually start out very innocently. When our initial innocence becomes overshadowed by an unconscious shift in behavior, it can lead us down a slippery slope, especially when filling our mental and emotional needs, desires, and habits without corrective measures. In navigating the complexities of temptation, it is imperative to recognize the motivations behind why we indulge while setting reasonable boundaries and effective strategies.

Jim and Lucy have cultivated a wonderful marriage over the past four years, filled with shared experiences, mutual respect, and deep affection. However, recently, their love story encountered an unexpected twist: Lucy's ex-boyfriend, a figure from her past, has retired from the military and moved back to their town. This change has introduced new dynamics into their relationship, requiring careful navigation and understanding.

Lucy's relationship with her ex-boyfriend, while part of a different chapter in her life, brings to the surface feelings and memories that can complicate the present. It is amazing how a familiar face can spark a wave of emotions and memories, especially after having deep-seated feelings for someone.

The local diner was just another routine stop for Lucy's morning coffee before an important 10 o'clock meeting. Little did she know, this was the day she would unwittingly change her schedule and perhaps her perspective.

As she settled into her favorite booth, the aroma of coffee brewing in the air, Lucy's heart skipped a beat. Ross, her ex-boyfriend, walked through the door. Without hesitation, the excitement caused her mind to race with memories of their shared laughter and bonds. 'Ross!' she called out with a loud voice of anticipation. They exchanged warm greetings while they were both clearly surprised by their chance of reunion. At that moment, Lucy made a quick decision, reaching for her phone to cancel her meeting.

Wall of Temptation

They settled into their fun-loving conversation over steaming cups of coffee, time slipping away as they reminisced, sharing fond memories of adventures, silly mistakes, and the innocence of young love. After three hours had passed, she finally told Ross that she was happily married, and he advised her that he was engaged.

As they parted ways, they exchanged contact information. Over the next couple of months, Lucy and Ross exchanged emails daily, but Lucy deleted her emails to ensure her husband did not see them. Lucy and Ross met for lunch several times, but she would always tell her husband she was meeting her girlfriends.

As reality begins to set in, Lucy starts to feel a little guilty, and she is not sure if she should tell her husband about Ross. Jim, though confident in their bond, may naturally experience feelings of unease or jealousy, wondering how this reunion could impact their marriage.

On the other hand, with this temptation, she knew if she got caught, it would damage her relationship with her husband. Plus, she also did not want to damage her relationship with Ross because he put her through college. She had no intentions of having an affair with Ross, but if she does not tell Jim about him, it would be considered an affair because she is being dishonest. As a result, Lucy spent a couple of days trying to figure out how to handle this situation.

So, she decided to tell her husband about Ross; she explained how he helped her through school after her mother died. For this reason, she did not want to be unkind to a person who extended kindness to her in her time of need. She also explained how she was afraid to tell him about the situation because she did not know how he was going to react.

Lucy reassured Jim of her commitment, reinforcing that their relationship is her top priority. Conversely, Jim's willingness to listen and share his concerns fostered a bond of trust between the two of them, as they willingly discussed boundaries related to interactions. In hopes of not burning any bridges, she wanted him to meet Ross and his fiancée. Her husband thought it was a great idea. They met, they got along, and they all became best friends.

Wall of Temptation

Lucy realized that if she wanted Jim to remain her husband, she had to be honest without putting herself in a position to become tempted to break *The Lady's Code*. Ross is now married, and he is really thankful to Lucy for teaching him a valuable lesson about honesty. They are all the best of friends, doing everything as a group.

As *Women of Stature*, we must protect ourselves when moving ahead in life. In addition, we must also be cautious of how things may appear. Not to please others but to set an example, *As It Pleases God.* When we move ahead, there will always be those who are designed to get us off track. Most often, it is through our environment or conversations that we lower our guard to people, places, and things that appear to have our backs.

For this reason, in *The Lady's Code*, we must evaluate our conversations carefully. Why must we govern our conversations accordingly? It is through the conversations we entertain that we get sidetracked, even if we are trying to do the right thing in our relationships.

Now, if there is some form of temptation that has the potential to cause you to suffer great loss, please do not, and I mean do not, put yourself in a position to become tempted or defiled. Sometimes, you cannot even entertain certain conversations with certain people because it is so easy to have an affair without having sex.

Secret meetings such as lunches, dinners, movies, vacations, etc., with a person of the opposite sex without the knowledge of your mate or spouse open the door to temptation. If you have to hide something like this, something is definitely wrong, and you need to reevaluate your intentions. Just entertaining such issues and thoughts lays the foundation for an affair to occur in the mind. Yes, you may be strong, but once again, you are human!

We do make mistakes! For this reason, in *The Lady's Code*, here are some tips to help you protect yourself as a *Woman of Stature*:

- ☐ Trust yourself to do the right thing.
- ☐ Know and understand what you are feeling and why.

Wall of Temptation

- ☐ Make sure you are doing it for you and no one else.
- ☐ Avoid sexually explicit conversations.
- ☐ Watch out for the intimate touching or feeling.
- ☐ Guard your heart.
- ☐ Do not go near a place you know that will entertain or feed your weakness.
- ☐ Do not consume your mind with lustful or perverted thoughts. Replace those thoughts with something constructive and positive.
- ☐ Focus on your self-control from the inside out, not the outside in.
- ☐ Keep yourself active and busy.
- ☐ Pray.

The taste of temptation is delightful, and regardless of what type of temptation we are faced with, if we are able to think our way into it, we are able to think our way out. With *The Lady's Code*, we must grow through our temptations to ensure we experience the fullness of life in our relationships.

Victorious living is within your reach; all you have to do is stay focused with a positive attitude while having an idea of what, when, how, where, and why temptations are designed to come your way.

Now, as a *Woman of Stature*, if you fall, the last thing you ever want to do is wallow in self-pity, self-defeat, or shame. From me to you, that is not your portion, primarily when it is so easy to gird up your loins and walk or flow in victorious living by repenting, forgiving, and moving forward in the Spirit of Excellence.

In *The Lady's Code: As It Pleases God*, it is not the way in which you tell your story when you are tempted that creates victory. It is the way in which you take the time to LIVE your story through the temptation that creates victory in the Eye of God.

Wall of Temptation

The Cheater Within - Brad's Writing on the Wall

Understanding is the best way to tame the cheater from within, as well as the cheater within someone else. If you bash cheaters, do you really think your spouse, mate, or partner would tell you if they cheated or are tempted to cheat? More than likely, they will not until they are caught. By then, the damage has already been done. Not only that, but when we have an understanding of our mate's wants, needs, and desires, we are better able to fulfill them.

The *Writing on the Wall* claims the best way to tame the cheater from within is to understand what triggers the urge to cheat. In order to truly understand the trigger, we must take the time to understand our behavioral patterns associated with the process of cheating.

In *The Lady's Code*, being equipped with this information, we become better able to pinpoint the release of the cheater from within, allowing us to exercise self-control. Actually, once we gain control over ourselves to understand our trigger points properly, then we are able to find the source.

In the Eye of God, our ability to find the source of our trigger points is really based on our values and belief systems associated with:

- ☐ Sexual Addictions.
- ☐ Traditional (Family) Addictions.
- ☐ Emotional Addictions.
- ☐ Drama Addictions.
- ☐ Deception Addictions.
- ☐ Passion Addictions.
- ☐ Attention Addictions.
- ☐ Trauma Addictions.
- ☐ Control Addictions.

Although these addictions can lead to other disorders, in *The Lady's Code*, we begin with these. In the Eye of God, there is always a reason why we do what we do, and until we take the time to

Wall of Temptation

understand the underlying meaning of our actions, we will not change. Unless the pain of not changing supersedes the pain of making the transition not to cheat. Yes, the pain that is associated with taming the cheater has a way of taming the most sophisticated cheater.

In Brad's *Writing on the Wall*, it unveils a valuable lesson associated with *The Cheater Within* a Playboy, having nothing to do with freedom, confidence, or charisma. In essence, the cheater is often not just someone who betrays a partner, but also someone who wrestles with internal conflicts, emotional struggles, and unresolved trauma, stemming from insecurities, longings, and fears. The Playboy may project an image of self-assuredness, yet it often masks a profound fear of commitment and emotional intimacy. This contradiction sets the stage for a cycle of deception and superficial connections, especially when having the audacity to brag about it openly as a badge of honor.

Beverly was the kind of girl who grew up surrounded by the sprawling hills, reading, riding horses, and dreaming of adventures beyond her little world. Her mind was one of imagination and exploration, where the pages of her favorite books transported her to lands of adventure, romance, science, and mystery. With each turn of a page, she envisioned daring pursuits and epic voyages, filling her mind with stories stretching far beyond the confines of her current situation. Each storyline inspired her to dream bigger—to fantasize about the life she could have, the places she could go, and the adventures she would someday embark upon.

Brad, on the other hand, was a smooth-talking city boy with an air of confidence hard to miss, living on the edge and straddling the fence in all areas of his life, while ironically hating reading. Books were not a part of his repertoire, and he could not see the forest for the trees. Instead, he preferred the thrill of the nightlife and the excitement of social gatherings, putting him on center stage. To him, reading was a boring afterthought, distracting him from being God's gift to women.

Brad downplayed the idea of reading, although he could read. But for some odd reason, he did not like taking the time to expand his mind in such a manner because he depended on others to keep

Wall of Temptation

him updated. His self-absorbed confidence stemmed from his understanding of people, his ability to navigate or dominate conversations, and his talent for making connections without ever thinking there is more to life than the fast lane.

At first glance, Brad and Beverly's worlds seemed incompatible, like night and day. Yet, there was an undeniable spark between the two, creating flames of dire interest. Beverly, with her gentle spirit and warm heart, was drawn to Brad's worldliness due to the presumed excitement and adventure it held. Despite their differences, He captivated her with energetic stories of city life, which were foreign to her yet still fascinating. She did not know where her venture on the wild side would take her; nonetheless, she welcomed the experience with open arms.

As fate would have it, their relationship blossomed, and Beverly began to dip her toes into the rich, vibrant life Brad shared; however, her life of simplicity was boring to him, and he wanted no part of the sprawling hills lifestyle. As the bustling city continued to call his name, Brad slowly began to remove his innocent, loving face to reveal the bad boy he indeed was.

As they forged their unique bond, getting Beverly right where he wanted her, he let it all hang out. It became clear that Brad was a man unafraid to embrace his identity as a self-proclaimed playboy with little interest in masking his intentions. He was comfortable showing his true colors; he had Playboy tattoos, Playboy accessories, and basically, he had Playboy everything. He even had a Playboy bungalow. This arrogant playboy even referred to women as his B...ches!

Brad became absolutely candid with Beverly about his pursuits, often discussing his wild escapades with a nonchalance that was both entertaining and repulsive. Beverly struggled to reconcile these qualities with her own more romantic ideas of love and partnership. Yet, it was unwittingly precisely what fueled their connection in the first place.

Sadly, what we envision in our minds from reading a book does not equate to living this type of love triangle adventure in real time. As the veil was ripped from Beverly's eyes, she realized that Brad was a womanizer at heart, flaunting his bodaciousness as if he were the best thing since sliced bread. This little smirk believed he had enough money to get any woman he wanted because he believed every woman had her price.

In addition, Brad also believed every woman wanted a luxurious lifestyle, and they would allow him to do whatever he wanted as long as he sold them a dream and gave them a little piece of the pie every now and then. And the ones who did not fall for the okey-doke, he demeaned by character assassinating, dumbifying them, or forcing them to run and hide from his brutal mouth. Undoubtedly, Brad's forthrightness about his lifestyle forced Beverly to question her perceptions of love, challenging her to reconsider what she truly desired in a partner.

As they navigated their evolving bond, for some odd reason, Beverly, the innocent country bumpkin, subconsciously thought she could change Brad into a good boy. She read enough books to know that beneath his Playboy persona was a man searching for meaning and sincerity, grappling with his own fears, doubts, traumas, and insecurities. She also knew his flirtatious antics were often a mask for his struggles with intimacy, commitment, responsibility, and a desire for an authentically real connection.

Although Brad did love her, his former lifestyle and habits clawed their way back into his psyche. So, every time they took a step forward, an underlying tension would pull them a step back. This cycle of advancement and regression became a defining aspect of their relationship, rooted in Brad's struggle against his own inner demons. By his refusal to read to keep his mind occupied with positive information, he battled with the constant cycle of relapsing back into his Playboy mentality with a constant loop of negative thoughts, trauma, and behaviors despite his intentions.

In a world overflowing with positive content to inspire and uplift, he opted out of the healing power of books, articles, and personal development resources. Reading could have provided him with the tools necessary to cultivate a more positive mindset, helping him to address his temptations and insecurities. Instead, he allowed himself to revert to his old Playboy patterns.

Beverly thought her beauty, encouragement, and support were enough for Brad, but she was sadly mistaken. It was not enough

Wall of Temptation

to keep a man who did not want to be kept. Ultimately, when dealing with the Power of Love, it requires not only commitment or attraction, but also continuous effort to GROW as individuals and together as ONE.

For Brad, understanding he needed to read, reflect, and cultivate a positive mindset would be crucial in breaking the cycle of tension and relapse; however, he hated reading. As a result, he opted to revert to his old lifestyle because it was easier for him. He chose to disregard the long-term benefits of personal development for the short-term comfort of his old lifestyle.

In a troubling turn of events, as a great big slap in the face, and after all the work Beverly put in to help him to help himself, he began to introduce her to his other girlfriends as if she were merely an acquaintance, diminishing the connection they had built.

In his reluctance to embrace change, Brad began to brush Beverly off more and more to be with other women who appeared to be prettier and more educated than her. She was devastated that it could be easier for Brad to detach and act as though those connections held little significance. Nevertheless, she finally concluded He did not want anything from her other than for her to let him do what he wanted and to get a little nookie on demand.

Beverly grew tired of being used by Brad, and she was no longer willing to share him with another woman. She was tired of being Miss Goody Two-Shoes. Moreover, she refused to be his little country bumpkin SECRET, that he places on the back burner while bringing other women who resemble her to the forefront.

When writing her story, I could not believe this man was placing a search for women who looked exactly like her...but who would be willing to do the bag girl things Beverly was not willing to do. He even paid them to keep their mouths shut about his extremely freaky, mischievous acts and not to expose those little, nasty rendezvous to Beverly. While at the same time, claiming he knew how to pick women.

Wait a minute here: Paying women and picking women are two different things. So, I asked Beverly, 'The same women he pretended to have are really paid sex workers?' Her response was, 'Yes.' All the women he brought in her face to make her jealous

Wall of Temptation

were paid to do so, while he pretended to be a playboy...it was all a lie. To her ultimate chagrin, he was buying pleasure, time, and favors from sex workers.

Beverly was not having this; dealing with a Playboy and prostitutes was a bit much for her; it was time to exit. She began this process by using the law of detachment; she detached herself from Brad mentally, emotionally, and physically—meaning 'NO SEX, NO SLEEP-OVERS, NO HANGING OUT, NO DATING, LIMITED CONVERSATIONS, and NO FUZZY WUZZY.'

She no longer had time for Brad's disrespectful foolishness. She became very secretive; she did not discuss her personal life with Brad, nor did she have a desire to listen to him, which meant no more free counseling sessions. When Brad calls, she uses the 30-second rule—she cannot hold a conversation with Brad for more than 30 seconds. She could not argue, fuss, fight, become angry, or react to anything Brad did or said; she could only use pleasant greetings while showering him with kindness.

After a couple of months of this, Brad began to act like an absolute fool. He constantly called her, and he started following her around, increasingly showing up in places where she was, seemingly uninvited. Actually, Brad became borderline psychotic when this country girl stepped up her game. He pondered the fact that not only was she attractive, but she was brilliant as well. He was definitely not accustomed to having wise women around him. Believe it or not, he began to see Beverly differently.

He begged her for a date, and she stood him up several times; she chose to occupy her time with more beneficial friends! Is Beverly a good girl gone bad? Brad could not believe the shoe was on the other foot.

He now understood how it really felt to be played. The pain of being thrown to the side by Beverly provoked the desire for him to change his ways. He begged Beverly to become his woman again; she refused. He even proposed to her; she refused.

The damage had already been done, and Beverly was not going to risk loving a newly reformed playboy. She was not going to risk being deceived a second time.

Wall of Temptation

Her mom embedded this analogy in her: 'Get me once, shame on you; get me twice, shame on me; get me thrice, I get what I deserve!' After all of the begging and pleading, she stated to Brad, 'Although I am a country girl, I am not stupid, and you cannot undo my broken heart, and your type of love is not good enough for me anymore.'

Even though Brad and Beverly did not get back together, she did indeed contribute to having Mr. Playboy Brad readjust his Playboy Mentality. Brad is indeed a player at heart, but now he is a player with limits, boundaries, and respect. He is now a pastor and faithfully married. He no longer engages in the act of cheating, but he must put the cheating spirit under the subjection of the Holy Spirit daily.

Beverly is married as well; she has a wonderful husband whom she met soon after she detached herself from Brad. If she had not detached herself from Brad, she would have missed out on her perfectly chosen triple-braided cord soul mate.

Wall of Relations

Who wants to be around someone who cannot relate to them? I do not! I will find the quickest exit! I am indeed a social butterfly; however, if someone is resistant to my relatability, I do not force it; I simply move on. Even if you are not the most beautiful, handsome, brilliant, wisest, influential, affluent, charming, or funniest, you can become relatable.

In order to truly master *The Lady's Code: As It Pleases God*, you must sharpen your people skills, being able to relate to anyone on any level and at any time. As a *Woman of Stature*, this gives you flexibility when dating, mating, and relating in a relationship or marriage.

If communication is not your strongest asset, you can work on it every day. In my younger days, I had poor communication skills. Ironically, they were so bad that I would shut down and not talk at all for days. However, I turned my weakness into my greatest strength, and so can you. I am living proof; thus, I am not telling you something I have not experienced myself. I have learned how to take a negative situation and create a win-win situation out of

Wall of Temptation

it, becoming a master communicator with excellent people skills to bring forth *The Lady's Code: As It Pleased God*.

Nevertheless, I have a little secret...okay, a big SECRET. The secret sauce to my communication skills is that I learned the power of asking fact-finding and relevant questions. In order to spark an interest in you, you must become interested in what other people are doing. It is not a fix people session; this is simply showing interest in what they are doing by asking questions.

Even if you do not have a clue about what they are doing, keep in mind the *What, When, Where, How*, and *Why* questions, and you will always have something to talk about. Once you become interested in them, by default, they will become interested in what you are doing. Of course, it may seem a little awkward at first, but the more you do it, the more it will become second nature for you. Just keep it fun without breaking eye contact with them. Clearly, this is not considered flirting; it is called relating!

When you can relate, you can build a circle of friends that you can connect with. When getting to know people, it is not always about you. Building connections creates a network that must give back to you in due time. In the Eye of God, this is called the Law of Reciprocity....the give and receive concept.

When you learn how to relate, you will also learn how to share relations with others to create BLESSINGS for them, as well as yourself. Listen, as you already know, not everyone is for everybody, and by the Law of the Land, if you connect to love, love has to connect back with you. Once you create this flow, you can pick and choose the desires of your heart.

According to your Divine Design, you are created to love and be loved. In *The Lady's Code*, you must never become your worst critic by thinking you do not deserve it; go for it! With this in mind, once you become an expert on authentically relating to love...You will become a POWERHOUSE in your own right!   Here are a few characteristics that will keep you on top of your game:

- ☐ Believe in yourself.
- ☐ Exude confidence.
- ☐ You must learn and educate yourself on a continuous basis.

Wall of Temptation

- ☐ Always appear charming and flattering—keep yourself up.
- ☐ Your attitude must represent strength and honor.
- ☐ Always have a plan of action.
- ☐ Be very strategic if you have to, creating a win-win situation out of everything, regardless of how it may appear.
- ☐ You must be very courageous and go after what you want.
- ☐ Never look at yourself as a loser.
- ☐ Do not associate with people who would cause you to lose. If you are going in different directions, part ways immediately.
- ☐ Do not take NO for an answer; be proactive enough to get yourself closer to a Yes.
- ☐ Set and accomplish your goals by exhausting all of your resources.
- ☐ You must stand behind your beliefs and find people who would contribute to your belief system.
- ☐ You must exhibit faithfulness by not being easily swayed by others.
- ☐ You must become a person of diversity who does not mind sharing your way of doing things.
- ☐ You must become very resourceful.
- ☐ Learn how to gain an alliance of people who would help, nurture, or coach you.
- ☐ You must become passionate about your own truth.

In *The Lady's Code*, the groundwork for GREATNESS starts with you. As *Women of Stature*, we banish the superficial limitations and relational distractions to embrace all God has for us as we become personal magnets of Divine Appeal in the Eye of God.

In conclusion, my sisters, my friends, and my successors, let nothing stop you from achieving what God has placed inside of you. Remember, this book, *The Lady's Code*, is for you! I have laid out the roadmaps, charts, and blueprints for you with all simplicity. Please use them for the GREATER GOOD, set a guard

Wall of Temptation

over your heart, and do what you have been called to do, *As It Pleases God*, and in the Spirit of Excellence.

Above all, exercise caution when living your best life, and understand that the *Writings on the Wall* are written for a reason. Every story in this book serves as a reminder of how the enemy works to get you off course or get into your head. When in doubt, pick up this book, and the VOICE will guide you, *Spirit to Spirit*, illuminating the way, Guaranteed! My love rests upon you, many BLESSINGS as you GROW GREAT!

Dr. Y. Bur

www.DrYBur.com

www.ingramcontent.com/pod-product-compliance
Lightning Source LLC
Chambersburg PA
CBHW071653160426
43195CB00012B/1455